Kitchen Think

Kitchen Think

*A guide to design and construction,
from refurbishing to renovation*

by Nancy R. Hiller

First published by Lost Art Press LLC in 2020
837 Willard St., Covington, KY 41011, USA
Web: http://lostartpress.com

Title: Kitchen Think
Author: Nancy R. Hiller
Publisher: Christopher Schwarz
Editor: Megan Fitzpatrick
Copy editor: Kara Gebhart Uhl
Distribution: John Hoffman
Copyright ©2020, Nancy R. Hiller

ISBN: 978-1-7333916-4-1

This book was printed and bound in the United States.
Signature Book Printing, Inc.
8041 Cessna Ave.
Gaithersburg, MD 20879
http://signature-book.com

Table of Contents

Dedication VII
Preface IX

Mary Lee and Herb. In their kitchen on Drayton Island.

Dedication

This book is dedicated to my forebears, whose kitchens have made indelible impressions on my sense of what a kitchen should be:

To Rose and Louis Adler. Thank you for the fish and vegetables fragrant with dill, served from your tiny apartment kitchen after you retired from a life-time serving others.

To Flora and Simon Rau, who lived in a ground-floor apartment with a modest post-war kitchen and always had a dictionary and magnifying glass in the living room. Thank you for the latkes and matzo ball soup.

To Stephanie Hiller, who lived far away, as a result of which we didn't visit her kitchen, but who always pressed pen and paper on us at restaurant tables to make sure we wrote the letters to cousins that we would otherwise not have written, and who insisted that the parsley garnish was the healthiest part of the meal.

To Arthur Adler, for taking such good care of us all, for the ceviche, and for the potato gratin.

To Esse Rau Adler, whose high-ceilinged kitchen in the Spanish Colonial Revival house on Garden Avenue is burned into my memory, as is the more compact one on Collins Avenue, where she greeted my sister, Magda, and me, along with our cousin Jean, on Saturday mornings with frozen Sara Lee cupcakes; who, having grown up as one of many siblings on a working farm where her family made everything from scratch, loved the freedom Bisquick provided; and who relished her opportunities later in life to dine out, especially on frogs' legs or snails while in France, or, once or twice, on trout at Gravetye Manor.

To Herb Hiller, for the many generations of sourdough bread, the emphasis on quality beer, the always-innovative salads and brown rice, and for demonstrating that in extremis you can cook great meals with a kettle, toaster oven and two-burner hotplate set up on a folding table in the bathroom.

To Mary Lee Adler, for her can-do example in all things construction, as well as a life's worth of shopping, cooking and cleaning up, and for making Magda and me chip in with those essential activities from an early age; and especially for the spring onion and Gruyère quiche, and the apple crumble.

Preface

A general note: This book is intended to be useful primarily to members of the following groups:

• Woodworkers, whether professional or not, who would like to expand their minds on the question of kitchen design, the culture of remodeling, materials and techniques used in kitchens

• Homeowners with some woodworking and home-renovation skills who would like to remodel their own kitchen, including building their own cabinets

• Homeowners who want a deeper understanding of what goes into a thoughtful kitchen remodel done by professionals

• Homeowners and others (who may not own a home) looking for design inspiration and unconventional, non-consumerist ways of thinking about kitchen design and remodeling.

I offer one method of building cabinets – the one I use regularly, which is a hybrid of methods learned while I worked in others' shops with many of my own additions. There are lots of books on kitchen design and cabinet building, as well as videos with instruction in how to build doors, drawers and other cabinet parts. I see no reason to replicate much of that material here in an effort to be comprehensive. Instead, I offer perspective on kitchen remodeling as a cultural phenomenon and driver of often wasteful economic activity, along with ways of thinking about particular aspects of kitchen design that are generally taken for granted.

If you're working on a kitchen in a turn-of-the-20th-century or early 20th-century style, read "Bungalow Kitchens" (Gibbs Smith, 2001) by the late Jane Powell. It's a systematic reference for restoring or building new in the styles that were popular from roughly the 1890s through the 1920s. One of Jane's most valuable contributions to the field of period-style kitchen design is her detailed guidance in standards of period authenticity; for every aspect of the job, from appliances to cabinet hardware, she provides options for "compromise"- or "obsessive"-level work.

Another must-have reference is "Kitchen Classics" (Active Interest Media SIP) by Patricia Poore, longtime editor-in-chief of *Old-House Journal*, *Arts & Crafts Homes and the Revival* and other period design publications, and one of the United States' foremost authorities on residential period design. "Kitchen Classics" expands the range of period styles, beginning with Colonial and extending through mid-century modern, with big-picture historical context and practical guidance for weighing all sorts of options for period-sensitive kitchen design. (The publication is currently out of print.)

My third recommendation for references on kitchen design is a pair of books by English kitchen designer Johnny Grey. "The Art of Kitchen Design" (Cassell, 1995) and "Kitchen Culture" (Firefly Books, 2004) will get you thinking about the history of kitchens as gathering spaces for family and friends, as well as inspire you with examples of Johnny's unconventional, artistic designs.

When it comes to instruction on building cabinets, there are too many books and other resources available to be worth summarizing in a survey such as this one. As a comprehensive guide to layout, materials and methods for building cabinets of your own, I can't recommend any book more highly than Jim Tolpin's "Building Traditional Kitchen Cabinets" (Taunton, 2006).

MRS. CHRISTINE FREDERICK
Noted Household Efficiency Authority
Long Island

MISS ALICE BRADLEY
Principal of School of Cookery
Massachusetts

MRS. FRANK AMBLER PATTISON
Domestic Efficiency Engineer
New Jersey

MRS. H. M. DUNLAP
Domestic Science Specialist and Lecturer
Illinois

MRS. JANET McKENZIE HILL
Head of Summer School of Cookery,
Editor and Author, New Hampshire

MRS. ALICE R. DRESSER
Consultant of Household Administration
Massachusetts

MISS FAY KELLOGG
Household Science Architect, New York

MRS. NELLIE KEDZIE JONES
Household Consultant, Wisconsin

*Hoosier's Council of Kitchen Scientists
That Aids You Every Day Through the Hoosier
Kitchen Cabinet*

Kitchen scientists. From the Hoosier Manufacturing Company's 1918 catalog, "You and Your Kitchen."
COURTESY OF HENRY COUNTY HISTORICAL SOCIETY, NEW CASTLE, IND.

Introduction

Among woodworkers, kitchen cabinets are the poor step-sister of the furniture world – the homely one with a sixth-grade education who processes fish for a living and always seems to have that smell.

"He builds cabinets," sniffed one of my woodworking friends, referring to an acquaintance a few years back. The statement was nowhere near as straightforward as those three simple words might suggest. He spoke with a pained expression, lowering his voice to a near-whisper when he got to "cabinets." Apparently this was some kind of shameful secret; building cabinets made the acquaintance – well, you know...not a real woodworker.

"Why would I want to build plywood boxes when I could be building 18th-century highboys?" remarked another woodworking friend, this time in the late 1990s. The question was rhetorical, more a way of announcing that he'd broken into the East Coast market for period Americana and thereby escaped the obscurity of the rural workshop where he'd spent years building cabinets, millwork and furniture for his regional market.

Kitchen cabinets are the Nestlé's Chunky Bar to the highboys' Godiva signature truffle – a species of work beneath those with higher skills and refined taste.

This snobbery doesn't just stem from an abhorrence of sheet goods joined with biscuits or Domino fasteners and screws. It also reflects the residential kitchen's longstanding identity as a woman's realm. When it comes to work done by men outside of the home versus that done by women inside, the outside world, in public view, wins every time.

There's no real controversy in this claim, at least as it applies to much of Europe and North America during the 19th and 20th centuries. In middle-class homes of the 19th century, especially that century's early years, kitchen work was typically done by servants; migration from rural areas to cities in response to industrialized production and changing markets had translated to plentiful domestic help. For women of the working class it was common to combine meals and lodging with employment in the homes where they cooked, cleaned, laundered clothes and tended fires.

But as factories proliferated, demanding more and more workers, servants began to leave their employers' homes. As some explained to family members and friends, factory work, however hard or monotonous, was vastly preferable to domestic work because it came with boundaries that too many housewives refused to acknowledge. There was an end to the workday, whereas domestic workers could be called on at any time, day or night, and bore the brunt of their employers' bad moods. "A man knows what he wants, and doesn't go beyond it," wrote one young woman who had gone to work in a jute mill, "but a woman never knows what she wants, and sort of bosses you everlastingly… I tell every girl I know, 'Whatever you do, don't go into service. You'll always be prisoners and always looked down on.'"[1] I wouldn't use this sexist quote to illustrate the flight of domestic servants to factories were it not typical of the sentiments expressed by many of the writer's contemporaries.

When servant help became hard to come by, middle-class women were forced to resume cooking and cleaning for their families – tasks that had now become not just low-status, thanks to their long association with women of the working class, but completely unfamiliar. Imagine being expected to make a dovetailed drawer when you have never used a handsaw. That's a reasonable comparison to finding yourself responsible for cooking a Sunday roast when you've never handled raw meat, let alone tended a wood-burning oven.

Many of these women newly bereft of domestic aid were educated and read widely. Through lectures and articles in women's magazines they found a champion in Catharine Beecher and her sister, Harriet Beecher Stowe, who wrote "Uncle Tom's Cabin"; the sisters came from a family of social reformers led by their father, New England Congregationalist minister Lyman Beecher. Motivated by a mission to educate women and improve the conditions in America's homes, the sisters leveraged the higher value placed on men's work in the fields of business, government and education to elevate the standing of work done by women in the home. How? Simply by pointing out that domestic labor, so easily taken for granted when it was done by cheap hired help, formed the foundation of all work recognized as valuable, not just to the family, but to local commerce, the state and even the nation.

In the preface to their 1869 book "The American Woman's Home," the Beecher sisters traced the problems faced by middle-class women to the lack of appreciation for "the honor and duties of the family state."[2] They had an insightful fix. Instead of assuming that women should be born knowing how to clean and boil a calf's head, prepare quince jelly or bake bread from scratch and berating them when they proved unable to do these jobs proficiently, they

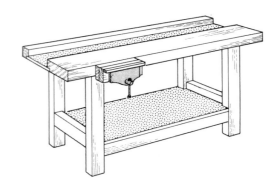

Bench basics. The benches I grew up with were simple affairs like this one from Robert Wearing's book "The Solution at Hand."

From the past. A simple and solid bench, built to the plan in André-Jacob Roubo's 18th-century "l'Art du menuisier."

would share the latest advice about diet and household management based on research done by experts in Europe and the United States. They fleshed out these principles with methodical instruction for all household tasks, right down to the construction of a hydrostatic couch for the sick, a vessel with a disturbingly similar appearance to that of a coffin.[3]

This wasn't so different from the way Christopher Schwarz spearheaded the elevation of the workbench – in the 1970s and '80s, typically a sturdy table of simple design, fitted with a vise – into a focal point of study, expertise and craft based on research into centuries-old methods that have since garnered international interest.

The bottom line, as the Beecher sisters appreciated, is that any occupation important enough to warrant formal training will be respected; the fact that people must be trained to do it validates its importance.

As the sisters and an ever-larger squadron of kitchen scientists wrote and lectured their way around the country, the building and appliance industries coalesced as major economic forces based on an understanding that the kitchen was a potentially lucrative source of business.[4]

Fast-forward to the 1960s, when the kitchen began to open up to family and friends. Tiny pass-throughs between kitchens and dining rooms morphed into open peninsulas with breakfast bars.

Gradually it became less uncommon for men to participate in everyday family cooking. I witnessed this shift personally. Around 1965 my mother, who did all the cooking in our house when we were little, was hospitalized for a few days with pneumonia. Our father, who worked in public relations, was left taking care of us at the end of the day. He probably took us out for hamburgers at least one night, but the only dinner I actually recall was the one he prepared at home: tuna salad.

There was just one problem with Dad cooking dinner, even allowing for the fact that tuna salad is more a matter of mixing than "cooking." Like those 19th-century housewives who were clueless about cooking calves' heads or shopping for sirloin, Dad did not know how to make a meal. He managed to find the can opener and a mixing bowl and spoon. He knew that tuna salad was made with mayonnaise; salt and pepper were also good guesses. But after mixing those basics together he said he really didn't know how to make the dish, so he was going to add a little of every seasoning in the kitchen. In went a spoonful of curry powder, along with some ketchup and mustard. Soy sauce couldn't hurt; nor could Worcestershire. Tabasco would add some zing, and he followed those with a dash of every herb and spice in the rack. It was the best tuna salad I'd ever tasted.

But by the late '70s, our father had become an accomplished cook. After being introduced to a less gendered division of household tasks by the hippies who came to live with us circa 1968, he'd start-

ed to bake bread and make churned ice cream from scratch. When our parents split up and our mother took my sister and me to live in England, he bought a series of international cookbooks published by Time-Life. I remember on visits home during summer breaks his pulling gorgeous loaves of yeasty bread from the oven, parchment collars supporting their lofty sides. Our mother had bought an ancient butcher's block for $10 a year or two earlier. It was 2' thick, made of hard maple blocks set vertically, their edges locked together with dovetails. She'd spent weeks sanding out the deep scores and gouges in its 3'-square end-grain top. It was the centerpiece of the kitchen, where Dad chopped piles of vegetables to steam with fresh herbs and serve on brown rice. Cleaning up the kitchen after dinner – washing dishes by hand, taking kitchen scraps out to the compost pile and thoroughly sweeping the floor to control the population of cockroaches that would otherwise invade any south Florida home once the "exterminator" had been cancelled – had become one of his satisfying, self-imposed rituals.

The 1990s saw a new development: the kitchen as a sociable space completely open to the public areas of the house. Most influential in this shift was kitchen designer Johnny Grey, nephew of British cookery author Elizabeth David. Trained as an architect, Grey was brought up visiting his aunt's kitchen and began writing about a phenomenon that many had experienced but not bothered to analyze: When guests come over, everyone wants to be in the kitchen. Grey's 1994 book, "The Art of Kitchen Design" (Cassell), provided a history of kitchens that restored the kitchen's centuries-long role as center of the home and relegated the shrouded kitchen of the 19th and 20th centuries to an anomalous historical blip.

Most furniture makers who build cabinets do so for the same reason as our predecessors built coffins in addition to tables and chairs: They offer a source of income that helps even out the road between freestanding furniture commissions. It's easy to look down on built-ins when your livelihood doesn't depend on woodworking, or when you are retired, your woodworking venture is subsidized

3

Kitchen bliss. Advertisement for Sellers cabinets in *Ladies' Home Journal*, June 1921. The accompanying text reads, "Have you pictured it in your mind, June Bride – that first tasty dinner in the new home? … How anxiously you will prepare the good things– on your snow-white Sellers Mastercraft – the housekeeper's unfailing friend…. And then, after it is over, hubby will follow you to the kitchen to help you with the dishes. What matter a few smashed pieces?"

COURTESY OF MANUSCRIPTS SECTION, INDIANA STATE LIBRARY

by a spouse's income or you've tapped into a vein of market popularity. Not everyone is so fortunate.

How did the lowly kitchen cabinet become a friend to many who trained as furniture makers, imagining we'd spend our days hand cutting dovetails and French polishing meticulously inlaid cutlery canteens? The answer has as much to do with publishing, advertising and banking as with wood and tools. Ultimately it boils down to the commodification of the home.

Home ownership today is light years away from that of 200, 100 or even 70 years ago, when the people who owned what's now my acre of semi-rural land cut down some trees, dug up some rocks and built themselves a simple board-and-batten-sided cabin worthy of Snuffy Smith. Today a massive industry surrounds home ownership, from Realtors (that term is trademarked and officially requires an upper-case "R") and appraisers to title companies, banks and building inspectors. There has been a radical shift over the past century in how many of us think of our homes: A home no longer simply represents shelter and a central base for family. It's the largest financial investment most of us will ever make – one that, with luck, may increase our wealth at a rate far greater than that of inflation.

As with any investment, we're urged to put ourselves in the hands of expert advisers. And there's an army of them out there. Take the wildly popular hosts of home improvement shows on HGTV – that cast of smiling, perfectly groomed characters eager to instruct you in the magical art of transforming a hovel into an "urban oasis" or liberating yourself from the corporate rat race by hitching a ride on the house-flipping bandwagon. Take the legions of salespeople at home stores, who will gladly guide you through one cabinet display after another until you're dizzy from over-exposure to CNC-routed fretwork, dedicated mixer cabinets with lift-up stands and decorative wine racks. Take the web-based magazines with their daily examples of designer ideas to "steal" and big-name-brand "hacks" or that modern means to keep yourself forever in debt, the home equity loan, advertisements for which have long encouraged us to treat our houses as ATMs.

To be a contemporary homeowner is to feel an almost moral obligation to spend money on your house. Never mind how your friends may judge your taste on seeing you still have that Laura Ashley Dandelion wallpaper from 1983; there's a sense that if you're not religiously "updating," you may be losing financial ground.

One result of this mindset is that customers are generally more willing to shell out big bucks on something they believe will increase the value of their house than on a piece of freestanding furniture. In some locales, built-in cabinets even fall into a different category in the world of sales tax: "improvements to real estate." People rationalize them as an investment. That artisan-made sideboard? Arguably a frivolous buy in comparison.

Of course, you can only get the value of a kitchen remodel out of a house so many times. Property values in most regions don't increase at anything like the rate that would be necessary to cover the tens of thousands spent on kitchens. And then there's the troublesome fact that new cabinets installed as part of a kitchen update undertaken to help sell a house are routinely ripped out by new homeowners, only to be replaced by something more in line with their own taste. Never mind the so-called green design professional who encourages you to tear out your laminate counters and replace them with a "sustainable" composite incorporating recycled glass (or whatever the "green" product du jour may be). The preoccupation with updating results in a mind-boggling amount of waste. These are real-world caveats that some of us point out to prospective clients as we urge them to think about what they really want and need, as distinct from what other experts (and friends, and relatives) are telling them they should want.

That said, who doesn't occasionally long for a change of scene, a shift in tone? There are ways to rework your kitchen without spending a fortune or adding significantly to your local landfill. The first requirement is simply to think. In this process, context, broadly understood, is your friend – where you are in life, what resources you have access to in terms of money, interesting materials, or time, the architectural style of your home and so forth. For the past two decades I have made my living largely by working with clients turning limitations into creative opportunities. This book offers a variety of examples, in addition to guidance in designing and furnishing the kitchen.

I embarked on my woodworking career at the age of 21, expecting to support myself by designing and building custom furniture. I'd completed the first year of a City and Guilds of London Certificate in Furniture Craft and was looking for a workshop with living accommodations that would be affordable to someone who wasn't yet making minimum wage. In the course of this search I ended up working for Roy Griffiths, an artist who had started a design-build kitchen cabinet company called Crosskeys Joinery in Wisbech, Cambridgeshire. Roy quickly disabused me of the romantic notions I'd had about making a living by traditional handcraft. In Roy's shop, good design, efficient fabrication and a high-quality final product reigned supreme. Although we made our cabinets with wooden face frames, drawers and doors, and hung the doors on solid-drawn brass butt hinges, we built our carcases from melamine-coated sheet goods, the parts joined together with shop-made plywood splines. Toe kicks were recessed. Doors and drawers were inset, with drawers running on mechanical slides. Working for Roy was a valuable education in the realities of running a business. When the cabinets for a particular kitchen were finished, fitters delivered them to the jobsite. I never saw my work again.

Roy's business placed little emphasis on the satisfactions of craft for his employees, though he made up for this in various ways – by encouraging a respectful and friendly atmosphere, expressing his appreciation and paying everyone on time.

In my next woodworking job, these values were shuffled around somewhat. This time I was working for a country workshop run by a pair of business partners. They made kitchen cabinets, but custom furniture commissions made up a hefty percentage of their business. They were no less focused on the bottom line – a necessity in any business – but their operation was smaller than Roy's, and traditional methods of joinery and finishing were central to their brand.

In this shop we built kitchen casework out of panels made by gluing together tongue-and-groove pine made for subflooring, an attractive material that allowed the owners of the business to describe the cabinets honestly as being made from solid wood. We built our drawers with hand-cut dovetails at the front and fitted them on wooden runners with kickers supported by back rails let into the cabinet sides. Here, as at Roy's business, toe kicks for kitchen cabinets were recessed. Doors and drawers were inset, with doors hung on butt hinges. This experience provided me with further lessons in running a professional shop.

My third experience of working in someone else's shop was at a company in Vermont that built striking contemporary furniture, primarily for offices on the East Coast. I don't remember any kitchen cabinetry being built while I worked there, but the casework – bookcases, desks, credenzas – was built using methods that were readily transferable to kitchens. We built case goods out of MDF panels covered with gorgeous architectural veneers and edges finished with heat-sensitive veneer banding. We joined the parts with biscuits (my first experience of biscuit joinery) and wood screws. When I started working there, we used biscuits for drawer joinery, though the foreman added router-cut dovetails to the repertoire soon after. We hung the drawers on Accuride full-extension ball-bearing slides and used European hinges for doors (my first experience of those, as well). All of our doors and drawers were full overlay, with precise architect-specified margins between them.

I mention these three shops by way of illustrating the variety of materials and methods appropriate to building cabinets. These are just three examples in a field that supports and also benefits from the development of ever-changing equipment and joinery systems, adhesives and composite materials. There is no "right" way in this work; what's best for you (and if you're a professional, your clients) may strike your neighbor as laughably inefficient. My current method for building basic kitchen cabinetry, which draws on lessons learned from all of the shops where I've worked and goes several steps further in terms of materials and techniques, is outlined in Chapter 3. It combines materials and techniques from the world of traditional furniture making with some conventional (and some less conventional) methods from the universe of kitchen cabinet shops and allows for enormous variations in style, in addition to being adaptable to built-ins for other rooms such as offices, living rooms and baths.

And to those who consider "cabinets" an inferior species of work, I say enjoy building your Shaker side tables, Federal hunt boards or sculpted credenzas. I've learned to relish the diversity of styles and construction methods I'm fortunate to work with as someone who mixes kitchens with freestanding furniture commissions. It's an honor to work with people who trust that I will listen to their ideas and create a room where they will spend time preparing meals every day.

A Trio of Influences on my Thinking About Kitchens

1978, Newington Green, London

My boyfriend and I moved to a post-war working-class housing project where the flats had been condemned, at least temporarily, as unfit for habitation. Thanks to a housing co-op, we were allowed to rent one of the flats for several pounds a week, the only place we could afford. The flat would have been considered wretched by middle-class standards, but we were thrilled to have somewhere to live.

The kitchen intrigued me. It was a small room, I'd say no more than 6' wide (including the space occupied by cabinets) by 10' long, with a few built-in cabinets – extremely simple affairs made of plywood with plywood doors and drawer faces. There was a small stove – tiny by American standards – and a sink with a drainboard. Most fascinating of all, the room was designed to be used without a fridge. A cupboard on the exterior wall was fitted with shelves and had a screened opening directly to the walkway outdoors – a larder! For most of the year, at least in those days, the temperature outside stayed within a relatively small range; in winter it didn't go much below freezing, and in summer it rarely got above the low 80s. A masonry building with concrete floors and walls stayed cool enough to store fresh vegetables, eggs and cheese for two or three days. Storing milk was not a problem; milkmen still routinely delivered bottles to the doorstep. We didn't worry about keeping beer cold; no one seemed to have beer at home – that was what pubs were for. Nor did we worry about keeping ice cream on hand; we bought our Wall's Cornetto at the corner shop and ate it while sitting on a park bench enjoying a rare bit of sun.

1996, Bloomington, Ind.

I stopped by a jobsite in town to visit a carpenter friend. He was part of a crew working on the restoration of a miniaturized Second Empire-style mansion built by a tinsmith in the late 19th century. The job included excavating part of a crawl space to make it deep enough for modern mechanicals, but the opening and existing headroom were too tight to accommodate any large power equipment. As a result, my friend and his fellow carpenters were digging the subsoil out by hand and removing it by the bucketful passed from one man to the next.

I was stunned. It was the last decade of the 20th century and we were in an economically thriving city in the United States. Did people really still work in such seemingly medieval ways?

As I thought about the bucket crew over the next few days, it occurred to me that efficiency is relative. Perhaps a different contractor would have enlarged the opening and excavated the nearby ground to create an opening large enough for heavy equipment. But that would have increased the disruption of the site and might have required adding a support beam to the wall above the crawlspace opening, in addition to more work to put the side yard back together. Compounding the potential complexity, the work was taking place on a narrow lot with very limited space between the clients' house and the neighbor's.

After working in cabinet shops where the emphasis was as much on efficiency as on high standards, it hit me that in some circumstances, doing things step-by-step the old-fashioned way might in fact be most efficient.

1996, Greene County, Ind.

I drove out to the countryside on a hot summer day to see another house where my carpenter friend was part of a crew working on the restoration of a Civil War-era I-house. As he took me into the kitchen, which was nearly complete, I was transfixed by the sight of a tall, narrow, painted cabinet. It had a single door – a simple frame and flat panel – and was hung on brass butt hinges inset in a face frame.

The cabinet shouldn't have struck me as special. I'd spent several years making similar doors in English shops, then later in the shop I'd shared with my former husband when we ran our own business. But I recognized that we were relatively quixotic in a local market dominated by slab-built furniture and kitchens with raised-panel doors; my eyes were scarred by the tyranny of red-oak-everything I saw in new construction. This cabinet was a revelation: There really could be alternatives to the prevailing "professional standards" of design and construction.

1

What is Custom Cabinetry?

The word "custom" gets stuck to virtually anything these days, often as nothing more than a marketing device to enhance a product's cachet. What, for example, is custom drywall? Sure, drywall can be finished in a variety of textures, but that variety has been part and parcel of the mudder's art since drywall became North America's go-to wall surface in the mid-20th century. This historical fact has not kept drywall businesses around the country from incorporating "custom" into their names. Custom running shoes? Those you can order online, selecting your preferences for lace color, tread and decorative top patterns from a wide variety of offerings. In some cases you can even upload your own images and patterns. It seems you can customize practically anything today, from candy and candy wrappers to underwear and toilet tissue – even condoms.

All such uses of "custom" are legit based on the widespread understanding of the word, which "Langenscheidt's New College Merriam-Webster English Dictionary" (Langenscheidt, 1998) defines as "made according to personal order." Before the mass production of practically everything we use in our homes and workplaces, it was commonplace to have clothing, toys, tools, household furniture – even houses themselves – and many other objects of daily use made by members of one's family or community, if not to make them oneself. Since the early 19th century, more and more stuff has been made in factories, where the rigorous application of scientific management and subsequent improvements in efficiency decreased the unit cost by such dramatic orders of magnitude that it no longer made sense to make them any other way. The word "custom," at least in this sense, came into widespread use against the backdrop of overwhelming standardization resulting from mass production.[5]

Most custom goods you'll find through internet searches are themselves produced not by individual artisans, but by computerized design and manufacturing, which make changing the color of a shoelace or the logo on a label as simple as pressing a button to switch from blue dye to red, or uploading an image file to a screen.

So much for a basic definition. But if you want to get serious, the examples above are what truly custom-anything is not.

According to the "Oxford English Dictionary" (O.E.D.), our word "custom" is derived from the Latin noun *consuetudo*, a custom or habit, and its related verb *consuescere*, to grow accustomed. Note the implication of a repeated or habitual practice; this is not about one-time transactions.

Until 1681, custom was also a verb; it meant to

frequent a business. One who buys from a business repeatedly (or commissions work) is a custom-er – i.e., one who customs. To be a customer is to be part of a relationship, to do business with someone on more than one visit – perhaps even to make a habit of doing so – in the process of which customer and merchant (or service provider) learn about each other and develop mutual respect.

One more dimension of this word is worth mentioning in this excavation of nuance. Our word "custom" is also related to the French "costume," derived from the same Latin roots. According to the O.E.D., a costume relates to "fashion proper to the time and locality in which a scene [in a play, for example]" is set. In other words, custom work takes into account the context for which it is done. Clearly this is a different universe from the one in which you type your preferences onto a digital order form.

Consider an old house – say, a Craftsman bungalow from the early 1920s. This is not to say that everything made for the house has to match the original millwork, but it should at least be premised on careful observation of existing fabric that defines the place's character – and I am talking about the particular place, not some vague notion of "Craftsman style" gleaned from HGTV. As with any style (or sub-style), Craftsman was expressed in widely varied ways. Even if you decide to build something completely different from what was there originally, it's important that you open your eyes and think about what's around you, rather than simply imposing your ego. Sometimes this entails seeking out precedent for some detail you'd like to include; sometimes it means crafting a narrative based on available, relevant evidence, to provide a rationale for your design.

Furthermore, as with costuming or custom clothing, custom cabinetry is made to fit. Whether or not it is actually attached to the walls, floor or ceiling, it is sized with its destination in mind, not built to standard dimensions.

Beyond dimensions, custom cabinetry is customarily shaped to conform to irregularities in its surroundings by means of a process called scribing. More on this in Chapter 3.

Finally, custom cabinetry should be made to serve

"Yes, Madam, We Have the HOOSIER in Your Height"

How high? Hoosier Manufacturing Company advertisement from *Ladies' Home Journal*, 1922.

the needs of its users. By this definition, incorporating a wine rack into a set of kitchen cabinets for a couple of teetotalers, as one respected designer in my town proposed to do several years ago, is not custom work; nor is designing cabinets with a counter height of 36" when your client is 6'7".

At this point you may think I am arguing for a definition of custom work so exclusive that few would be qualified to use the word. You may also infer that custom work is only for the wealthy.

Neither is true. The understanding of custom work elaborated here has deep roots in history and encompasses work done for family, love or barter. The level of care involved in genuinely custom work has made "custom" a buzzword for marketers only thanks to our contemporary backdrop of near-universal standardization. While such care takes time, close attention to a customer's particular needs and preferences, along with details of the context for which you are working, can result in a job that costs less than some products that are not custom made.

How is this possible? Budget is a critical dimension of context. To use my own business as an example, as long as a customer's budget is within the broad realm of possibility based on my experience (I have kept detailed records of job costs for the past 25 years), I can tailor my design for a dining table, sideboard or kitchen accordingly. While some see custom work as an opportunity to inflate their charges, others (I am one of these) want our work to be affordable to people in our own tax bracket.

Space reclaimed. The 8-1/2"-wide cabinet (left) holds baking sheets.

Shared structural elements maximize usable space. I combined the sink and trash cabinets in a single unit to maximize usable space by having them share the stile of the divider face frame.

Case Study 1.1

A Truly Custom Kitchen

A recent kitchen commission of mine offers a good example of what I call custom work. The kitchen is relatively small (approximately 10-1/2' x 11'), and the clients were intent on utilizing the space well while keeping a clean, open look. The original 1920s kitchen had been completely remodeled in the 1990s with new cabinets in cherry, full-overlay doors and drawers, all built in standard sizes. Standard sizes were not in sync with the kitchen's dimensions, so some impractical compromises had been made.

More waste of space, now with claustrophobia-inducing extras. The dishwasher and fridge wall before work commenced.

On the east wall, the trim for the doorway to the pantry allowed for a cabinet depth of just 16". Because the previous homeowners wanted the stove to be on this wall, they used a 45° cabinet that went from 12" to 24" deep on the right of the stove, with another on the left. The cabinets wasted a lot of space and loudly announced "compromise." On the opposite wall, the space between the dishwasher and its neighboring cabinet was filled with a whopping 8"-wide filler strip.

When you build your own cabinets (or build for others), you can make them fit the space. No more space-wasting filler strips or purportedly ingenious pull-outs for condiments that promise more usable space than they deliver; no more 45° corner cabinets that seem brilliant but actually waste a shocking amount of cubic footage due to their tiny openings.

Designing cabinetry for a kitchen is an exercise in weighing priorities, budget and available materials – in other words, a puzzle. In my work, aesthetics, too, play an important part; I am often designing built-ins for old houses, and matching the proportions of original millwork.

Only three of the base cabinets in this newly remodeled kitchen are a standard 24" deep. One is the sink cabinet, which has a flanking section with a pullout for trash and recyclables.

The second cabinet of standard depth is an 8-1/2"-wide cabinet for baking sheets; the clients decided they wanted it after protracted discussion of pros and cons. Considering that it replaces the 8"-wide filler strip in the kitchen's previous iteration,

A classic example of space-wasting layout. The east wall of Nandini Gupta and Rick Harbaugh's 1990s kitchen.

it would have been hard to argue that it was not a practical use of the available space.

The third standard-depth base cabinet is a set of large drawers to the left of the stove for silverware, kitchen utensils, pots and pans etc.

The remaining two base cabinets are anomalous. One is a 19-1/2"-deep peninsula cabinet to store bakeware, potholders and so on.

Why 19-1/2"? We wanted to keep the cabinet as shallow as possible, to avoid encroaching on the dining room. At the same time, we wanted the drawers to be as capacious as possible. My preference is for Blum Tandem drawer slides, which come in 75mm (3") increments. The drawer faces are inset, so in principle I could have used an 18" slide for a 19"-deep cabinet (allowing 18" for the slide, 1/4" for the

plywood cabinet back, and 3/4" for the applied drawer face). However, the slide lengths are nominal; I learned the hard way that the actual slide length is about 1/2" greater than the stated size. Hence the cabinet depth of 19-1/2".

Most of the cabinets in this kitchen, uppers and lowers, have face frames, doors and drawer faces that finish at 1" thick for stability. But I made the face frame and drawer faces for each of the final two base cabinets 3/4" thick to maximize the usable depth.

The final base cabinet is made to fit on the east wall, where the door trim begins just over 16" from the corner. This cabinet is 16" deep. Knowing that my clients are serious about utilizing the available space, I suggested that we use ball bearing slides here. Why? The longest Tandem slide that would fit (without excavating 1/2" from the plaster wall behind the cabinet, which the contractor was loathe to do) is 12" once you factor in the 75mm increments and the 1" sum of the drawer face plus cabinet back. (No doubt some bright spark will suggest dispensing with the cabinet back, but I have learned that a well-fitted back is important in discouraging varmints from easy access to a cozy nest filled with a ready supply of edibles. Although many rodents are capable of chewing through 1/4" plywood if they are highly motivated or desperate, its presence is at least a deterrent — another gem I have learned from experience.) The ball bearing slides I use come in 2" increments, which meant we could have drawers 14" deep. Two inches may sound insignificant, but when you consider that the interior depth (front to back) of a 12" drawer with 1/2"-thick sides, front and back is 11", versus 13" for a drawer that's 14" deep, and multiply this 2" difference by the cabinet's height and width, you're talking about roughly a cubic foot of potential space. Just as significant is the question of what the clients may wish to store; many kitchen items are more than 11" but less than 13" deep, which can mean the difference between those items fitting where you want them or having to store them in a less convenient location.

At this point, if you're paying attention, you may have some questions, so let me answer them.

Liberated from convention. This peninsula cabinet is a non-standard 19-1/2" deep to better fit the space.

1. Why not move the doorway over a couple of inches?

If this were your own home, you could certainly do so. For that matter, perhaps your customers would be game. But in this case, other important considerations were in play – one, an adjacent bathroom on the other side of the doorway, which militated against moving the doorway; two, the clients' desire to contain costs; and three, the reality that the clients were out of the country while we were remodeling their kitchen. Although we kept in touch and sent photographic updates, in addition to asking their opinion on critical decisions, there is a limit to such communication. Deadlines, budgetary constraints and the demands of our own professional schedules all argued for working within the existing limits of the basic jobsite.

2. Why not make some of the drawer faces full-overlay?

Doing so would have screamed "compromise," not to mention it would encroach on the adjacent door trim.

3. If you really cared about maximizing useful space you should have dispensed with face frames on these particular cabinets.

You can do this in your own kitchen if you like, but I wanted to keep the cabinetry looking as intentional and cohesive as possible.

4. Why not make your own wooden drawer slides? Then you could make the drawers as shallow or deep as you wanted.

Please see above for discussion of budgetary constraints, and let me add that full-extension ball bearing slides are a pleasure to use in a kitchen.

In our first phone call, these customers made two goals clear. First, while they didn't want to be wasteful by getting rid of their perfectly usable cabinets, they did want better traffic flow and more practical storage. Second, while they appreciate the historic character of their home, the sharp division between the kitchen and dining room did not serve their three-generation family well. Their concern to avoid waste and their respect for the historic character of their house spoke to me. These people were not just following design trends, which would typically dictate removal of the entire wall between the kitchen and dining room to create a single space.

The city's historical survey lists the house as a Colonial Revival built circa 1930, which might mean anywhere from, say 1923 to 1934 (though my money would be on 1925-30). The exterior is limestone; a pair of elegant stone columns support the roof of the porch at the entry. Inside, public rooms are spacious and light, with original oak floors (sanded and refinished to their natural pale color), lightly textured plaster and metal casement windows. The doorways are cased with dark-stained trim and a backband moulding. The baseboards are plain, with an eased top edge. The windows are recessed in plastered openings without trim. The effect is a warm, minimalist "black and white."

After several meetings, we had a plan. Here's a summary.

1. Respect the Windows

Windows let in natural light and define architectural character. The customers would have preferred that this window come down lower than it does; its height above the counter is probably due to the original sink, which almost certainly had an integral backsplash that came up to the underside of the trim.

The position of everything on the west wall was determined by the original kitchen-sink window. In the original architect's drawing, the sink and window were centered on the west wall, but a previous homeowner added a bump-out to augment the half-bath with a shower. The new sink, a narrow apron model, will be centered on this window. After discussing the feasibility of reclaiming that bathroom space for the kitchen and deciding that doing so would be more costly and complicated than desirable, our clients decided to work with the existing footprint.

Windows are precious assets. The position of everything on the west wall was determined by the original window.

Seamless connection. Aaron McDaniel painstakingly toothed the new rift-sawn and quartersawn oak boards for the kitchen into the existing dining room floor to minimize the visibility between old and new. (This image was shot before the floors were sanded and finished.) The ceiling fixture in the dining room is original to the house. A pair of matching sconces are on the north wall.

2. Regard the Home's Historic Character as a Guide

The kitchen previously had a swinging door into the dining room. Now there would be a cased opening about 8' wide. Kitchens in homes of this vintage were not open to adjacent public rooms; they were workspaces for servants or the woman of the house. We decided to use the original cased opening between the dining room's south wall and the entry hall as a precedent for the design of this one; the remaining sections of the wall would honor the original division between them, while preserving valuable space for storage on the kitchen side.

3. Listen to the Customer

It seems obvious, but too few builders do it: Listen to your customers. Respond with pros and cons so they can make informed decisions. Then do what they want – because it's their house, not yours.

I usually urge people to consider putting their trash can in the sink base instead of using precious cabinet space to house garbage, but many prefer to have a dedicated space. These customers wanted a pull-out that would house trash and recyclables and could be opened hands-free.

Fitting the sink and a trash pull-out into the limited available space while centering the sink on the window took careful planning. For this job, the most functional and cost-effective solution for trash was a ready-made unit by Rev-a-Shelf.

After searching for taller cans to avoid wasting vertical space (none of those available fit the width we had to work with), I broached the possibility of adding a drawer above and provided an estimate of cost. The cabinet now includes that drawer.

Whose kitchen is it? My preference is to put the trash can in the sink base; my customers preferred a dedicated cabinet space for trash and recyclables.

4. Enjoy Your Freedom

Custom work liberates you from the tyranny of standard dimensions. Sure, you still have to work with the specifications required for appliances, plumbing fixtures etc., but apart from these, you can size your cabinets to fit the space and your (or your customers') preferences. In this kitchen, the upper cabinet to the right of the sink is about 14" deep, to accommodate extra-large dinner plates behind 1"-thick inset doors.

Because the peninsula cabinet is not an authentic early-20th-century feature, it was in the "con" column of my list of pros and cons. But the customers wanted a peninsula; it would be an ideal place for their children to draw or do homework right there with them in the kitchen. We settled on a plan to make the dining room side of the cabinet more dining-room worthy and less kitchen-like in appearance by finishing the end and back. Instead of just plonking cabinet doors onto the peninsula's exposed sides, as many conventional manufacturers do, I designed the end and back panels to extend to the floor, increased the proportions of their rails and stiles so that they would appear more structural, and allowed for the two panels to be mitered at the dining room/

Sneaky space. I was aware of the space behind the wall (at far right here) that would go unused unless we added a recessed cabinet accessed from the dining room side. The customers decided against that. Until the builder installed the peninsula cabinet, however, I didn't realize that the area between the jamb of the cased opening and the inside corner of the peninsula (space required for the peninsula cabinet's drawers to bypass the stove and its handles) would accommodate a cabinet about 15" wide by more than 16" deep.

kitchen corner for a seamless look. Finally, instead of topping the peninsula with the same stone as the other counters, we agreed to use solid wood stained to match the house's original trim.

Once the contractor had installed the cabinets, I noticed a chunk of space I hadn't thought about before. I checked with the customers, who agreed it was worth modifying the peninsula's back panel in order to use it.

Now what appears to be the right panel of the peninsula's finished back is a door with adjustable shelves inside. We discussed adding drawers, but they would have increased the cost far more than a single door and would also have made this side of the peninsula look more kitchen-like than the customers preferred.

Some on-site assembly may be required. Because the face frame and finished side panel of this upper cabinet for pantry storage would extend down to the counter and up to the ceiling, we didn't install it until after the counter had been fitted. That's the only way to ensure a good fit at the counter.

5. Think

The 8-1/2" space between the dishwasher and cabinetry on the north wall used to be occupied by a filler strip. Now it stores baking sheets.

We discussed installing a pull-out unit to store condiments or spices. My experience with these is that they utilize less space than promised; side bars on the shelves make reaching contents relatively inconvenient and restrict the usable width, while the limited adjustability of the shelves further restricts the amount of space available for practical use. These units make sense for some applications, but this was not one of them.

The upper cabinet that would go with the still-unattached face frame (above) has a top section for pantry storage and a lower section that would be left open, housing a microwave. Because the lower section was designed to be open, I built it separately in cabinet-grade plywood that does not have a prefinished side. This way it could be painted to match the rest of the cabinet faces. After assembling the two cabinets, I screwed them together through the ceiling of the microwave section for ease of installation.

The cabinet stands across from the fridge, so it is designed to hold the kinds of things used for storing food (storage containers, food bags, wrapping materials) and function as a tea- and coffee-making area, with a drawer for boxes of tea, coffee filters, etc. The shelf above houses the microwave. We discussed whether the microwave should be out or behind doors; given the way this family uses the kitchen, the decision was to leave it in the open, as this corner is not visible from the dining room.

Details
Bona Fide Custom

Use available space. *What appear to be three static panels at the back of the peninsula are two with a secret storage cabinet behind a touch-latch-operated door.*

Truly custom details. *The minimal top trim is scribed to the ceiling.*

Upper cabinets flanking the stove appear symmetrical, as well as the same depth. The cabinet right of the stove is partially recessed into the wall so that it appears to be the same 4" depth as the spice cabinet left of the stove. Why not make the cabinet 12" deep? For two reasons: First, a deep cabinet for storing spices just ends up being annoying. Most spice containers are less than 2" deep. Storing them more than one-deep means having to rifle through to find what you're looking for. Second, the customers wanted to maximize the diffusion of light from the north window across that wall and into the rest of the room. Keeping this cabinet as shallow as possible does the trick.

The shelves in the spice cabinet are 1/4" glass with ground edges, a material that takes up minimal vertical space and is easy to clean.

The 12"-deep cabinet on the right makes use of additional depth offered by a recessed alcove that housed the original cookstove. When we discussed whether to increase the cabinet's depth to take advantage of existing space, I pointed out that the cabinet's contents would be a challenge to reach once the stove and adjacent peninsula cabinet were in place. The customers wanted to go ahead anyway; space that's hard to reach can still be worth building to store items used less often, such as holiday glassware.

The panel between these upper cabinets conceals the exhaust vent, located in the original recess. Finally, the clients wanted to minimize the protrusion of the stove, so it is installed a few inches into the recess to make it as close as feasible to the depth of the cabinet at its left.

Of a piece. *The back and end panels of this peninsula are mitered where they meet at the outside corner for a smooth, integral look. Mitering is arguably less important when cabinets will be painted, but over time the panels' stiles will experience differential movement, resulting in a difference in plane. A glued and nailed miter prevents that.*

See the light. A laser level is enormously helpful for accurate measurement, especially in rooms with a floor or ceiling that's out of level.

2
Getting Started

Whether you're planning a kitchen for a newly built house or remodeling an existing kitchen, there are some basic steps to getting started. The first step is to break what may feel like an overwhelming task into manageable components.

Here are a few examples of kitchen remodeling scenarios:

- Gut the kitchen. Whether you're gutting the space to beef up structural elements, enhance insulation or simply to get the ceiling, walls and floor level, flat and plumb, a hardcore gut usually entails new cabinets. This doesn't necessarily mean cabinets that are newly built; some complete remodels incorporate salvaged cabinets, modified to work in their new space. But the idea here is that you're starting from scratch.
- Partial remodel: Keep the best of what you have and add to it. This scenario encompasses kitchens that have a few original cabinets that are charming and perfectly fit the character of the house, but there are too few of them (or they have impractical counters, or they need to be refinished and have various parts tuned up etc.).
- Refacing existing cabinets in cases where the existing cabinets are in good shape and were well made, but you want to change the aesthetic of the kitchen.
- Modify existing cabinets to make them more functional, as when old drawers were poorly made and slid on wooden runners, and you decide to replace them with newly made drawers that are easy to clean and mounted on full-extension slides.

Assess the Situation

Think about how you use the kitchen and what you would like to change. Do you live alone, or are you the only one who cooks? Do you work with someone else in the kitchen – i.e. do you need space for more than one cook? Your answers will have a bearing on considerations such as the space you need between cabinets or appliances and central features such as tables or islands.

Do you have children in your kitchen, whether they live with you or visit often? If so, think about how you can avoid creating sharp corners, especially those at children's eye level. Also choose hardware without tight spring closures that can hurt little fingers, and plan to keep poison or alcohol out of reach.

Do you really cook or do you just want a nice-looking kitchen? How much do you really want to spend on appliances and fixtures marketed as "professional" or "high performance?"

Now list the best features of your existing space. These may include

- Proportions and shape of the room
- Natural light from windows or skylights
- The view through windows
- Existing cabinetry, counters or other elements, such as a lovely old wooden floor.

Make a wish-list of elements you'd like to add.

Now list the things you consider detractions. Examples may include

- The room is dark
- There's no window over the sink (nor is adding one an option)
- The room feels cold
- The room is tiny and has too many doorways that eat up what might otherwise be usable space
- The existing cabinets are not well designed to utilize available space.

The goal of this exercise is to begin defining priorities.

Next note any constraints imposed by the existing space. While some may be able to be changed, time and budget permitting, others may not be. Instead of viewing what you can't change as an obstacle, think of how it could be an opportunity with the benefit of some creative thinking. For example, if your kitchen is tiny, as architect Christine Matheu's was (see pages 342-345), take note of that – then think about whether there are ways to make it feel lighter and more spacious. In Christine's case, the answer was to add new skylights, enlarge the window on the exterior wall and install a large window on an interior wall that overlooks the entryway to her house. But the ultimate genius move by Christine was to open up one portion of the wall between the kitchen and dining room to create a space for the cook to converse with family and friends while preserving a clear distinction between the work and public spaces.

If only it were this simple. This 1936 advertisement for "Porta-Bilt" furniture from the Mutschler cabinet company attempts to make kitchen planning as easy as child's play.

MACY'S PORTFOLIO-EXPOSITION ★ FALL & WINTER 1936-7

OUTFIT YOUR KITCHEN SHELVES — **WITH MODERN KREAMERWARE!**

Let the clean, uninterrupted lines that distinguish modern living rooms and bedrooms, follow you right into the kitchen. Kreamerware is the last word (so far in heavy, richly enameled tin accessories — in white with red accents; or cream, red, green or white with black. Bread box with removable tray, cake cover with chrome serving tray, waste basket, step-on can with galvanized insert, 5-piece canister set. *Famous Housewares—Basement.*

LET'S *"play blocks"* . . . . . AND PLAN YOU A TRULY MODERN KITCHEN

It's more fun than a game—and it makes sense—for it makes you your own kitchen architect—no college degrees, no poring over blue prints. We'll sit you down with a squared off pad and a set of specially scaled blocks, and you'll plot out just the kind of labor-saving kitchen you want. Then we'll show you our fine new **PORTA-BILT** furniture made by **MUTSCHLER,** not just pictures, but the actual pieces — no waiting for special plans! You can have yours straightaway — all the modern cabinets and shelves you need for a functional food-preparing work shop. And the prices are just as sane as the idea and as low as our *Famous Housewares — Basement.*

Now move on to looks.

The steps above are general; they make no mention of your kitchen's aesthetic. Think about how your kitchen looks now and how you want it to look. Do you want it to feel more in sync with other rooms? If so, you may take your design cues from those. But if you're leaning toward a period style, keep some caveats in mind (see pages 295-301); also, if you want a period kitchen to be convincing, you need to bone up on some kitchen history, bearing in mind that kitchens of yore were not public spaces, but the servants' domain.

Measure the Space

One of the first steps in turning your aesthetic vision into reality is drawing the room to scale. But before you start to draw, you need to measure your space.

Measuring entails more than simply stretching a tape across the room in two dimensions, then checking the distance from floor to ceiling. While these basic dimensions are important, fitted cabinets demand far more detail. Walls, floors and ceilings are almost always irregular. Floors sag, often toward the center of a room, where there is no support other than joists, in contrast with the edges of the room, where the floor may be supported by bearing walls. The same goes for ceilings. Walls are rarely perfectly plumb.

And there's more. Never assume a wall is flat. Many walls have sections that are concave, convex or wavy. In drywalled rooms, you can expect a greater buildup of finishing compound, also known as mud, in the corners. For these and other reasons, it's important to measure at several different points. Here's how.

Measure the width of a wall at floor level, then measure at the height of the counter. Now, preferably with the help of a second person, measure the same dimensions at the point where the front of your cabinets will be, for example at 24" from the rear wall for a standard base cabinet, or 12" for a standard upper. Note all of these measurements. Typically, the cabinets at the ends of a run will have a face frame that protrudes from the cabinet side, allowing you to scribe it to fit the wall. The mea-surement at the rear wall, then, is just a guide; the measurement across the front of the faces is equally important.

In rooms with floors, ceilings and walls that are seriously out-of-level or out-of-plumb, a laser level is invaluable for getting an accurate read. When the tool is set up level and plumb, it spins rapidly, casting an unbroken line on all the walls simultaneously. You can measure from this line up to the ceiling (or down to the floor) at any point along a wall to create a map of the precise contours, allowing you to customize your cabinet design accordingly.

For example, the ceiling of a kitchen where my erstwhile employee, Daniel O'Grady, and I did the cabinets in 2006 sloped almost 1-1/4" from the wall to the center of the room. To deal with this slope on the upper cabinets, which were designed to go all the way up to the ceiling, I planned a taller piece of simple trim that could be scribed (a technique you'll learn in Chapter 3) to hide the gap that would otherwise have been left over the upper cabinets.

Use a level (the longer the better; a 4' level is the minimum practical length for this work, but an 8' level will give you a more accurate read) to gauge the slope and contour of the floor. Pay attention to the depth (from the rear wall to the front of the cabinets) as well as the length. This will enable you to design a toe kick appropriate for the space. If your kick will be recessed, as most are (this has been the convention since the 1930s), you can plan to shim up the base cabinets until they are level, then conceal the recess (and the shims) with an applied piece of trim called the toe kick.

If you are building cabinets with a flush kick, as in the method that follows, determining the slope and contour of the floor will allow you to adjust the height of the kick depending on how much scribing you will need to do in fitting it to the floor.

The same principle applies concerning the walls. Use a level to see how plumb the walls are, as well as gauge their contours. This will allow you to plan your face frames. The more irregular the walls, the wider you should make the face frame stiles that will go against the walls so that you can scribe them to fit. Even if you are going to apply trim to conceal the gaps instead of scribing, you need to make the face frame stiles wide enough so that there will be

Go with the flow. The crown moulding on this cabinet is an example of applied trim that had to be scribed to the contour of the distinctly undulating ceiling in a 1915 kitchen.
SPECTRUM CREATIVE GROUP

room to nail on the trim.

Take all of these measurements into account in your scale drawings.

Commercial cabinets come in standard sizes, but when you're building your own, you don't need to worry about that. Plan the cabinets to fit the space. Got an area 11-13/16" wide? No problem. You can build the cabinet to fit.

One caveat regarding the customization of dimensions: Don't forget about appliances and plumbing fixtures. While designing your cabinets to fit the vagaries of your particular space, you also need to accommodate the dishwasher, sink, stove and any other fixtures and appliances you plan to use.

Manufacturers provide specification sheets and installation instructions with their products, but to-

day these documents are also typically available online; you can search for them under the manufacturer's name and the specific model. However, based on experience, I recommend that you have the appliances and fixtures on hand before making final measurements to build the cabinets, because the published specifications are subject to change. Deviations from specs can be costly to accommodate once the cabinets are built. Save yourself headaches by having all of these parts on hand before you finalize the drawings. (More on this on pages 75-93.)

Drawing

I draw by hand, using a scale rule, usually working at 1/8":1". It's most helpful to have a plan view – i.e., a layout of the entire room as viewed from above – in addition to elevations (the drafting term for a straight-on view of the cabinets).

The more information you have about the space, the better. Be sure to take all features of the room into account, such as the width of door casings, location of HVAC vents, existing or planned electrical receptacles and gas pipes protruding through a wall or floor.

The drawings illustrate the importance of visualizing the cabinets as a system, even if you're going to be building them one at a time.

From Drawings To Ordering Materials

It's easy to feel overwhelmed by the scale of a kitchen cabinet plan and at a loss for how to begin putting together a materials order. As with most daunting prospects, the key is to break the job up into manageable pieces. Here I'll walk through the process to translate drawings into a materials order.

This kitchen in a circa-1910 house in Indianapolis was remodeled in the 1980s. My client bought the house in 1990 but moved for a job in another town. Rather than sell the house, which she adores (and bought at a very affordable price when the neighborhood was down on its heels), she rented it out until she retired in 2015. A serious advocate of historic preservation and lover of period kitchens, she decided that she wanted to remodel the kitchen in a way that would reflect her home's history.

For the cabinets, we took our cues from an original cupboard built into a small hallway between the kitchen and dining room, modifying that design based on an example in the 1927 "Universal Millwork Catalog," adding a couple more doors at the top. Because Nancy already had an antique Hoosier-style cabinet that she'd had restored, we incorporated it into the plan for the room.

Number the cabinets for easy identification. I number base cabinets separately from uppers when I build them individually, as in this case.

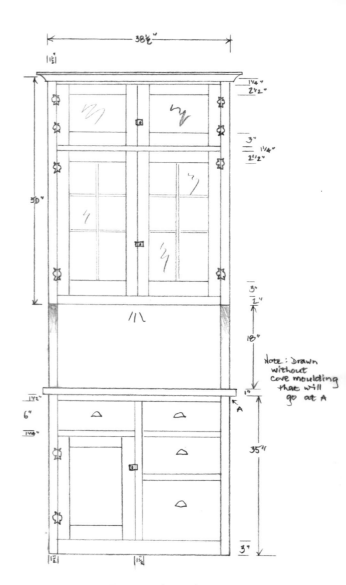

Simple does it. An elevation (above) and a profile view (right) provide the information you need to create a materials list and cutting list for the components.

For Ordering

I begin with the sheet goods and make a list based on parts, starting with a stick-figure drawing that indicates the basic plywood components and how they will relate to the face frame – i.e., will the outside faces be flush with the outside edges of the face frame, or will the face frame stiles overhang to create a scribe strip or allow me to apply a finished end panel?

For a materials order, dimensions can be rough; just make sure you don't underestimate. For the base section of the cabinet shown here, my list for plywood parts would go like this:

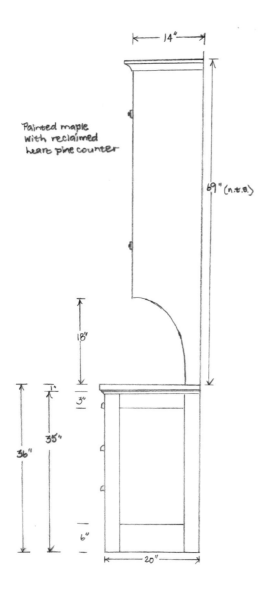

Painted maple
with reclaimed
heart pine counter

14"

69" (n.t.s.)

18"

1"
3"

35"

36"

6"

20"

faced plywood for backs that will be painted on the interior of a cabinet with clear glazed doors.

After I've listed the sheet goods parts for all the cabinets, I quickly plan how I'll cut them out of the sheets, which are nominally 48" wide x 96" long. (In fact, they tend to be closer to 48-1/2" x 96-1/2".) I make a crude sketch based on 4' x 8' sheet good sizes to figure out how many sheets I need at different thicknesses.

Next I move on to solid wood, which typically involves one species for the faces and visible end panels, and a secondary species for interior parts such as drawer boxes. I work with rough-sawn lumber that I mill myself. This allows me to control the quality of the milling – too often, sawmills simply run boards through a planer instead of flattening them first.

So, for this upper, my list will look like this:

Face species
5/4 stock§:
• front of base cabinet: 1 @ 35" x 38"
• doors in upper¥: stiles: (10") x (48")
• rails: (12") x (38")

4/4 stock:
• upper end panels: 2 @ 13" x 69"
• base cabinet end panels: 2 @ 19" x 35"

§ *for face frames, doors, drawer faces.*
¥ *for glazed doors I just add together the approximate widths of all the stiles and rails and multiply by their lengths to come up with a net board footage, then I factor in my allowance for waste and working around unsuitable portions of boards.*

Because the upper cabinet has minimal face frame material, I'm going to count on getting that out of the waste allowance.

Calculate the board footage (thickness x width x length, divided by 144, is your net board footage, noted as "bf"), then add up the board footage for each thickness of lumber and multiply by your waste factor. For most jobs, I include a waste factor of 50 percent – not because I waste 50 percent of the material, but because in my experience this allows me enough

• 3/4" prefinished plywood sides: 2 @ 18-3/4" x 35"
• top and bottom: 2 @ 18-3/4" x 35-1/2"*
• divider: 1 @ 18-3/4" x (32")**
• 1/4" prefinished plywood: back: 1 @ 37" x (32")
• drawer bottoms: 4 @ (17") x (18")

I will use a strip top for these base cabinets, but I still note the dimensions for a solid plywood top, because I will use this as my cutting list later on. More on this below.

**I put approximate dimensions in parentheses. This makes it easy to allow for the quantity of material I'll need for parts I'm going to cut based on direct measurements of the partially built casework. Also, I use poplar-*

stock to match grain as appropriate, cut around defects, and deal with widths and lengths of rough-sawn boards that aren't always ideally matched to the dimensions of my job.

- 5/4 stock: approximately 30 bf
- 4/4 stock: approximately 33 bf

Finally, I do the same for drawers. When figuring out the lumber for a drawer stack, such as the three on the right side of this cabinet, I simply treat them as one, using the approximate interior height of the cabinet for the "width" and the sum of 2x the depth plus 2x the opening width for the "length," i.e.

- 4/4 poplar for drawers: 1 @ 32" x (18" + 18" + 17"+ 17") = 32" x 70"
- 1 @ 6" x 70"

Because these drawer box parts for this job will come out of 4/4 material, I don't bother noting the thickness – it would be 1.

Work out the board footage – in this case, 23 bf including waste allowance for the drawer stack and 4 bf for the single drawer on the left.

Now you have your basic lumber order:

Face species
- 5/4 stock: 30 bf
- 4/4 stock: 33 bf

Secondary species
- 4/4 poplar: 27 bf

Sheet goods
- 3/4" prefinished plywood: 1 sheet
- 1/4" prefinished plywood: 1 sheet
- 1/4" poplar ply: 1 sheet

Note that although this single cabinet will need less than one whole sheet of each type of 1/4" plywood, a full sheet is the minimum you can buy from wholesale suppliers. In reality, I will need quite a bit more for this kitchen, but I'm using the quantities for this single cabinet as an example.

Cutting List

Depending on how precise you were when preparing your materials order, you may not need a separate cutting list. But it's still important to go through the drawings and check that your dimensions are correct.

I start with the sheet goods and make a list based on parts, making a quick stick-figure drawing of the front and top view to give me the overall dimensions and dimensions between parts depending on how the face frame fits relative to the plywood carcase.

For the drawing here, my cutting list would be as shown on page 33.

Again, I use parentheses to indicate approximate dimensions. For most base cabinets, I don't bother with a full top – it's going to be covered with a counter. I need enough of a top surface to hold the sides together and support whatever material ends up being applied as a counter. Avoiding a full solid sheet for the top saves material and reduces the cabinets' weight, an important consideration during delivery and installation.

Go through all the drawings, making a basic list this way. Pay attention to any variation in the construction of particular cabinets, such as cabinet sides that may be rabbeted for backs instead of having the backs simply planted on.

Now you have your basic cutting list for the cases. At this point I usually go ahead and build the carcases. When the carcases are constructed, I move on to the face frames, putting together a cutting list based on the stick-figure drawings as follows:

Face frame cutting list
Base
- Stiles: 2 @ 1" x 1-1/2" x 35"
- Rails: 1 @ 1" x 1-1/2" x 35-1/2"
- 1 @ 1" x 1-1/4" x 35-1/2"
- 1 @ 1" x 3" x 35-1/2"
- Vertical divider: 1 @ 1" x 1-1/2" x 30-1/2"

Upper
- Stiles: 2 @ 1" x 1-1/2" x 50"
- Rails: 2 @ 1" x 1-1/4" x 35-1/2"
- 1 @ 1" x 2" x 35-1/2"

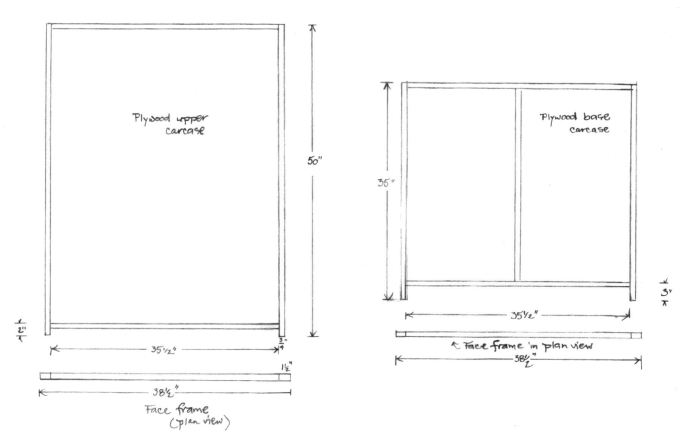

A quick study. A rough stick-figure-type sketch of each plywood carcase seen from the front, with its face frame seen from above, lets me see at a glance how the face frame rails and stiles relate to the sides, top and floor of the carcase and thereby determine lengths.

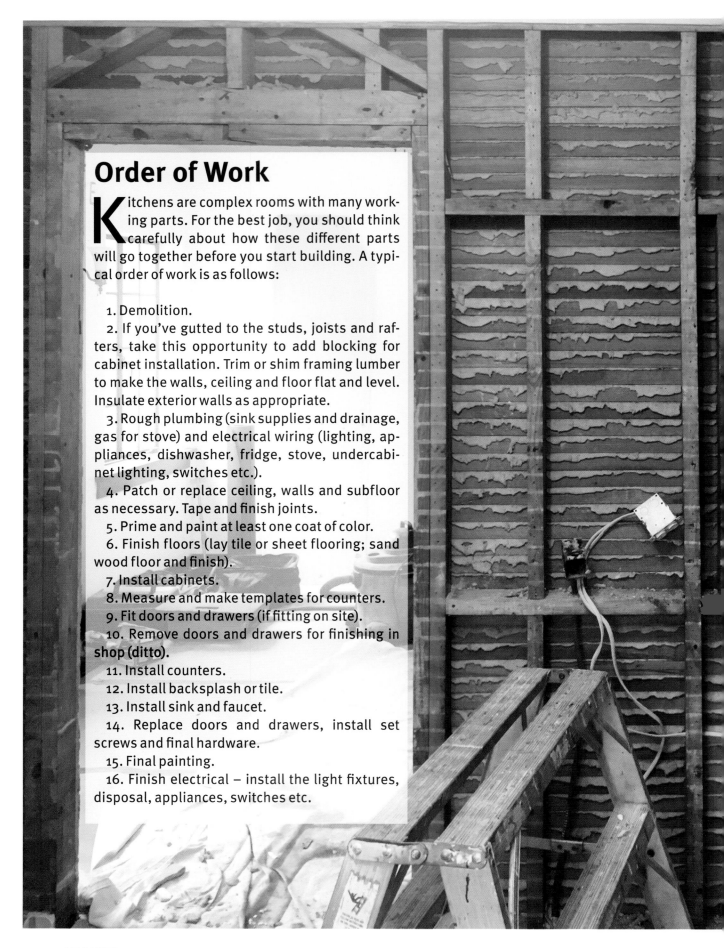

Order of Work

Kitchens are complex rooms with many working parts. For the best job, you should think carefully about how these different parts will go together before you start building. A typical order of work is as follows:

1. Demolition.

2. If you've gutted to the studs, joists and rafters, take this opportunity to add blocking for cabinet installation. Trim or shim framing lumber to make the walls, ceiling and floor flat and level. Insulate exterior walls as appropriate.

3. Rough plumbing (sink supplies and drainage, gas for stove) and electrical wiring (lighting, appliances, dishwasher, fridge, stove, undercabinet lighting, switches etc.).

4. Patch or replace ceiling, walls and subfloor as necessary. Tape and finish joints.

5. Prime and paint at least one coat of color.

6. Finish floors (lay tile or sheet flooring; sand wood floor and finish).

7. Install cabinets.

8. Measure and make templates for counters.

9. Fit doors and drawers (if fitting on site).

10. Remove doors and drawers for finishing in shop (ditto).

11. Install counters.

12. Install backsplash or tile.

13. Install sink and faucet.

14. Replace doors and drawers, install set screws and final hardware.

15. Final painting.

16. Finish electrical – install the light fixtures, disposal, appliances, switches etc.

3

A Simple, Strong Method for Building & Installing Cabinets

"Have the haters started?" asked a visitor one Saturday when I was at the Lost Art Press storefront for a book release. "I mean in response to your article on kitchen cabinets," he added, seeing my mystified expression. I hadn't seen any negative feedback to the article, which was published by *Popular Woodworking Magazine*, nor have I since then, but the apparent lack of criticism has honestly come as a surprise. (It's probably out there in an online forum, but I don't go looking for such things.)

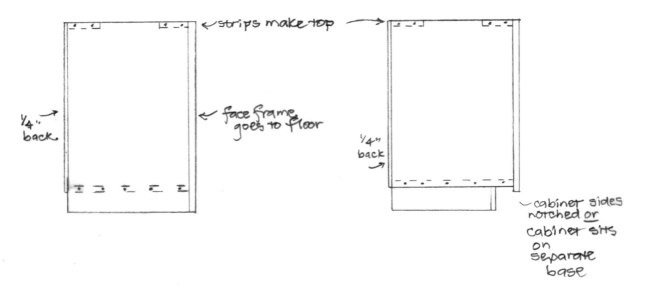

Basic types of toe kick seen from the cabinet's left end. The base cabinet at left has a flush kick. The one at right has a recessed kick.

In the 25 years since I started my own business, I have selectively adopted new materials and methods. The method I use most often for built-in cabinetry combines simplicity and strength for the basic casework with materials and techniques for doors, drawers and finished panels that owe more to the world of furniture than that of contemporary commercial cabinetmaking. The technique that follows is a hybrid, drawing on what I learned at the different shops where I've worked. I have chosen materials and methods that make sense for my business, given my clientele and the styles in which I specialize.

I have worked on kitchen remodels managed by general contractors, but more often I'm working directly for clients. This is at least partly because installing the type of cabinets I most often build for kitchens is more labor-intensive and finicky than a lot of contractors want to bother with. They want to get their job done and return the kitchen to their clients as quickly as they can while doing high-quality work.

I get it. Before my husband and I were romantically involved, we were acquainted as tradespersons in the town we'd both made our home. The first job on which we collaborated was a wall of built-in bookcases. The clients had contracted with me to design and build them; Mark and his crew were going to do the installation. When we discussed the

job initially, I asked about scribe rails for the sides where the bookcase face frames would meet the walls. "Life's too short," Mark commented. I was happy to be let off the hook and have him install the casework with applied trim, as he saw fit.

As time went on and we worked together on several kitchens, his attitude shifted. He still prefers not to scribe cabinets to their surroundings – it's fiddly work that involves a fair amount of heavy lifting. As you get older, it hurts. But despite the aches, Mark has become expert at installing this type of cabinetry. A couple of years ago he even said he'd come to appreciate why I design and build kitchen cabinetry the way I do – it's far more truly handmade than the majority of custom cabinetry. It allows the cabinetmaker (in this case, Mark's wife) to use materials and techniques that are no longer common in this line of work, which translates to opportunities for the kind of satisfaction John Ruskin argued was every worker's birthright.[6] And in my experience, it's clear that many clients appreciate the extra attention to detail, along with the awareness of history and craft that underlies it.

This is not to suggest that building and installing cabinets according to the following methods will be for everyone. It obviously isn't. But considering how much flak I've had for my approach from fellow professionals over the years, it's worth pointing out that a growing number of craftspersons and clients value this way of working.

The cabinet in the following example was designed for the kitchen of a 1912 house. I planned to scribe it to the floor and to the wall at its left; that's why the face frame protrudes beyond the cabinet's left side.

Unless you're running a production facility where you build things in multiples to standard sizes, you should take the building work in stages instead of cutting all your parts at the start, based on a cutting list taken off drawings. That way you'll have a chance to adjust the different parts to fit what you've made so far, instead of finding that your face frame is 1/16" too narrow or you cut the recess for your kick 1/4" too high.

Some people start with face frames, then build their carcases to fit. I work the other way around: Once the basic cases have been assembled, I move on to face frames. Then come doors and drawers.

Get Going

Now you have your scale elevations at hand and have made a cutting list based on them. My typical material for kitchen casework is 3/4" maple-faced veneer-core plywood, prefinished on one side. The prefinished side goes to the cabinet interior; it saves a lot of time, which helps make my work affordable. That said, some jobs call for painted interiors or other finish treatments, so I always choose the sheet material to suit the job.

The next step is to cut your basic parts (sides, tops and cabinet floors) to size. Because I'm building each job to genuinely custom dimensions, some base cabinets may not be designed to end up 24" deep or 34-3/4" high. (For example, I love a 38"-high counter. It should go without saying that the carcase height must be adjusted to allow for the thickness of whichever counter material you'll be using.) And even if most of the uppers in a kitchen job will be 12" deep, one may be a 5"-deep spice cabinet, while another may be 16" deep.

Rip all of the sides and floors to width. The edges and corners of sheet goods may not be square, and they often have minor damage, so it's ideal to make the first rip slightly overwidth, then turn it around

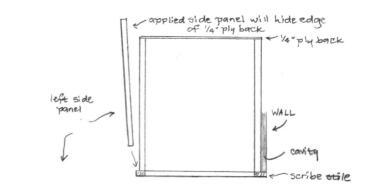

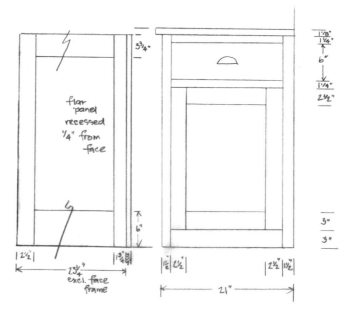

Keep in mind how parts relate. Plan view of cabinet sides and back with face frame overhang (top). Front elevation showing face frame, door and drawer (bottom).

and rip the other edge to the size you require. That way you'll have two square, clean edges for joinery.

After ripping, cut the parts to length. There are various ways to do this. Aside from cutting each part accurately to length, it's important to cut the ends square. You can do this with a track saw if you have one. Alternatively you can use a straightedge and a pattern cutting bit to rout one end square, then crosscut on a table saw, running that end along the fence. (The same technique will work with a radial arm saw for the second cut, which trims the piece to length.) My current method is to crosscut one end of each piece using a slider on my table saw,

Let rip. I store my plywood on sturdy sawhorses near the table saw so that I can grab one end of a sheet over to the edge of the saw, adjust it against the fence and rip.

Be there & square. A sliding table set at 90° makes it easy to cut the first end of each casework part square. You can then cut multiple parts to the same length by crosscutting with stops.

Simple & strong. Clamp the spacer in place at the bottom of the cabinet side and attach with 1-1/4" twin-thread screws. Four or five are plenty for each side of a typical base cabinet. You can drill and countersink or use an impact driver, as I did here.

then cut it to length using the fence. Be sure you mark each part clearly as you cut it.

My method for joining cabinet floors to sides may not be refined, but it's quick, simple and strong. I use a spacer made from scrap 3/4" plywood to position the floor and support it. Twin-thread screws run in through the cabinet sides will fasten the whole thing together.

Your elevations will determine how high the kick needs to be and whether it will be flush or recessed. Calculate the height of the space that will be be-

Drill. Even though the screws will be run in from the outside of the cabinet, I drill pilot holes from the inside, because that way I don't need to measure for the holes' positions; the spacer tells me where the holes should be: 3/8" on center above its top edge. Then I flip the side over and countersink. Four or five screws are usually ample for a 24"-deep base cabinet.

Join the top. In most cases you can simply hold the strip in place and mark the centerline for each biscuit from the strip to the cabinet side.

Steady on. For safety and accuracy, clamp the cabinet side in your vise and hold the biscuit jointer firmly against the fence to make a square cut.

Keep things flat. Clamp the top (whether it's solid or strips) to your bench and hold the biscuit joiner firmly in place, then make the cut.

neath the cabinet floor and rip spacers from scrap plywood to this width, then cut them to length. If your kick will be flush, the spacer should be a hair under the width of the cabinet sides in length; if the kick will be recessed, the spacer should be a hair under the width of the cutout portion at the bottom of each cabinet side.

Next, drill for the screws that will tie the sides together with the floor.

Most base cabinets do not need a solid plywood top. A strip several inches wide at the front and back offers plenty of material to tie the sides together and support a counter, and using less material lightens the weight of these substantial cabinets while minimizing waste. Sink bases in particular do not need a solid top; the vast majority of a sink base's top will be cut out to accommodate the sink. For narrow cabinets (those 18" or less wide) it's usually quicker to go ahead and make a solid plywood top, following the same directions as those for a strip top.

The strips for a particular cabinet will be the same length as the floor for that cabinet, so cut them to length at the same time. The sides of the cabinet will be joined to these strips with twin-thread screws, but I also use biscuit joints, for increased strength as well as a positive means of locating the parts during assembly. Mark each strip with the cabinet name or number and "front" or "back," so you'll be able to identify quickly which end is right and left, and which long edge faces forward. It's a good idea to have at least two biscuits in each strip to help prevent the strips from twisting during assembly.

If you have ever found yourself on hands and knees, searching for that custard pan in the very back of a base cabinet, you'll understand why most cabinets today are made with drawers or pull-out trays on full-extension mechanical slides instead of with shelves concealed by doors. I rarely put shelves in base cabinets, but I do use them in upper cabinets and in shallow base units such as bookshelves.

When a cabinet will have adjustable shelves, I usually use 1/4" pin-style supports, which are unobtrusive, extremely strong (I have used them to store large shelves of LPs) and fast. Now is the time to drill shelf support holes, because you can clamp the cabinet sides together and mark them at the same time. Lay out the positions with a long square.

Shelf spacing may seem like a no-brainer, but even here it's worth paying attention to a few considerations:

• There is no point putting shelf support holes too close to the cabinet floor or top (or, in cases where there will be drawers above the shelf compartment, too close to the drawers) where there would not be enough room to store anything on the shelves. Think about what the shelves will need to hold and plan their spacing accordingly. If the bottom of the cabinet will be holding flower vases that are 12" tall, there may not be any point putting shelf support holes lower than about 13" above the cabinet floor.

• Holes at the back of the cabinet should be about 1" forward from the back edge to allow enough space for fingers when inserting and removing supports.

• Holes near the front of the cabinet should be positioned close enough to the front edge of the shelves that they prevent the shelves from tipping when someone is putting an object away or taking it out. At the same time, take any lipping at the front edge of the shelf into account. In general it's a good idea to center the front shelf support holes about

Note shelf support hole locations
Front: just behind applied lipping
Back: 3/8" – 1" from back of sides

applied crown
cabinet top
1 3/4"
3/4" floor
1/4" back
2" bottom rail leaves 1 1/4" cavity for task light
1"
1"
12"
2"
3/4"

Safety first. Drill shelf support holes close to the front and back of the shelf, where they will give the necessary support.

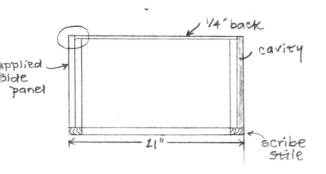

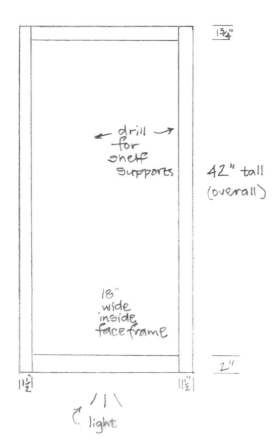

applied side panel

1/4" back

cavity

21"

scribe stile

1¾"

drill for shelf supports

42" tall (overall)

18" wide inside face frame

11½"   11½"   2"

light

Be sure to allow enough width for crown (if using) & face frame reveal

A typical upper unit. The top shows a plan view; at bottom is an elevation.

5/8" on center behind the back face of a shelf lipping that hangs below the underside of the shelf.

• Consider how much adjustability is really necessary for the shelves in a given cabinet. For cabinets that will store shorter items such as juice glasses and dishware, closer spacing may be warranted; I often lay these out at 1-1/4" on center. For cabinets storing large items such as tall jars of dry goods, 2" on center may be more practical. The point is to allow as much versatility in positioning the shelves as may be needed while avoiding the visual busy-ness of too many holes.

Assembly Time

With the basic carcase joints cut and shelf support holes drilled, you're ready to glue up the cabinets. Run a bead of glue along the top edge of each floor spacer, then stand the sides on the floor, front edge facing up. (You can lean each side against a workbench, stationary machine or sturdy trash can to hold it temporarily.)

Set the cabinet floor in place between the sides, and clamp loosely. Depending on the size of the assembly and whether you have a helper, it may be more practical to hold the floor and sides together by clamping the floor to the bottom spacers (see image on page 44, bottom left) instead of clamping across the cabinet's width. At this point the clamp is just to hold the parts together while you insert the top (or top strips); there will be time to adjust the fit and get things square.

Now apply glue to the biscuit slots for the top (or top strips), insert the biscuits, and set the top in place. Apply a couple of clamps to hold the assembly together while you adjust the fit.

After squaring the cabinet, sight across the top edges to check for winding. Shim at the bottom as necessary to remove twist, then drill and screw. Let the cabinet sit until the glue has set, per the glue manufacturer's instructions.

Vertical Dividers

Plywood that's prefinished on both sides comes into its own for vertical dividers. I measure for dividers at this point and fasten them in place with screws.

Thoughtful gluing. Apply a bead of glue to the top edge of the spacer and where the biscuits will go. Don't waste your time or glue on the prefinished surfaces; it won't bond to them.

Gluing tip. Make sure the bottom face of the cabinet floor is tight against the top edge of the spacers; the bead of glue along the spacers' top edge will contribute to the cabinet's strength, especially if you are using plywood that's prefinished only on the interior face and so offers few opportunities for gluing.

Adjust the clamps and square up. I find light clamps useful in holding the floor against the spacers while getting things adjusted. Here I am tightening the clamps at the top, having flushed up the front and back edges. Next I will move to the cabinet floor, tapping it down firmly onto the bottom spacer before I insert a clamp under the back edge to tighten everything up.

X marks the sweet spot. If you are working alone on a relatively large assembly, it's sometimes helpful to insert one screw at each side before the carcase is fully squared up to keep the parts joined together. You can remove that screw if necessary, then redrill and replace it once the cabinet is squared. The carcase is square when the diagonals are equal.

Drill, then screw. Drill pilot holes for the screws using a bit just smaller than the shank of your screws. Then countersink to prevent breakout. Insert screws with a driver.

Direct measure. Determine the length of dividers by holding one end against the cabinet floor, then marking the other. Because it's typical for floors and tops of wide cabinets to sag or bow, measure for dividers at the nearest end. That way your divider will even up the height of the cabinet near the center.

Instead of using a tape measure, I cut a couple of pieces of scrap plywood (one for the bottom, the other for the top) to the distance between the divider and the nearest cabinet side. Clamp the scrap in place and you have an instant way to drill the pilot holes, 3/8" on center from the edge of the scrap. This method also makes locating the divider a snap when you're ready to screw it in place.

Of course, you can't insert that divider until you've cut it. Don't precut dividers to size; cut them to fit. Otherwise you may find that your divider is too small. The most accurate way to determine a divider's length is by setting one end in place and marking the other.

Wide cabinets should have support feet below or near vertical dividers to prevent sag. Make these from strips of 3/4" plywood cut to the same height as the spacers supporting the cabinet sides. Screw a batten on each side of the foot through which you can fasten to the underside of the cabinet floor.

Face Frames

After using several kinds of joinery for kitchen cabinet face frames, I now regard a pocket screw jig as my go-to. Pocket screws are quick, simple and strong. If you make a mistake, you can often remove the screws and replace a part.

Mill the stock for your face frames to thickness and width but don't cut anything to length until the cabinets are assembled. Direct measurement is the quickest, most accurate way to go. Start with stiles, setting a squared end on your shop floor for face frames with stiles that go to the floor; for cabinets with fully recessed kicks, start at the top and mark the location of the cabinet floor's underside, then add 1/2" (or however much you want the face frame to hang down, which will hide the joint between the cabinet and an applied kick). Clamp the stiles in place, then hold one end of the top rail against one stile and mark the position of the other. Repeat with the bottom rail.

For vertical dividers, wait until you have the main part of the face frame screwed together so that the spacing of all the parts is locked in. Then continue with direct measuring. Hold one squared end of the divider stile in place and mark the other, then cut. Hold the skeleton face frame against the cabinet and transfer the position of the divider onto the edge of the top and bottom rails. Drill pocket screw holes at the ends of the stile and insert the stile.

Drawer Rails

Even if your drawers will slide on mechanical runners, you may want to install drawer rails for a more traditional look (at least, traditional for built-ins from the late-19th through the mid-20th century). With the vertical divider in place, repeat the same steps to size and install these rails.

When you have completely assembled your face frame, give a light sanding to the inside edges. This is much easier to do before the frame is glued against a prefinished surface that you won't want to mar. Brush glue on the front edges of the carcase, spreading it over the surface, and apply the face frame. Make sure that the top edge of the bottom rail is flush with the floor of the cabinet; do the same with any critical inside or outside edges. Then clamp.

Hanging Cleats

The next parts I usually tackle are the hanging cleats, by means of which the cabinets will be screwed to the wall. Then I cut the backs. After these steps, the structure of the cabinet will be finished and I can turn to the fun parts – doors and drawers, both of which deserve their own books and articles, and have been covered well by others.

Note that for safety, the attachment cleat must be firmly fastened to the carcase; otherwise a cabinet could be separated from the cleat and fall off the

Scrap spacers save time & enhance accuracy. Use a piece of scrap plywood to lay out holes for vertical dividers and locate them for fastening. Then rely on the scrap to locate the divider while you drill pilot holes with a countersink/drill bit and screw it in place.

Intermediate support. A batten screwed to each side of the foot allows you to attach it to the cabinet's underside. I stagger the battens, putting one toward the front, the other toward the back, so that I can screw into them from the opposite side of the support foot.

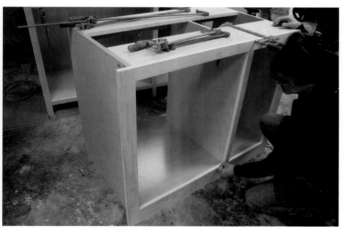

More direct measuring. With one end of each face frame member squared, it's quick and accurate to determine all of the parts' sizes by direct measuring off the carcase. Start with the stiles, clamping them in place dry.

Pocket screw. A pocket screw jig such as this Kreg model makes strong face frame joints quickly. You can buy a special clamp to hold the rails and stiles in plane, but I clamp the parts together on my bench, making sure they're square.

Looks matter. Cabinets made with mechanical drawer slides don't need rails to hold runners and kickers, but if you're after a period look, you may want to consider including them.

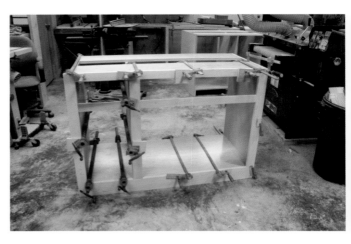

Let's face reality. Clamp position is important. Put the clamps where they will do the most good. For joints that will be seen from the inside of the cabinet, such as the one between the cabinet floor and the bottom rail of the face frame, put the clamp inside. Sometimes, such as when the face frame is flush with an outside face that will be a finished end, it's preferable to put the clamp on the exterior. Cauls protect the face frame.

wall, with potentially fatal results. I make a sturdy cleat from solid wood or 3/4"-thick veneer-core plywood and attach it to the carcase with wood screws run through the top and sides. The cleat becomes part of the cabinet structure, not only supporting the weight of cabinet and contents from beneath the top, but also resisting the kind of leverage (such as that imposed when a child leans on an open cabinet door – please teach your children not to do this) that could pull the cabinet sides away from the cleat if gravity alone were holding it in place.

It should go without saying that a cabinet designed to store pantry goods, appliances or dishware must be attached to the wall through studs or heavy-duty blocking, not just fastened to a wall with molly bolts or drywall anchors.

Backs

Many people think backs are optional for built-ins, but backs are almost always worth incorporating. A good back will help a carcase resist racking, in addition to providing a more finished interior look.

For kitchen cabinets I typically apply a back cut from 1/4"-thick veneer-core maple plywood, prefinished on one side. The prefinished side goes toward

the interior. Measure the width of the carcase and cut the back to that width, then measure the height from the underside of the cabinet floor to the top of the cabinet and cut the back to that dimension. Fasten the back to the cabinet with #6 1" or 1-1/4" wood screws after drilling countersunk pilot holes.

Shelves

In most cases, kitchen cabinets will be vastly more functional if made with shelves that are adjustable, rather than fixed, allowing you to customize their locations to make the best use of available space. I generally make shelves from the same 3/4"-thick veneer-core plywood as the carcases and add a solid front lipping to finish the edge and increase rigidity. (For a handy guide to dealing with load, span and other shelf-construction basics, see http://www.woodbin.com/calcs/sagulator/.)

For shelves, as with vertical dividers, it's nice to use stock that is prefinished on both sides if you have it available. Resist the urge to make your shelves a perfect fit. They need to have a gap of about 1/32" to 1/16" on each end in order to be easily adjustable.

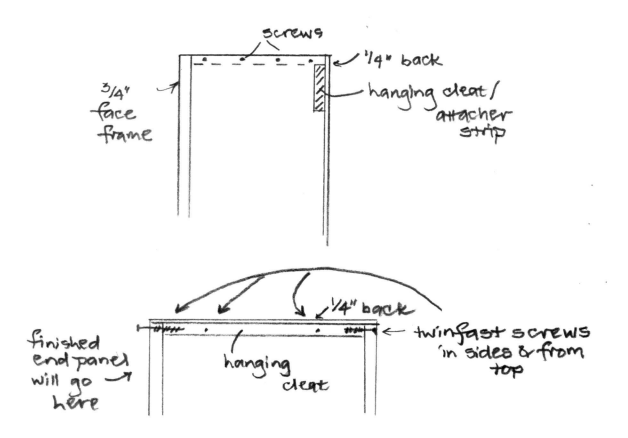

Don't rely on gravity. Hanging cleats, seen from the cabinet's right side (top) and in plan view (bottom), need to be integral to the cabinet's structure. Attach them with screws through the cabinet sides and top.

Toe Kicks

If your cabinets have a flush kick, as does this one, you're home free – at least until it's time to scribe the kick to fit the floor. If your kicks are recessed, mill them to thickness but leave them over-width and over-length until your cabinets are installed. Then cut them to fit.

Finished End Panels

The basic cabinetmaking method above will work well for cabinets that are trapped by walls at both ends. But it's also designed to allow for finished end panels. I find it more efficient in many cases to build and install the cabinets, whether uppers or bases, then carefully fit and apply finished ends. Regardless of whether the finished ends will be frame-and-panel construction, solid-wood sides, or sheet goods custom-veneered to match the cabinets, I cut them roughly to size in the shop, then scribe them to fit on site. The end panels will cover the 1/4" back, which would otherwise be exposed.

Crown Moulding & Other Trim

Applied trim goes on after the cabinets have been installed. That way you can cut it to fit the room.

Installing Built-ins

Keep the following three points in mind.

1. Kitchen cabinets need to be level and plumb. They also need to provide adequate support and attachment material for counters. Stone counters and solid-surface composites have support requirements that vary according to the product; some, such as those with heavy veins of quartz, are more prone to breakage. The amount of unsupported overhang will also vary depending on variety and thickness, so be

sure to check with your supplier when designing islands or other pieces with significant overhangs.

2. When designing your cabinets, take into account the type of kick you plan to use. If the kick is recessed, you can "build up" – i.e., locate the highest point of the floor, set that cabinet first (or at least mark its height on the wall), then shim the other cabinets up to that. Any shims will be hidden when you apply the recessed kick.

If your cabinets will have a flush kick, like the base cabinet in the scribing example that follows, you need to think the other way around. Find the lowest point of the floor and set that cabinet first (or mark its height on the wall), then scribe the other cabinets so that they fit snugly to the floor with their tops lining up at that level.

Whether you'll be shimming up or scribing down, you'll need to take the amount of upward (or downward) shift into account when planning the length of the base cabinet sides if having the majority of the counters at a particular height is important to you (or your clients).

3. Even though fitted cabinets are usually built as units (sometimes called modules), then screwed or bolted together, you need to think of them in multiples in order to end up with a row of cabinets with faces and tops that line up in a flat plane. This means that in addition to thinking about leveling relative to the floor, you must also consider fluctuations in the surface of the wall behind the cabinets. It's not uncommon to have areas of slight concavity or bulge.

To take this into account, use a long straightedge to assess the plane of the wall horizontally as well as vertically, before you start setting cabinets. Mark the point of greatest protrusion and base your cabinets' location on that; you can shim the others out so they'll line up. As with the height of the cabinets (in section 2, above), you can mark this position on the floor across the entire run of cabinets, then use it to guide their placement.

Where cabinets will be screwed to each other, as distinct from areas where they will be interrupted by a stove, dishwasher or fridge, it's often helpful to clamp, then screw them together once they are scribed to the floor (or shimmed up from it). Treating a row of cabinets as a unit will often simplify the process of shim-

ming them at the back wall so that you end up with an even plane across the faces.

Scribing

Rooms are virtually never square, level or plumb. Ceilings tend to sag toward the middle of their rooms; floors usually do the same. Plaster walls are rarely flat; drywall builds up at interior and exterior corners.

Designing built-ins is an art that takes contextual imperfections into account and makes dealing with them as easy as possible. A common way of handling these points of intersection between a cabinet and its surroundings is to cover them up with trim. Think cove moulding, quarter-round, shoe moulding, crown. Applied kicks are another example. But some historical styles call for minimal applied trim. In these cases, it's customary to handle the gaps between built-ins and their settings by scribing, a method of marking a built-in precisely so that it can be trimmed to fit its surroundings.

Here is a method for scribing a base cabinet to an adjacent wall and the floor. Note that in most real-life scenarios, we would not be installing a single cabinet, as we did here, but a bank of cabinets that are fastened together. The same basic principles apply in such cases.

1. Assess your surroundings

In an ideal world, we would start with an empty room – no carpet, furniture or existing built-ins. A clean space is the ideal situation in which to check the ceiling, floor and walls for plumb, level and square. Before heading to the drawing board, we would note the conditions outlined in the following paragraphs as a guide to planning the width of face frame members that might need to be scribed.

In reality, we usually have to assess a room's conditions while our customers (or family members) are still living in the space. That was the case with the kitchen in this example, as a result of which we encountered a couple of surprises during the cabinet installation.

Whatever the conditions when you start the process by measuring, you'll have the room cleared out by the time you're ready to install your built-ins.

Go big. For this sink base we used an 8' level to check the contour and slope of the floor at the back wall and also at the point where the front of the cabinet would land.

Check all planes. To gauge the slope of the floor from the cabinet's front to back, we used a 2' level. Note that we removed the floor protection temporarily, because it would have given us an inaccurate reading.

Use a level to check the status of the floor and walls. You're not just assessing whether the floor is level – it's probably not. Few are, so note the direction of slope and the amount of fall. You're also appraising the contour. Is the floor flat? Don't assume that it is. It may dip toward the center of the room or have high spots – for example, over a beam.

Check the floor at the back wall and at the point where the front of the cabinet will be. Cabinets, unlike drawings, exist in three dimensions; we need to take depth into account as well as width and height.

Do the same in the other direction, i.e. from the back wall to the front of the cabinet, assessing the floor at several spots along the width of the wall where the cabinet will go.

Now repeat the process with the walls at the back and side(s) of where your cabinet will go, holding a long level against the wall to see how plumb and flat it is.

Multiple levels are handy for installing cabinets. Here we used a long one across the cabinet's width and a short one across its depth at the same time.

2. Shim the cabinet level and plumb in the location where it will be installed

Use carpenter's shims to get the cabinet sitting level and plumb. You may need to move shims around, adding more than one and wiggling them back and forth until the cabinet is sitting level across its width and depth and plumb at its face.

Find the gaps. With our cabinet shimmed level and plumb, we found there was a gap at the wall (note the shadow line at the upper part of the left face frame stile).

Mind the gap. Trace the width of the gap on the cut shim.

3. Assess the gaps made by shimming

You probably now have a gap between the cabinet at the wall and another at the floor. The object of scribing is to remove the material that's causing those gaps. Although you're dealing with wood, not fabric, the process is analogous to that of fitting a piece of clothing to a model.

4. Make a scribing guide

With the cabinet shimmed level and plumb, make a scribing guide. You can use a log scribe or dividers, but usually I find it perfectly reasonable to make my own guide from a carpenter's shim. Find the widest part of the gap between the cabinet and the wall (or floor). Insert the thin end of a shim into the gap at this point, until it fills the space – don't push it in tight or you'll move the cabinet and end up with a scribing guide that's too thick. Mark this point on the shim with a pencil, then pull the shim back out and cut along the line with a utility knife.

5. Scribe

Now hold the cut end of the shim in place against the cabinet with one hand (see top right image), hold a pencil against it with the other hand, and in a smooth motion, trace the width of the gap from the

Simple scribe. To make a simple scribing guide I insert the thin end of a shim into the widest part of the gap between the cabinet side and the wall until the shim fills the gap. I mark that point across the shim with a pencil. The cut end of the shim is the scribing guide.

Roll over. We turned the cabinet on its back. You can see the line scribed on the bottom rail; it fades to nothing at the cabinet's right side.

Trim time. Plane the cabinet face frame to fit. If there's a lot of material to remove, you can start with a jigsaw, then clean up the line with a handplane.

A more sophisticated alternative. Mark used a Lee Valley log scribe, setting it to the widest point of the gap between the bottom of the cabinet kick (in this case, with a flush kick, this means the lower edge of the face frame's bottom rail) and the floor.

floor to the top of the face frame stile. When you reach the widest point of the gap – the point you used to make your guide – your line will die out to nothing.

6. Cut to fit

Turn the cabinet so that you can work on it as necessary, then plane down to your line. It's helpful to angle the cut toward the back of the cabinet, where the fit need not be as snug, to create a nice sharp edge at the front where the face frame meets the wall.

7. Proceed to the next plane

Push the cabinet tight against the wall and check the fit. Remove more material if necessary. When you have it fitting well, move on to the next step: the floor.

With the cabinet against the wall but still shimmed level and plumb, repeat the same basic process you used to scribe the face frame stile to the wall. You can use a shim, as we did in the example above, or a log scribe, as Mark did here. You can even use a pair of dividers. The basic principle is the same: You are extending a mark equal to the widest part of the gap all the way across the bottom of the face frame.

Step down. The small gap at the floor was created by a ledge left from floor sanding years ago. It was simplest to remove the ledge with a chisel.

Oscillating saw for the win. Mark used a Fein oscillating tool fitted with a coarse saw blade to trim the bottom of this cabinet side.

Time for the other side. We had determined at the start of the process that the same amount of material had to be removed at the back of the left side as at the front. Mark used a level as a straightedge to transfer this line from the front to the back of the left side, then removed the material with a jigsaw.

Who said no one uses hand tools on jobsites? Finish up by hand with a handplane.

Perfect fit.

When fitting a base cabinet to the floor, there are two parts to the process. First, the sides of the cabinet must be trimmed to conform to the floor across the cabinet's depth. We do this with a jigsaw or oscillating tool. Then comes the front of the cabinet, which in this case has a flush kick.

The cabinet sides will not show once the piece is installed, so there's no need for special finesse with those; you really just need to remove material. Nor do the sides need to sit firmly on the floor all the way from front to back; it's fine to have just a couple of sturdy sections (each at least an inch or so wide), one toward the front and one toward the back, making contact with the floor. That's plenty of support for most cabinets.

8. Cut again
Repeat the process of removing material as necessary.

9. Test the fit
Replace the cabinet and check the fit. Make sure that it is level and plumb. You may need a few more strokes of the plane to adjust the fit.

A Method for Making a Door

As with carcase construction, the world of door making encompasses great variation in materials and joinery. One of the kitchens in this book has painted plywood doors from the mid-20th century. These are made of veneer-core ply laid up tightly without voids (and in some cases joined with adhesives that have long since been banned). The edges are typically exposed, not finished with solid lippings or veneer, then rabbeted for half-inset application. I am not going to tell you how to make those here.

There are boarded doors joined by means of bracing at the back; you can see this kind of door in the kitchen on pages 244-247. Again, I am not going to tell you how to make this kind of door; there are instructions elsewhere (in Christian Becksvoort's "Shaker Inspiration," for one).

Other doors are slab-made. Solid slabs are made by joining several boards, just as with a tabletop, trimmed to size and hung with hinges. Slab doors today are most commonly made of plywood or MDF

Rusty inspiration. Inspired by a mid-century metal cabinet she'd spotted rusting in a garage, Lynette Breton made her kitchen cabinet doors in solid maple. She used quartersawn maple for stability, because she didn't want to rely on battens at the backs for reinforcement. The doors and drawer faces have proved surprisingly stable over the years.
MARGARET STEVENS-BECKSVOORT

with veneered or lipped edges and fully overlaid on top of face frames (or the front edges of frameless cabinets).

You can build a frame-and-panel door with traditional mortise-and-tenon joints, shop-made floating tenons, Dominos or dowels. You can use a rail-and-stile cutter set with a router table to make doors with a moulded frame (such as those in my kitchen on pages 186-193). You can even join rails and stiles with pocket screws or biscuits, though I wouldn't recommend doing so.

For this example we are going to make a flat panel door with mortise-and-tenon joints. The same basic technique can be used to make a door with a raised panel; just fit the panel with the protruding part facing the front of the door instead of the back, and raise the panel with a handplane, table saw or router.

Start by measuring the widths and heights of door openings. Make a list, clearly identifying which door will go where in relation to the cabinets.

For half-inset doors that will be rabbeted to fit

3/8" over the face frame, add about 5/16" on each side to the net opening sizes. In other words, if the opening is 15" wide by 28" high, you will make the door about 15-5/8" by 28-5/8". You might even want to go a little smaller. The key is to allow enough of a gap around the edges of the part that goes inside the face frame for the door to open and close. If you fit the door too tightly, you won't be able to operate it. Be sure you also factor in an appropriate allowance for seasonal movement and whichever finish you're going to apply. For example, if you're painting with primer followed by two coats of oil-based enamel, you'll need more space around the inset portion than if you're using a penetrating finish such as Osmo.

I usually make inset doors to the full opening size; this gives me enough material for fitting.

Cut the stiles to length and add a face mark, as well as an identifier for each part (such as "1 L" for door number one, left stile).

The doors for this kitchen have a 1/2"-deep groove

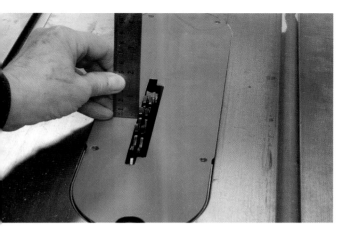

Start with the groove. I use a steel rule to check that the height of the dado set is 1/2", for a 1/2"-deep groove. You can use a digital gauge if you prefer. Make sure you measure to the top point of the alternating bevel teeth when the teeth are at their highest point in the blades' rotation. The groove need not be centered in the thickness of the parts, but centering it will make your life easier for some of the steps that follow.

hat's 5/16" wide, cut with a dado stack on the table aw. To determine the lengths of top and bottom ails, take your full door width (15") and subtract the vidth of the stiles, in this case 2-1/2" x 2 = 5" to get he net distance between the stiles, 10". Now add the llowance for your tenons. The traditional rule is that tenon's length should be two-thirds of the door's vidth, but for most kitchen doors I make tenons 1" ong. I have never had a problem caused by the rela- ively short tenon length, and it's one way to simpli- y a process that is full of potential for mathematical nd other errors.

Now cut the rails to length.

Set up the table saw blade and fence to groove the nside edges of all your stiles and rails.

Groove all your frame stock, keeping each piece ›ressed firmly against the table and fence. Use a ›ush stick to finish each cut.

Next lay out the mortises. One benefit to grooving he parts first is that the mortise position relative to he stile's face is already marked; just line the hol- ow chisel up with the groove. These doors will have ι haunch, a square cut-out at top and bottom to fill he groove, so the mortise will start 1/2" from each ›nd of the stile. When laying out the inside edge of

Lay out the mortises. I hold a rail precisely level with the end of the stile to determine the location of the mortise's inside edge. Then I square this point across all the stiles at top and bottom.

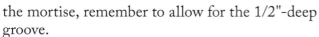

Easy does it. The groove makes it easy to set the mortise chisel, relative to the stile's face. Set the depth of cut a little deeper than the length of your mortise to save you the task of cleaning up the bottom. The joint gets most of its strength from the tenon cheeks, haunch and shoulders. The end grain at the tenon's tip is not important here.

Chop, chop. Chop all the mortises. If you don't have a full-size mortiser you can use a benchtop model or cut mortises with a router.

Direct measure. Set the dado stack at the correct height for cutting tenons by showing it to a grooved rail.

the mortise, remember to allow for the 1/2"-deep groove.

Finally, set the mortiser to cut to the chosen depth, in this case about 1-3/16" to allow for the rough bottom of the mortise. Then chop all the mortises.

The tenons will be cut on the table saw with a sliding miter gauge, a method I learned from Daniel O'Grady after years spent cutting tenons vertically with a tenoning jig. If you have a tenoning machine, as did the cabinet shops where I worked in England, congratulations.

To set the table saw for tenon cheeks, I start by placing a rail face-down on the table next to the dado stack so I can line up the tip of the outer blades' teeth to the groove's edge. The goal is to cut the tenon so it fits snugly; there should be a thin shaving left on the grooved section after you cut the cheek. (Steve Latta recommends cutting tenons

Fence for length. Set the table saw fence to determine the tenon length.

Trial cut. This is how my trial looked after the first pass across the blade. See the little bit of remaining waste at the shoulder? It's on the skimpy side. After this trial I moved the blade down a hair to reduce the amount of material I would be removing.

Fill that groove. To determine the top cut for the haunch that will fill the groove at each end of the stile, clamp a stile vertically in your vise and hold a tenon against it (not pictured). Square a line from the groove across the tenon. The lower edge of the tenon has already been made by the groove. Determine the top edge of the tenon by laying a tenon on the corresponding stile's edge.

last thing in the day, then leaving them overnight. The newly exposed material when you cut the tenon cheeks will lose a bit of moisture; he says the tenon will fit perfectly in the morning.)

Next set the fence to determine the tenon's length. For a 1"-long tenon cut with a 5/16" dado stack, I set the fence at 11/16" from the blade's far edge, i.e. the edge that will make the shoulder.

Test the set-up on a scrap piece. Start by laying the scrap "rail" against the miter gauge fence and slide it toward the blade (when the saw is still off) about 1/4". Turn the saw on and move the piece forward, keeping the "rail" firmly against the fence.

Repeat the cut until the end of the scrap tenon is touching the rip fence, at which point you will have a 1"-long tenon.

Cut the face cheek of all your tenons, then repeat the set-up for the back cheek. (If your groove is centered in the rails and stiles, you shouldn't need to change the set-up.) Test the cut on your scrap rail and make sure it fits before you cut the back cheeks on your workpieces.

When all your cheeks are cut, move on to the haunches. You can cut these at the table saw using the miter gauge, but I prefer to cut them by hand.

I cut the haunches with a tenon saw.

Check the fit and trim if necessary.

Measure each door for its panel and cut the pan-

Test clamp. Fit the door parts together dry to make sure they go together as they should.

Preserve panel thickness. The rabbet will be 1/2" deep so that there's about a 1/8" margin around the protruding part of the panel when the edges have been set 3/8" deep into the groove on each side. To determine the width of the rabbet, lay the panel on edge with its front face flush with the front edge of the groove. The amount protruding at the back must be removed, leaving a scant 5/16" to fit into the groove.

els to size. Be sure to allow for seasonal expansion or contraction depending on prevailing conditions. For a 1/2"-deep groove I typically allow 3/8" of panel on each side.

The panels for this kitchen are rabbeted so that they fit into the 5/16"-wide grooves. I cut the rabbets on the table saw in two cuts.

Check the fit and trim as necessary. Dry-fit each panel into its frame before gluing; this is especially important if your doors are different sizes. Before assembly, sand the front face of the panel. If the back of the panel will not be flush with the back of the frame, sand it, too.

Apply glue to the tenons. Take care not to get glue on the panel edges as you set them into the frame parts.

Fitting an Inset Door

This door is going to hang on traditional butt hinges. The width of the gap around the door should be

Depth first. Set up the depth of the rabbet with a steel rule. Be sure to include the thickness of the blade. For the first cut, I run the panels flat on the table with each edge in sequence against the rip fence.

Assembly time. Clamp, then check for square and twist.

Width second. After the first cut I adjust the height of the blade to remove the waste, leaving a 5/16"-thick tongue. I set up a featherboard to keep the panel firmly against the fence while I make the cut.

Guiding rails. For this kitchen, I aligned the hinge mortises with the top and bottom door rails.

the same on all sides, which means you have to factor in this space when setting up the mortise for your hinge leaves.

Start by laying the door in its opening with the hinge stile and bottom rail against the face frame. If the bottom of the door does not lie flat on the bottom rail of the face frame, note the width of the triangular gap at one end and make a mark at the other end. (Say the gap at the opening edge is 1/16" high when the hinge edge sits flat on the bottom edge of the face frame. You're going to make a mark 1/16" up from the bottom of the hinge stile on the door.) Extend a straight line from the corner of the opening edge to the mark on the hinge stile, then trim down to this with a handplane.

When the hinge stile and bottom rail of the door are firmly in contact with the face frame, insert a shim beneath it equal in thickness to the gap you want around the door. For painted kitchen cabinets I use a pair of pennies; for finer work, a pair of dimes. With the door on these shims, look at the top rail. Will it fit inside the opening, or is it still too tall? If it's too tall, make a mark on the edge of the hinge stile and opening stile indicating the point of contact with the face frame, then extend a line between them and trim until this third edge of the door will go into the opening.

The final edge to trim is the opening stile. This edge will be trimmed at a slight angle toward the back (i.e. the inside of the cabinet), to allow for the

Clean cut. Severing the grain by scoring with a knife will prevent breakout.

Gauge the width. Use a marking gauge to lay out the width for the hinge leaves.

Gauged. Depending on the type of butt hinge you're using your leaf layout should look at least something like this.

Gauge two. Set to the mortise depth – the distance from the edge of the barrel to the center of the pin, minus one-half of your desired reveal.

Chop it out. Use a wide chisel to chop the waste across the grain for easy removal.

slight arc the edge will go through when the door is hinged.

When the door fits the opening, mark the location of the top and bottom hinge on the door, using a hinge to transfer the top and bottom points onto the door face. Then square these marks around the hinge edge of the stile.

Score the ends with a marking knife.

Set a marking gauge to the hinge leaf width. When using extruded butt hinges such as these, the measurement should go from the edge of the leaf to approximately the center of the pin.

Now use the marking gauge to score the door edge.

Set a second marking gauge to the depth of the mortise, which will be equal to the distance from the edge of the barrel to the center of the pin, minus half the amount of the gap you want to end up with. This is a critical measurement, as it will determine the size of the gap between the hinge stile of the door and the face frame.

Gauge this line on the face of the door between the end marks.

Use a 3/4" or wider chisel and a wooden mallet to break up the long grain between the outside ends of the mortise.

Waste removal. Use a wide chisel to remove the material you just broke up. Pare carefully as you near the gauge line on the door's face.

What I'm talkin' 'bout. This is what you're aiming for at this stage: a mortise that is mostly cleaned out but still has a bit of material left at the ends, back edge and on the door face.

Crisp and clean. One down, quite a few more to go.

Next use a wide chisel to remove most of the waste.

Pare out the remaining waste, taking care to avoid blowing out the thin ledge at the back. Check the fit by inserting a hinge leaf and remove more material if necessary. When the leaf fits, drill the outer two holes with a Vix bit and insert screws that are the same size or slightly smaller than those you will be using for the final installation. Leaving one hole yet to drill allows you the option of adjusting the hinge position by slightly enlarging the mortise, if necessary.

After you have mortised the door edge, shim the door in its opening and transfer the hinge positions to the face frame.

Repeat the steps above to cut the mortises in the face frame. At this stage I like to keep my options open for final fitting after the cabinets have been installed, so I use just one screw per hinge to attach the door to the face frame. For the most accurate representation of how the door fits, use the top hole of the upper hinge and the bottom hole of the lower one.

Set in place. Lay the door in its opening with your preferred shims at the bottom (I often use dimes or pennies, depending on how large a space I want around the perimeter), then mark the position of the hinge's top and bottom with a knife.

Time to remove more waste. If you can lift the cabinet onto a bench, do so. This one was too unwieldy for me to lift alone, so I worked on the floor.

Hang it. Done (for now).

Drawers

The overwhelming majority of kitchen cabinet drawers today are mounted on mechanical slides. These slides come in a wide variety of forms designed for different purposes. The two types I now use most often are Blum Tandem and Accuride 3832. Each type of slide requires specific accommodations in the dimensions of drawer parts, so it's crucial that you get the appropriate installation information and follow it closely.

Blum Tandem slides can be fastened to the sides of the carcase or at the front and back by means of a rear mounting bracket. They are full-extension, operate silently and are hidden in the cavity beneath the drawer bottom, which makes them invisible in use. They also offer vertical, lateral and tilt adjustability, which makes them especially attractive for drawers with inset faces.

The Accuride 3832 is a side-mounted slide with full-extension, ball bearing operation.

The kitchen in this example called for Blum Tandem slides, so the method that follows will refer to those.

Rabbeted Drawer with Wire Nails

About 15 years ago I was shown the specs for a house that was to be built through a local affordable housing program. Looking through the kitchen specs, I noticed that the cabinets were required to have dovetailed drawers.

A little knowledge can be a dangerous thing. I'm not suggesting that the beneficiaries of affordable housing programs deserve cabinets or other house parts of lower quality, but that this is a good case of some well-intentioned professional imagining that dovetails are the only joinery good enough for durable drawer construction.

It's just not so. Contemporary kitchen cabinets, whether mass-produced or custom built, typically have drawers mounted on mechanical slides that run so smoothly there's no friction to stress the joints. The primary structural need is for joinery capable of resisting the force on the joints between the drawer front and sides when a drawer filled with heavy contents is pulled open and pushed shut.

Fence for width. Set the fence to produce the width of the rabbet.

Blade height for thickness. Set the blade height.

Cut away. Make the first cut using a sliding miter fence.

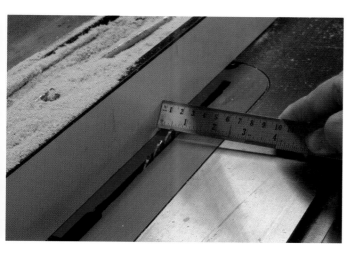

Time for grooves. Set the rip fence for the bottom grooves in the drawer sides and front.

Multiple passes. Cut the grooves in repeated passes. When adjusting the fence, be sure you maintain any distance below the groove that your slides require.

While dovetails are ideal for this, they are not the only appropriate joint. A drawer made with biscuits or shop-made splines joining the front and back to sides that extend the entire length of the drawer will work fine. So will a drawer made with rabbets and wire nails, as in the following example.

At one shop where I worked, the foreman did an experiment comparing a drawer made with dovetails and one made with biscuits. Each drawer was glued and clamped; there were no nails to reinforce the biscuit joints. For worst-case scenario value, he tested each drawer by dropping it to the floor so that it fell on a corner. The dovetails out-performed the biscuits. So if you are planning to take your drawers out and throw them around the kitchen, you should definitely consider dovetails.

For what it's worth, I have nothing against dovetails, whether hand-cut or made by machine. I simply have a problem with dogma and conceitedness, both of which seem to attach themselves to dovetails like iron filings to a magnet. Most of my kitchens have dovetailed drawers. There's a universe of literature available on how to cut dovetails, whether half-blind or exposed, with a router and jig, so the editors and I decided not to reproduce that information here.

If you want a quick, durable joint that also happens to be historically appropriate for early 20th-century kitchens, here's one way to build a drawer.

Mill your drawer parts, cutting the parts to size based on how your drawers will be mounted. If you're using wooden runners, you have virtually no limitations. If you're using mechanical slides, follow the hardware manufacturer's specs.

After cutting the parts to size, rabbet the sides. I do this at the table saw using a Forrest finger joint blade that's ground to produce a groove with a flat bottom. The rabbet will be as wide as the thickness of the drawer face and back – in the case of my drawers here, 1/2". Don't measure; simply use the drawer part to set the fence.

Now set the blade height. I wanted to remove 5/16", leaving a lip of 3/16".

Use a sliding miter fence to make the cuts. Always keep the stock firmly against the fence for safety.

After cutting the rabbets in the front and back

Treat the waste as the workpiece. When ripping the back to width, use a push stick to support the offcut. Do not push the drawer back itself, as doing so can cause injury.

Sample Charts on Installing Blum Drawer Hardware

Calculating outside drawer width					
For drawer side thickness	**16** (5/8")	**15** (19/32")	**14** (9/16")	**13** (1/2")	**12** (15/32")
Deduct from opening width	**10** (13/32")	**557** (21-15/16")	**12** (15/32")	**16** (5/8")	**18** (23/32")
Example: For 21" opening width and a 5/8"-thick drawer, 21" minus 13/32" = 20-19/32" drawer width					

TANDEM plus BLUMOTION	Cabinet depth	Minimum inside cabinet depth	Drawer length	Maximum drawer thickness	Runner length
563H5330B	**610** (24")	**557** (21-15/16")	**533** (21")	**16** (5/8")	**548** (21-9/16")
563.5330B	**610** (24")	**557** (21-15/16")	**533** (21")	**16** (5/8")	**548** (21-9/16")
563H4570B	**533** (21")	**480** (18-29/32")	**457** (18")	**16** (5/8")	**471** (18-17/32")
563.4570B	**533** (21")	**480** (18-29/32")	**457** (18")	**16** (5/8")	**471** (18-17/32")
563H3810B	**457** (18")	**404** (15-29/32")	**381** (15")	**16** (5/8")	**395** (15-9/16")
563H3050B	**381** (15")	**328** (12-29/32")	**305** (12")	**16** (5/8")	**319** (12-9/16")
563H2290B10	**305** (12")	**266** (10-15/32")	**229** (9")	**16** (5/8")	**259** (10-3/16")

ends of the sides, use the same blade to cut the grooves for the bottom. My drawers will run on Blum Tandem slides, so the lower edge of the groove (i.e. the underside of the drawer's plywood bottom) has to be 1/2" up from the lower edge of the drawer sides and front. Depending on the size of your blade (mine is 1/8"), you may need to do this in two or more passes. Be sure you keep the bottom edge of each drawer part against the fence, otherwise you'll have a drawer with a lid instead of a bottom. Don't waste time grooving the back of the drawer; in this type of drawer construction, the back will be ripped so that the drawer bottom can be slid into the grooved sides and front.

To rip the back to width, keep the blade and fence at the same setting. Cut the first pass with the fence set as you had it for the top edge of the groove, then turn the drawer back over, keeping the lower edge against the fence, and use a push stick on the "waste" for safety. If you're only making one drawer, you can simply raise the height of the blade instead, but if you're doing multiple drawers you may want to keep the setting for other parts. (In my case, I was making several drawers with 1/4" ply bottoms and two with 1/2" bottoms, so I wanted to keep the setting for the 1/2" bottoms but wanted to complete the grooving and ripping for the other drawers so I could start gluing them up.)

When assembling the drawers, glue both edges of the rabbet. I glue these drawer boxes upside-down on the bench, for reasons that will become obvious when you try this method, and I clamp in both directions – lengthwise and widthwise.

When the glue has set, drill pilot holes for wire nails, then hammer them in. I use a simple technique my instructors called "dovetail nailing," in which the pilot holes are alternating angles like those of dovetails. If the glue should fail, the angled nails will resist pulling out.

Because this cabinet was made for a client who wanted a drawer with extra vertical capacity – and we wanted to keep the proportions of the drawer and door as you see them here – I made a false drawer rail that attaches to the half-inset drawer face. You can make the drawer faces before or after you make the drawers; what's critical is that you install the slides at the appropriate distance in from

False drawer rail maintains the look. To give this drawer extra interior height while preserving the horizontal line of its neighbor, I made the drawer rail beneath it part of the drawer face.

Sleight of hand. The drawer face with false rail attached.

Getting jiggy. I use a shop-made template to locate the slides at the requisite distance behind the face frame.

From the top. For cabinets with more than one drawer, I start by installing the top pair of slides. To hold them at the right height and keep them square to the face, which should be square to the cabinet floor, I cut scrap 3/4" plywood, stand the plywood on the cabinet floor against the carcase side and lay the slide on the top edge. When I have inserted two screws in each of the slides at this height (one near the front, the other near the back), I cut the scrap plywood to whatever length I need for the next drawer down. The last slides to go in are those that rest on the cabinet floor.

the cabinet face, depending on which kind of face you use.

For half-inset drawer faces such as these, Blum recommends mounting the slides 14mm in from the cabinet face. I made a simple jig to set the spacing.

Most kitchens I build have drawer boxes dovetailed with a Keller dovetail jig. Although the Keller cuts fronts and backs with one jig and sides with another, which means it takes longer than jigs that dovetail the sides, fronts and backs at the same time, I prefer the proportions of the resulting dovetails. Keller jigs come with clear step-by-step instructions. I am not going to explain their use here. The following images show a drawer made for a different kitchen, this time in Baltic birch plywood, rabbeted and fastened with glue and wire nails – a method

used widely for drawer construction in the early and mid-20th century.

Applying the Faces

Here I'm going to switch to a different kitchen with drawer boxes made of 1/2"-thick Baltic birch plywood joined with rabbets and nails for economy. This kitchen has full-overlay drawer faces, but the method for applying them is the same as that for inset faces; for inset faces you just have the added step of fitting the face to the opening as you would for an inset door.

At this point you've installed the drawer slide hardware and drilled the boxes for the rear tilt

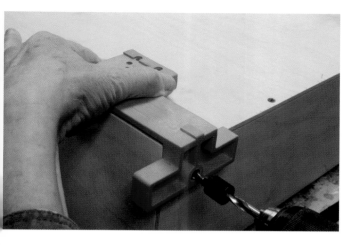

Prepare to attach the hardware. After you have assembled the drawers you need to drill them in two locations on each side. A jig supplied by Blum locates the position of holes for the rear tilt device.

Room for adjustment. Locking devices at the front of the drawer box are attached with screws. These allow for vertical and lateral adjustment.

mechanism and locking devices at the front. Put the drawer boxes into the cabinet.

One quick note: If your drawer faces will be inset, the front surface of the drawer box should be set behind the outside of the face frame by the thickness of the drawer face. If your faces are going to be half-inset, the front of the drawer box should be about 3/8" in (in other words, it should be set back from the outside of the face frame by however much your inset is). If your faces will be full-overlay, the front of the drawer box should be roughly even with the outside of the face frame.

The toughest part of applying a drawer face is holding it in place long enough so you can fasten it. If you have a helper, you're home free; he or she

Ready for faces. This stack of drawers will have full-overlay faces. Note that there are no intermediate face frame rails, as this is a more contemporary kitchen design.

About face. In most cases I apply the drawer faces long before the customer has moved in, but I did this kitchen for Sherry Holliday and Eric Mitter in stages. After drilling holes, I removed some of the drawers' contents and vacuumed out the dust.

can hold the face against the drawer box for you. If you're working alone, you can use double-sided carpet tape. Another method is to drill two holes of 3/8" or 1/2" diameter and apply the faces initially with panhead screws run through fender washers; this is handy because it allows you to make more adjustments to the drawer face than the Tandem hardware allows. In either case, it's best to clamp the face to the box so you can run in a couple of screws. I start with just two screws, in case I need to remove them and reposition the face.

When you have applied all the drawer faces you can fine-tune the fit, then drill for and install the final screws. Most drawers I build have solid-wood boxes and solid faces, so I don't worry too much

about problems caused by expansion and contraction. If you are attaching a plain-sawn face, especially if it's more than 5" wide (i.e. high, in the world of drawers), to a plywood drawer box, you should make provisions to allow for wood movement. You can do this by fastening the face with wood screws at whichever point is critical to the fit (top, bottom or center), then use panhead screws and fender washers with oversized holes to hold the face in position at other points.

I generally use four wood screws per small or medium drawer face. Drawers of 20" or more in width get another set in the middle of the width. If the drawer is 8" or more tall, I add a third screw at the center of the height to keep it flat.

Attractive and well planned. This corner of Bert Gilbert and Amy Dyken's kitchen is light, inviting and makes intelligent use of space.

4

Designer-Builder Beware

Experience, especially when it's hard, is the most effective teacher. For makers, it's galling to arrive with the cabinets on installation day only to find that the corner unit's too large to squeeze through the door. And for cooks, there's a world of difference between a kitchen with dark corners and wasted space, and one that's carefully planned for practicality and comfort. Here are 22 lessons I've learned the hard way.

1. Plan for Perspective

Drawings may be flat on the screen or page, but as adult humans, most of us see furniture and cabinets from the perspective of 3' to 7' above the floor. Ignore this perspective and your work will appear unhinged from gravity-bound reality.

My first woodworking employer, Roy Griffiths, came to furniture design with a background in fine arts and antique restoration. One of the first lessons Roy taught me was the importance of perspective. Explaining the proportions of a prototype kitchen cabinet door, he pointed out that the bottom rail was made from wider stock than that of the top rail and stiles, a device he compared to the tradition of the fine art framers' world of mat making. If you cut the mat evenly all around, he explained, the bottom section will appear narrower than the rest, which will give the viewer a subtle sense of unease. Mat heavier at the bottom.

The most graphic example of the perceptual phenomenon underlying this rule is the stack of kitchen drawers in which every drawer face is the same width (i.e. from top to bottom). The bottom drawer will look narrower than the others.

Another good example is cabinet doors and drawers with pulls that are centered. If you put a door knob in the actual center of a lower door's height, it will appear to be below the center; the same applies to drawer pulls. This rule also comes into play in upper cabinet doors with divided lights; space all your muntins evenly, and the bottom lights will appear shorter than the rest. In laying out hardware, muntins and similar elements, unless I'm following a particular example (such as when I'm adding cabinets to match existing originals), I will stand back and look at the piece in question from the perspective of a kitchen's user. If you're working with someone else, have him or her look, too.

While this general rule applies to door frame members, whether they will be above or below eye level, the opposite applies to certain other elements

You aren't graduating. Drawer cabinet with equal-width fronts.

ASTRID DRESSER, COURTESY OF NORSE INTERIORS

of cabinet design. Rules of classical proportion hold that some elements, such as crown moulding and cornices, should grow as they near the ceiling.

On the other hand, all rules have their exceptions. Some styles, especially in the mid- to late 20th century – when mass production, with its overwhelming regard for efficiency, was king – come with their own rules regarding proportions. What count as pleasing proportions will vary according to style, and sometimes that subtle sense of unease or outright jarring is key to capturing the essence of a particular look (as some of the more ponderous examples of Arts & Crafts furniture will attest). Just be sure you take perspective into consideration, rather than overlooking it or ignoring it on the grounds that it's not realistic to contemplate making a whole kitchen's-worth of doors with different-sized parts.

2. Inside Corners: You Really Can't Have it All

One of my stranger findings from years of working with clients to redesign their kitchens is that people will guard their cubic footage like an angry vulture with a road-killed skunk. Suggest they leave some portion of the space unused and they break into a cold sweat.

Most of the kitchens I work in are small, typically in older houses. That's my niche. My usual brief is to create a kitchen with 21st-century functionality in a space that was originally for servants whose comfort and aesthetic preferences were immaterial to those who planned the room. In later kitchens, those from the early 20th century, I'm often faced with a space that's small and shut off from other rooms so that women, who almost always were the ones doing the cooking, could work efficiently while sparing their families the realities of sausage-making. Transforming spatially challenged kitchens into rooms that function well and are a pleasure to work in has been my bread and butter, so I understand the potential value of every cubic inch.

But space comes in different varieties. Some space is primo – easy to reach and fitted with shelves or drawers that are appropriate for what you need to store. Some space is less than ideal for general-purpose storage but works brilliantly for specific items (think top cupboards in kitchens where the cabinets go all the way up to the 10' ceiling – the perfect spot to store that chafing dish you use just once a year). And then there's the kind of space you're arguably better off without: the kind that demands the moves you last performed at the age of 8 in a game of Twister. Agility and core strength are certainly worth cultivating, but there are better ways to apply them than navigating the dark recesses of a base cabinet to retrieve a can of baking powder that fell off the lazy Susan.

The problem with most inside corners is simple: There's a small opening into a large space. In prac-

It's lazy alright. Lazy Susans come in several configurations. This one is affixed to the backs of the doors, which rotate with the shelves inside the cabinet.
REV-A-SHELF

tice, this means you can easily get to things at the front, but beyond those first few plates and glasses you use on a daily basis, let's just say that's where you'll find the sippy cups from when your college-age daughter was a child, along with six insulated coffee mugs embossed with your electrician's logo and the "Eat Drink & Be Married" can cooler from a cousin's wedding.

Numerous specialty fixtures exist to help you utilize inside corners, especially in base cabinets, where

Two doors in one. Sometimes a bi-fold door is just the ticket for a small corner cabinet. The cabinet has two doors, but instead of being hinged independently, they are hinged together so that the doors fold back on each other and open as one. This cabinet, in the kitchen of Richard and Joy Harter, uses European hinges. You can achieve the same basic result with a length of piano hinge.

You lead; I'll follow. This corner has a lazy Susan accessed by opening two doors. In this case, the one hinged on the left is the primary door; once it's open, the user can reach in and open the one that's hinged on the right.

so much cubic footage is at risk. Here's a quick run-through (though it's not exhaustive).

The lazy Susan, which comes in a variety of forms (among them full round, kidney, pie-cut and D), is the most common solution for inside corners of base cabinets. These can be installed in various ways.

Pie-cut Susans are designed for installation on the backs of doors, in which case the doors spin around inside the cabinet with the lazy Susan. Kidney Susans spin around independently of each other.

Bi-fold doors offer another option for access to inside corners. A primary door is hinged on one side of the face frame, with a secondary door attached to it by a piano hinge or European-style hinge. Depending on your circumstances, you can fit the cabinet interior with shelves or a lazy Susan.

In some instances, two separate doors, hinged so that they open independently, can work well in layouts where one opening is wide enough to offer plentiful access to the interior and the other is nar-

row. In this case it's usually best to make the wider-side door the primary door, which allows access to most of the interior most of the time. This treatment really comes into its own for upper cabinets, which are typically shallower than base units and so make more sense with shelves.

For shallow upper cabinets it was long customary to span the corner diagonally, with a door hinged at 45°. The drawback here is that the opening is tiny, while the space inside the cabinet is much larger. In practice this means you have to remove the things at the front to reach those farther back.

There are also half-moon Susans that pivot on a central bar, then pull out a few more inches on slides. (See the case study on page 80.) Another popular option today is to install a stack of corner drawers that look like they've been punched in the stomach with a hockey stick; these are fitted into the corner cabinet so that they pull straight toward you when you're facing the corner.

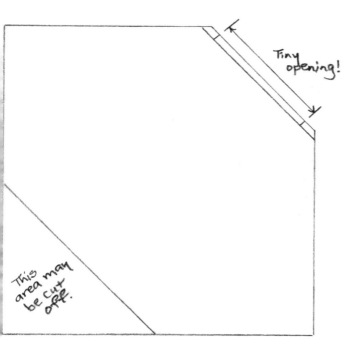

Tiny opening!

This area may be cut off.

Cavernous interior, tiny opening. Inside corners deserve careful planning. It's exasperating to know the bowl you need is at the bottom of a stack behind a mountain of pots and pans, each one of which you'll have to extract through the narrow doorway while kneeling on the floor.

Here, diagonally. Corner drawers are one solution to inside corners, but the amount of genuinely useful space they offer is lower than you might imagine.
KRAFTMAID CABINETRY

The ultimate inside-corner solution in the world of cabinet hardware is the "Magic Corner," with four trays that allow you to maximize storage in a blind corner.[7]

In analyzing what's best for your particular situation, you should start by considering the variables – the depth of the cabinet and the width of the potential opening on each side of the corner. Another important variable is whether the wall at the back of the cabinet can be accessed from an adjacent room. More on this last one later.

For now, let's reboot. Corner units don't have to conform to standard dimensions. In most kitchens, if you're building the cabinets yourself, you have the opportunity to build to custom dimensions.

One way to maximize efficiency is to build your own lazy Susan cabinet following a now-antiquated pattern in which circular shelves rotate within a circular carcase. Some manufacturers use thin fiberboard to make the carcase "back," which is af-

Cantilevered cabinetry. For blind corners, space optimizers such as this one make it far easier to reach things at the back that would otherwise require spelunking.
PHOTO COURTESY OF KESSEBOHMER

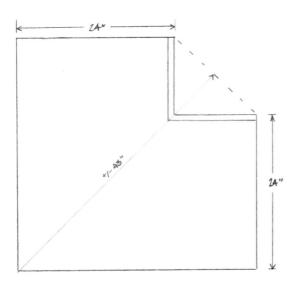

Inefficient. Many conventional lazy Susan base cabinets are 24" deep x 36" long, with doors approximately 12" wide (whether the doors are hinged independently or hinged together as a bi-fold). Note that even without deductions for the thickness of sides, back etc., each tier of this cabinet in the best of circumstances will offer at most 8 square feet.

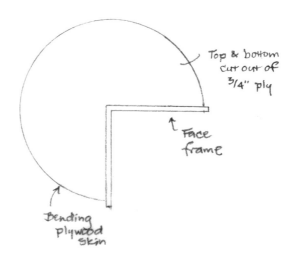

Mid-century marvel. Mid-century lazy Susans were often built as 3/4-round cabinets with a square face frame. You can build your own to this model using a standard pie-cut Susan.

fixed to a circular floor and top; bending plywood would also work. The advantage: Stuff can't fall off the edge, because the shelves go all the way to the back. However, as the rough drawing on page 82 illustrates, even this solution doesn't utilize as much of the available space as it may seem to; in a cabinet that's 36" x 36" to allow for just under a 12"-wide opening on each flank of the front, the full-round lazy Susan gives you access to about half the potential space in the "dead" corner.

Why not trade quantity for quality? If you're building your own cabinets or having them custom-built, you probably don't have to stick with a 12"-wide opening for each flank of the corner. You may have 14" on one side and 22-5/32" on the other. Perhaps the 14"-wide cabinet could be used to store trays and baking sheets with a narrow drawer above. On the other hand, even 14" is enough width for a stack of drawers, depending on what you need to store. And at 22-5/32", the other side of the corner is certainly large enough for drawers. One crucial caveat: Make sure your face frame stiles are wide enough to allow the drawers to bypass each other when you open them — and take the protrusion of the drawer pulls into account when making this calculation.

A (Literal) Case Study

I documented the modifications I made to the blind corner cabinet in my own kitchen. I had originally fitted the cabinet with a half-moon lazy Susan that rotated, then pulled out partway – not because I really wanted one of these fixtures, but because I thought I should try it out, so I could give future clients my informed opinion.

The half-moon Susan worked adequately. Because these fixtures are made to pull partway out through the cabinet door, you have to base the size of the fixture you're going to install on the width of the door opening. If the opening is relatively narrow (mine was 15") and you're installing the fixture in a cabinet with a standard depth of 24", you're going to see a lot of wasted space.

When I removed the cabinets to refinish them a few years ago, I dispensed with the half-moon Susan and retrofitted the cabinet with a set of carefully planned drawers. Everything that used to be stored on the two lazy Susan trays now fits into three drawers. (The middle two drawer faces are actually one face for a drawer tall enough to accommodate the coffee maker while keeping the proportions of the faces attractive.)

Taking stock. The contents of the two-tier half-round lazy Susan: coffee maker and related items (filters, coffee, etc.); baking stuff; boxes of tea; and a block of steak knives that someone gave my husband years ago (our equivalent of the long-unused sippy cup, considering that we never cook steak at home).

Unused space revealed. Here's the half-moon lazy Susan, about to be removed. You can see how much of the cabinet's interior was not being used.

Tea on top. The shallow drawer has more than enough room for all of our boxes of tea (left). The coffee drawer stores a coffee maker and ceramic filter cone, boxes of coffee filters and bags of beans (right).

As for the space in the corner between the mobile bakeware cabinet and the three new drawers – it's empty. If the pantry/mudroom on the other side of this wall had allowed, we would have created a built-in accessible from that room to use the wasted space; that's a trick I learned years ago from paying attention to architectural details in old houses. It's by far the most satisfactory way to utilize the space in an interior corner. Yet even without using that space we have every bit as much usable area now as we did before. The difference is that now it's a pleasure to use instead of a pain.

Baking goods below. The many smaller containers of such ingredients as almond essence, vanilla and baking powder are secure within the bounds of a drawer, whereas they routinely fell over the edge of the lazy Susan trays.

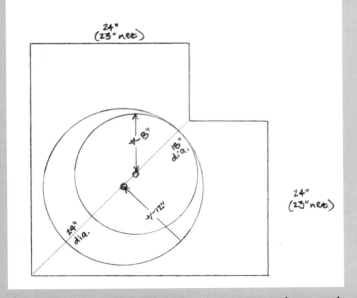

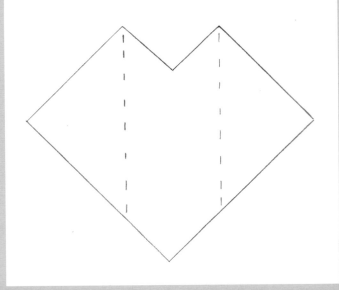

Not lazy, but less productive than you might believe. *A comparison of potentially versus actually useful space in a three-tier full-round Susan cabinet.*

Waste not. *Corner drawers may promise efficient storage, but they still deliver vastly less usable space than the cubic footage they typically take up.*

Geometrical Analyses of Typical Storage Solutions for Inside Corners

Say you have a standard 24"-deep cabinet with a counter 36" high that has 12" of width (overall) on each side of the corner. The precise cubic footage available will vary depending on how high the cabinet floor is, whether the doors and drawers are inset, the thickness of the counter, and whether the back has been angled off at 45° to allow the cabinet to fit through standard interior doors, which you shouldn't assume will be more than 32" wide. To make things simple for this thought experiment I'll use 23" for the depth x 30" for the usable height and assume that the back corner of the cabinet has not been angled off. This means the basic area of the cabinet floor will be between 1,000 and 1,150 square inches, give or take, depending on the dimensions of specific details.

Now let's say you install a three-tier 18"-diameter full-circle Lazy Susan in this cabinet. This will give you 254 square inches x 3 = 762 square inches of usable storage space.

The support post in the middle means that you can only store items that are no more than 8" wide in one direction. Also, you will need to determine the heights of the two upper shelves, which will then in effect be fixed.

"I'd up that to a 22"-diameter fixture," you object. OK, so that will give you a total of about 380 square inches per tier – 760 for two tiers or 1,140 for three.

You'll still have to take account of the post in the mid-

dle, which limits the size of objects you can store.

Let's compare this with a 24" pie-cut Susan with two tiers for the same size cabinet. Depending on the design of the unit, this will offer a maximum of about 402 square inches per tier, or 804 square inches in total.

The advantage of this one is that you can store taller items, but you will have just two tiers, and they will be fixed.

At this point you may be wondering why we don't routinely just put one or two big shelves in such cabinets and be done with it; that would certainly yield the maximum usable storage space. The reason, of course, is that with a small access area, reaching the stuff in the cabinet becomes a nightmare. Not only do you have to get on your hands and knees; you also have to pull out half the cabinet's contents to reach the stuff at the back.

Compare this scenario with the V-shaped/gut-punched drawers. Let's say you have four drawers.

In the end, the amount of usable space is no better. Drawers on full-extension slides allow full access to their contents, and if you make the back of the drawer V-shaped, echoing the front, you can even avoid wasting the triangle formed by a conventional square back. But even in a fantasyland where face frames and other cabinet parts don't eat up potentially usable space, you still end up using less than half of what's available.

Clearance. The left stile of the drawer cabinet's face frame is wider than the others to allow the drawers to clear the dishwasher handle. I considered making the face frame stile narrower for the lower drawers, where the dishwasher handle is not an issue, but it would have complicated the construction of this already-capacious cabinet more than it would have been worth.

3. Avoid Blockages

Pay close attention to inside corners where adjacent drawers, doors or dishwasher doors could be blocked. It's easy to factor in the protrusion of handles, only to discover, when your installation's complete, that a drawer won't open because the oven handle on the neighboring stove sticks out too far.

Pull away. I added a narrow stile at the right of the stove to make sure the oven door would clear the protrusion of adjacent drawer pulls.

Clearances vary. This fridge with a single wide door needs more than a foot of space on the hinge side in order to open sufficiently to allow the drawer to open. It's critical to design the area around a fridge so that you can open the fridge door (or doors) enough to remove drawers for cleaning.

4. Leave Room to Breathe

Fridges need space for air circulation, and microwave ovens produce steam. Always consult the appliance manufacturer's specs for recommended ventilation allowances.

When fitting cabinets and measuring for counters on either side of a stove, don't be tempted to go for zero clearance. At some point down the line you're going to have to pull the stove out for maintenance, repair or replacement. A little wiggle room – 1/16" to 1/8" on each side – will make your life easier and help keep you from damaging the appliance when you scoot it out. As for leaving no gap between the counters and the stove on the grounds that there won't be room for crumbs and spills, think again. In practice, the crumbs and spilled liquids will simply be wedged so tightly in place that you won't be able to clean them up.

5. I Need My Space

There's a fine line between too big, too small and just right. Kitchens are full of operable elements. Cabinet doors open. Drawers pull out – and a drawer that slides on a 21"- or 23"-long full-extension slide, the most common sizes in Blum Tandem and Accuride 3832 slides, respectively, come out a long way when fully open. Chairs around a kitchen table may be tucked in when not in use, but when an adult is sitting in them they can easily stick out nearly 24". Even if you don't have chairs around your island, it likely has its own protruding parts, such as drawers. If you want to be able to have your dishwasher door open while unloading the mixing bowls you want to stack in the pull-out straight across from it, you'll need to take into account the space occupied by those elements when they are in use.

Our kitchen is undeniably too small for the table at its center. Whoever is sitting on the sink side of the room has to move her chair in order for me to open the drawers that store the dish towels and napkins. We deal with it. We knew the table was too big for the room when we moved it in, so we were prepared for the inconvenience. But when you have the luxury of reworking a kitchen from scratch you should take the size of the room into account when designing central features such as islands or tables.

On the other hand, having too much space between work areas comes with its own inconvenience. Ideally you should be able to pick something up from one surface and reach the surface where you're headed without taking many steps – in fact, this is one of the reasons to have a central work table or island in the first place. Don't make the mistake of assuming it's better to have 5' or 6' between such features and the nearest counter unless there is a compelling reason to have this much space.

Beyond the cabinets, fridge and freezer doors need room to open fully. Always consult the manufacturer's installation guide; otherwise you may find that a door won't open far enough to allow you to pull out a vegetable drawer for cleaning. Better yet, read the installation guide, then experiment with how much space the appliance really needs to function fully once you have it on hand, before you build the cabinets…which leads me to the next point.

"Do as I say, not as I do." Our kitchen is arguably too small for two people. "Sorry, but I need you to move so I can get an extra napkin out of that drawer behind you" is an oft-heard statement.

Vintage ventilation. Mid-century sink bases were often built with dummy panels pierced with contemporary patterns to allow for air flow, preventing the cabinet interior from getting moldy – or worse, rotting.

6. Beware of Published Specs

Published specs and installation guides are a good starting point, but don't trust them without verifying critical dimensions in person at the jobsite. Specs are sometimes wrong. Even when they're right, they can change; manufacturers are constantly modifying designs to improve production efficiency as well as their products' performance. Have appliances, fixtures and sinks on hand before you start cutting materials. Yes, you may have to live with a stove and fridge in the garage for a few months (or stomach their company in your living room). It's worth the inconvenience to save the hundreds or thousands of dollars, not to mention delays, that can result when cabinets and counters have to be redone in the wake of discovering that despite your meticulous planning, some part of the puzzle isn't going to fit.

7. Don't be a Dummy

Fake drawer faces, sometimes known as "dummy panels," have long been standard on sink cabinets – a way to hide the basin on the inside of the cabinet while continuing the horizontal line of a top drawer that's standard in base units. Dummy panels are usually static, fixed in place. Some cabinetmakers mount them on hinges or stays that allow the panel to be pulled open and fitted with slim-profile containers to store sponges and other sink-related items, a nice idea in theory, but some of these containers end up being more effective at collecting smelly old sponges and grime than offering worthwhile storage space.

In some cases it's simpler and more cost-effective to forgo the panel and just build the doors for the sink base full height. Also, I've found that plumbers appreciate every inch of accessible space they can get.

Think about whether a dummy panel or fold-out will really enhance the aesthetic and functionality of your kitchen before assuming you need one.

An old angle. The overhang of this granite counter is supported by angled brackets spaced according to the stone fabricator's specifications.

8. Counter Support

Counters require site- and material-specific types of support. In general, the thicker the material, the greater the distance you can expect to span without support.

Some types of stone (or stone composites) need more support than others for overhangs on islands or peninsulas. One means of support is to add a 1/4"-thick (or thicker) length of flat steel, working on the principle of a cantilever. Rout a recess for the steel into the top of the cabinet so the steel is flush with the surface of the top, then screw it in firmly at several points along its length.

In other cases you may need steel angle; the flat portion can be routed into the top of the cabinet carcase, with a slot cut by hand for the vertical part.

Sometimes an angled bracket made of wood, aluminum or steel is the best choice, though you should think about how they may impinge on your knee room before you decide to install brackets.

Solid-wood counters need other kinds of support in addition to those that prevent breakage and sagging of overhanging spans. See the section on counters in "Elements of Design" for wood-specific information.

Be sure you consult the seller of the materials you're using for their advice. Otherwise, should the stone break or the butcher block split, you may find the warranty void.

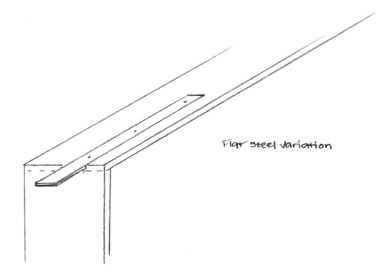

Flat steel variation

Stealth support. In cases where you don't want the visual intrusion of brackets, consider a length of 1/4"- or 5/16"-thick flat steel to cantilever the countertop. (I buy steel from a local welding shop.) This method depends on firm attachment to the carcase, so in such cases I build the base cabinet with a full veneer-core plywood top, instead of strips. I recess the steel in a routed groove so it lies flush with the top of the plywood, then screw it in place. Depending on how much support you require, you may need to reinforce the plywood top with a strip of solid wood below, inside the cabinet; you should use at least two strips of steel for a counter 25" deep and may need more for a top that's deeper.

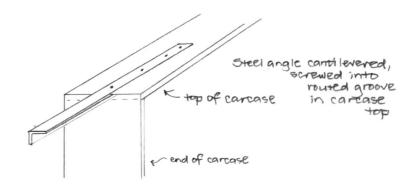

Steel angle cantilevered, screwed into routed groove in carcase top

← top of carcase

← end of carcase

Extra rigid. In some cases you may need more rigidity than flat steel can provide. A variation on the steel support method is to use steel angle, installing it as you would flat steel, but with an added notch in the carcase side for the vertical section. The obvious drawback here is that the vertical portion of the angle may be visible, depending on the counter's location.

Go low. Large items such as pots, pans and appliances are so much easier to lift out of a drawer, and then replace, when drawer sides are lower than their faces.

9. Lower Your Drawer Sides

Consider what will go into a drawer or pull-out tray before you build it. Objects stacked too high can fall out and get trapped behind a drawer, preventing it from closing fully; if a drawer is going to hold a lot of smaller items (or Tupperware, which many people tend to store in a jumble rather than organize with care), think about building the drawer with high sides. On the other hand, large items don't need high sides to keep them in place. In fact, high sides are a liability when you're lifting a tall pasta pot or bulky food processor. In these cases, drawer sides may only need to come up 3" or 4" above the drawer bottom.

10. Nominal Versus Actual Dimensions

The nominal size of a piece of hardware is not necessarily its actual size. A 24" Blum Tandem drawer slide should logically fit inside a 24"-deep base cabinet, right? Nope. The dimension refers to the net size of the drawer box, before you add a separate face. Also, don't forget to factor in the thickness of your cabinet's back, in most cases at least 1/4".

Beyond this, with Blum Tandem slides the hardware protrudes another 3/8" or so behind the back of the drawer. So in reality, the longest Tandem slide you can use in a 24" cabinet is the 21" model. If it's critical that your drawer be deeper, use a different type of slide; for example, Accuride 3832 slides come in 2" increments that allow you to use a 22" slide on a drawer with an inset face in a cabinet that's 24" deep.

On the other hand, if you want a drawer box that's 24" deep (bear in mind that this will be the drawer box's outside dimensions, yielding an inside depth of approximately 23", depending on the thickness of your drawer box's sides, front and back), increase your cabinet's depth to allow for it. Just bear in mind that this will affect counters and may have a bearing on nearby appliances.

11. Avoid Unattractive Surprises in Cabinets with Glazed Doors

When building cabinets that will have glass in the doors or at the sides, think about how the internal hardware is going to fit. Do you really want that massive 165° European hinge (or electrical transformer for undercabinet lighting) showing through the glass in the doors?

12. Plan for Reality

Walls, floors and ceilings are rarely level, square or plumb. Drywall mud builds up in corners. Plan your cabinets with face frames and other elements that allow you to scribe them to fit or provide enough surface to attach a moulding that will conceal the gap. (For more on scribing, Chapter 3.)

Uninviting. Unless you are a child (or a dog or cat), cramped spaces that are dark and awkward to use, such as the corner section of counter here, will tend to go unused. Wherever possible, avoid creating them.

13. Avoid Siberia

Don't design spaces that are uninviting – small, dark and hard to reach due to protruding chimney breasts or appliances.

The contents come to you. When Lee Sandweiss filled these drawers, she remarked that it was a pleasure not to have to hunt around inside a base cabinet, as she had for years previously.

14. Drawers Below

Full-extension hardware makes drawers the most ergonomic solution for 24"-deep base cabinets. No more getting on your hands and knees to search through piles of stuff on shelves.

Base cabinets that are shallower than normal may be reasonable candidates for doors with shelves, especially in cabinets that store large items such as baking sheets or mixing bowls.

Stow it in the overhead bin. Denise Gaul incorporated a cabinet over her fridge in plane with the pantry section to the right, minimizing the apparent depth of a cabinet that's extraordinarily capacious.
DENISE GAUL

15. Go Deep Over the Fridge

The long-standing convention of putting a 12" upper cabinet over a fridge is stupid. People invariably put things in front of the doors, preventing them from opening. If you're going to install a cabinet above a fridge, make it close to the depth of the fridge. A deep cabinet over the fridge can be a great place to store large items such as trays and baking sheets, which you can reach from the front without needing a step stool. It's also a good place to keep things you rarely use.

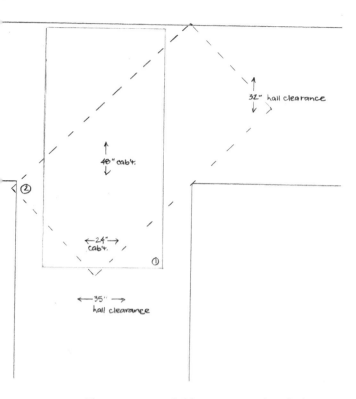

Plan your route. Cabinets are not bendy-buses.

16. Consider Delivery

Will your cabinets fit through the existing doorways? This is especially important with corner units, which tend to be extra deep. There's a reason why commercial corner bases are mitered off at the back.

Measure all doorways, taking account of the thickness of doors (which may have to be removed) and pay special attention in cases where your route may involve dog-leg turns, such as the end of a hallway. Design the cabinets accordingly, or you may need to perform surgery on the jobsite.

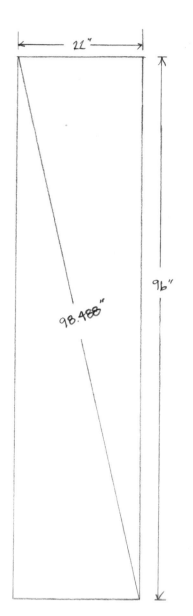

Height matters. You cannot tilt a 96"-high cabinet into a 96"-high space.

17. Pythagoras Rules

Just because you have, say, 96" available from the floor to the ceiling does not mean you can make a 96"-high cabinet. When you go to stand that cabinet up, the hypotenuse will exceed the ceiling height. If you have to maximize your use of vertical space without an opening between the base and upper cabinets, it's better to build in two or more sections. Install the base first, then stack the other units on top. This way you can lift them to the required height and slide them in.

Learn from my mistake. Because of how we installed this pantry cabinet, I was left with a face frame stile at the far end in this image that was too narrow to accommodate the full width of these hinges' leaves. I had to trim them with a hacksaw and file.

LAURI HAFVENSTEIN

18. Decorative Surface-mounted Hinges Take Up Space

Make sure you allow enough width on the face frame and door stile to accommodate them. Otherwise you will have to trim them with a file or hacksaw.

19. Shelves Have Thickness

Don't forget to take into account the thickness of shelves, drawer cabinet face frame rails and the like. It's easy to think the entire inside vertical space of a cabinet you're going to fit with shelves will be available for storage. It won't. If the combined height of your olive oil bottle, peanut butter jar and box of Cream of Wheat, each of which you plan to store on its own shelf, is 28" and you've designed a cabinet with a 28-1/4" tall interior, you're in for a rude surprise. Whether you're using 1/4"-thick glass shelves in a shallow spice cabinet or 3/4"-plywood shelves with appropriately sized solid lippings for pantry goods, you must take the shelves' thickness into account. And while you're at it, give yourself a few inches of extra vertical space to make it easier to reach things.

20. Drawer Slides & Other Hardware Require Vertical & Side Space

Pay attention to hardware specs. Blum Tandem drawer slides, for example, require a 1/2"-vertical cavity between the underside of a drawer bottom and the lower edge of the drawer sides and face. Also, as in Nos. 18 and 19, drawer bottoms occupy space. When designing drawers to accommodate particular items, such as pasta pots, spice inserts or appliances, take these dimensions into account.

21. Glass is Fragile

Avoid putting glazed doors in locations where they are likely to be broken. In general, it's advisable to avoid base cabinets with glazed doors. It's also a good idea not to put glazed doors where they are liable to be hit by the knob of a room door.

When you design with glass, consult local codes (or at least a knowledgeable professional at your glass supply store) regarding the thickness and type of glass you should use for specific applications, whether single strength, 1/8", tempered or other.

Finally, when ordering glass for cabinet shelves, ask to have the edges ground for safety.

22. Hidden 'Treasures' & Be Ready to Think on Your Feet

Everything seems to be going smoothly on the job until it isn't. In an ideal world, we would gut the room before measuring for the new cabinets and starting to build them. In reality, we often have to design the job, and even start building the cabinets, while the existing kitchen is still intact, because the homeowner would (understandably) prefer to minimize the length of time she'll have to cook in a Crock Pot and wash dishes in the bathtub.

I often wish I had X-ray vision; then I'd know about the supply pipe hiding in the wall where I'm drilling holes to attach my cabinet to the studs – the pipe some hapless former homeowner decided to notch into the studs just behind the drywall instead of running it through holes at the center of the studs' width, per convention. Did I mention that she or he also neglected to add a protective plate to keep my drill bit from piercing said pipe and leading to a soggy mess?

My current job was moving along swimmingly until this morning, when I heard from the carpenter handling demolition and other aspects of the job. Having removed the last bank of cabinets, which housed the kitchen sink, he discovered that the oak floor, which is staying in place, was laid up to the toe kicks of the previous cabinets instead of all the way across the room. The new cabinet design called for a deeper toe kick, so there would be a gap – more like a chasm, really – between the toe kick and the floor. Fortunately I still had the cabinets in the shop, so it was a simple matter to move the nailer for the toe kick forward on each of the base cabinet sides.

That panned out. Jan Bulla-Baker and her husband, Jack Baker, bought this pot rack for $8 at a yard sale many years ago. Suspended above the kitchen table, it makes a handsome and hardworking focal point.

Max out. The original owners of this kitchen, Carol and Roger Parks, needed more space than usual to store their impressive stock of international spices and herbs. This cabinet is roughly 3' wide by 8' high and stores jars one-deep. Carol suggested the lacquer red interior.
SPECTRUM CREATIVE GROUP

5

Elements of Design

Mention the word "kitchen" and the image that pops into most minds will be a fixed set of built-in cabinets with a sink, stove and fridge wedged in. But kitchens vary widely in their composition. Before the 20th century (and to this day, in many parts of the world), "kitchen" was, in effect, less noun than verb – more about the activity of food preparation than a space dedicated to that work. In the majority of homes (i.e., not those of the wealthy), a kitchen was a cluster of working furniture in the midst of un-

Fit for the Gilded Age. Butler's pantry at the home of Mark Twain's family in Hartford, Conn.

THE MARK TWAIN HOUSE & MUSEUM, HARTFORD, CONN.
PHOTO BY JOHN GROO

differentiated living space – a table, a basin or dry sink, some pegs for hanging utensils, a bin or two for sugar and flour - the primary locating factor being the presence of a hearth. If you were lucky, you might own a pie safe. Electricity? Gas? Indoor plumbing? Stop with the humor. Even today many a kitchen is made with freestanding furniture, rather than built-ins. This chapter will help you consider the pieces that make up the puzzle.

1. Freestanding Cabinets Versus Built-ins

Though many people imagine that kitchens have always been synonymous with built-in (or in Britain, "fitted") cabinets, built-ins have been the norm for only a little over a century.[8] Built-ins certainly existed in the mid- and late-19th century, but they were assembled on site and largely limited to butlers' pantries in wealthy households or institutions such as clubs. Other forms of built-ins found in earlier kitchens are presses – shallow cabinets fitted with shelves behind doors, such as those found in the communal kitchens of Shaker residences.

The kitchen cabinets most people think of today

Press fit. Kitchens at Shaker settlements, such as this one in Pleasant Hill, were typically furnished with freestanding pieces such as those here. The red cupboard is a form known as a press; recessed into the wall, it is fitted with interior shelves and doors.

PAM WATTENBARGER

are descendants of those manufactured by companies that specialized in architectural millwork in the early 20th century. These companies made everything a builder might wish to incorporate into a house – door and window trim, baseboards, crown moulding, telephone niches, china cabinets, interior and exterior doors and cabinets for kitchens. What spurred the development of built-ins was the realization that cabinets could be made in modular form, which allowed them to be assembled in all sorts of arrangements, depending on the dimensions and layout of a room. Economies of scale in using materials, as well as efficient manufacturing processes developed leading up to the turn of the century,

made modular cabinetry, built into the kitchen, the norm, as it remains to this day.

But just because built-in cabinets are the norm doesn't mean you have to have them. You could instead furnish your kitchen with freestanding pieces such as those found in a pioneer kitchen – a wooden coffer for dry goods, a pie safe (useful for storing anything you would ordinarily keep on shelves in a shallow cupboard), a large worktable – add drawers for handy storage – and a sink cabinet or sink on legs.

Alternatively, you may want to consider a kitchen that combines freestanding pieces with built-ins, as kitchen designer Johnny Grey has done in so many of the kitchens his firm has designed.

KITCHEN CUPBOARD U2816

IT WOULD be difficult to arrange a more convenient working space than suggested in this design. The large work table is directly beneath the windows, with cupboards, drawers, tilting bin and sink within easy reach. Even the space above windows is utilized for storage cabinet. A breakfast nook as suggested will save many steps.

Complete cupboard includes design as illustrated (except windows and room trim), with doors glazed D. S. glass, three adjustable shelves in upper section, one shelf in each bottom compartment and over broom closet, tilting bin and one bread board. Countershelf $1\frac{1}{16}''$ thick. Length along right wall, including broom closet, 7–6. Angle forming work table projects 4–6, and section over windows extends about 6–10. Height to top of countershelf 2–10, open space above 1–2. Depth of top compartments 1–1, broom closet 1–3, and bottom sections 1–8. No backs included unless specially ordered. Furnished for standard 8–6 ceiling, if no other height is given. Hardware never supplied. Made of any wood and other sizes. Always furnished unpainted.

Measurements given are outside body sizes and do not include projection of mouldings and countershelf.

FOR COMPLETE PRICE INFORMATION SEE UNIVERSAL PRICE SUPPLEMENT.

[258]

Catalog copy. Historic millwork catalogs such as those published by the Universal Catalog Bureau are a rich record of modular built-ins' early years.
UNIVERSAL MILLWORK CATALOG 1927

Furnished with antiques. For the kitchen of her pre-Civil War house in rural Indiana, Edith Sarra kept things unfitted, combining elements from the decades after her home was built. The double-drainboard sink is part of a cabinet built by her carpenter, Ben Sturbaum, of Golden Hands Construction. Simple shelves hold spices, utensils, mugs and dish towels. A vintage tablecloth covers an old painted table and another smaller table beneath a window provides additional prep space. The cabinet at right is a late-19th-century antique that stores a variety of kitchen items. A recessed press (a shallow set of shelves behind doors, original to the house but not visible here) holds additional goods. The stove here is also an antique. The fridge (not visible) is a retro style model from Big Chill.
SPECTRUM CREATIVE GROUP

Unfitted par excellence. This kitchen by designer Johnny Grey combines built-in cabinets with a multi-section island and free-standing furniture for lounging or dining.
BENEDICT GREY PHOTOGRAPHY

Hoosier. The battle between freestanding furniture and built-ins was fought fiercely by the makers of Hoosier cabinets in the early 20th century. Manufacturers such as The Hoosier Manufacturing Company, Sellers and Coppes claimed that their cabinets consolidated storage and preparation areas to make the ideal furnishing for the kitchen. They marketed the cabinets as more modern than site-constructed built-ins that had preceded them, and when modular cabinets were introduced to the home-building industry, these companies countered that their cabinets were a better investment because you could take them with you when you moved.

This cabinet is one I made in solid elm salvaged from the City of Bloomington Urban Forester's "No Log Left Behind" program. The design is based on an original Napanee Dutch Kitchenet. The counter is made of locally quarried limestone that I darkened by rubbing a slurry of water and black tinting powder into the porous stone. After the first coat had dried, I rubbed in a second, and when that was dry I coated the stone with mineral oil, allowing it to soak in before wiping off the excess.
SPECTRUM CREATIVE GROUP

Toylike appeal. The late Patsy Powell grew up with this Hoosier cabinet, which belonged to her mother. She learned to read by playing with the "Need List" on the open door; its shiny red buttons slide from a column with a list of kitchen staples to one titled "Need."
SPECTRUM CREATIVE GROUP

Freestanding or built-in? Although most of the cabinets in this kitchen are fitted, the base and upper at the left of the sink area are designed to look similar but not identical to the others. This decision was prompted by the challenge of making an L-shaped inside corner on the mahogany counter; a miter would potentially have opened up over time, while running the short leg of the L across the grain of the main sink counter would eventually have resulted in an irregular surface due to wood movement. The solution chosen by Tasha Vorderstrasse and Brian Muhs was to make the short leg of the L a separate counter and modify the details of its companion base and upper cabinets to make this section of the kitchen seem as though it had been added at a different time from the rest.

The kitchen also has genuinely freestanding elements: a worktable over the radiator, a baker's cabinet (see page 322) and an antique scrollsaw table used for breakfast.
SPECTRUM CREATIVE GROUP

Open corner. Although I could have made a built-in for this corner of our kitchen, I chose a steel and glass cabinet instead, to give the small room a more spacious feel.

Kitchen workbench. David Berman uses an antique workbench with swing-out seats as a kitchen island.
DAVID BERMAN, TRUSTWORTH STUDIOS

Shallow storage. A long wall in our former kitchen had previously been covered with a 4' x 8' sheet of softboard to display family pictures, postcards and children's art – sweet, but not a great use of space. I built this set of 12"-deep cabinets that combine open shelves with doors below that hide mixing bowls, less attractive kitchenware and small appliances. The base of the center section comes out a few more inches and is fitted with drawers.
The counter is elm.
SPECTRUM CREATIVE GROUP

1927 Inspiration. In our former kitchen there was a short L-shaped run of built-ins between the stove and the fridge. At the left of the stove I built this cabinet based on early 20th-century millwork catalog examples. Made in red oak with dye, stain and shellac under oil-based polyurethane, it has a solid-wood counter. The back of the upper section is papered with "Bamboo" wallpaper from Trustworth Studios. Door and drawer hardware came from Rejuvenation. And yes, those wires for the undercabinet lighting are just hanging loose; we hadn't yet installed the fixture when this photo was taken.
SPECTRUM CREATIVE GROUP

Island ancestor. Historically, the kitchen worktable was an indispensable element of kitchens – from primitive frontier cabins to fashionable upscale homes, such as this one at Standen in Sussex, England.
©NATIONAL TRUST IMAGES MICHAEL CALDWELL

2. Islands & Peninsulas

Before built-in cabinets became the norm, kitchen work typically centered on a worktable, with or without drawers built into the apron. Some worktables also had a low built-in shelf. Nineteenth-century worktables usually had solid-wood tops; many in the early 20th century had enameled steel, which is durable and easy to clean. In kitchens used by servants, worktables were also places for those workers to eat meals; the same went for farm hands in rural locations.

Contrary to widely circulated claims, islands are not descended from the Hoosier cabinet. It's more accurate to say that the kitchen island and Hoosier cabi-

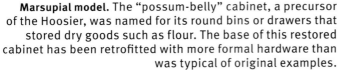

Marsupial model. The "possum-belly" cabinet, a precursor of the Hoosier, was named for its round bins or drawers that stored dry goods such as flour. The base of this restored cabinet has been retrofitted with more formal hardware than was typical of original examples.

COURTESY OF CORY NEWMAN

Gathering place. An island on legs in the kitchen of Bert Gilbert and Amy Dyken hides a microwave. Also on the stove-facing side are drawers for onions and potatoes, hot pads and storage for cutting boards. With a counter of polished black granite purchased at discount (it had been cut the wrong size for another job), the island provides a great serving area when friends gather in the kitchen.

net share a common ancestor, the possum-belly cabinet or table, which combined a work surface with one or two semi-circular bins below for storing flour and sugar. But why stop with the possum-belly table when we have plentiful examples of earlier kitchen worktables that combined drawers and sometimes a spacious lower shelf with a counter at which to chop, slice, mix, knead and roll?

Today's islands typically provide enclosed storage, as well as work space; some even house sinks, dishwashers and other appliances. Some people also use their island as a place to eat.

An island can be made as a freestanding piece of furniture designed with work and storage in mind or an arrangement of cabinets that would ordinarily be built in, topped with a counter.

Whether or not you use it for taking meals, a central table or island can be an excellent way to bridge the distance between the stove and fridge, as well as increase work space. It can also be a good way to share the kitchen with friends while preserving the main prep space for the cook.

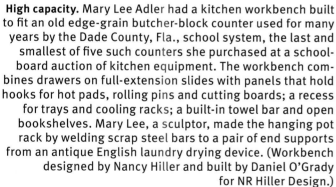

High capacity. Mary Lee Adler had a kitchen workbench built to fit an old edge-grain butcher-block counter used for many years by the Dade County, Fla., school system, the last and smallest of five such counters she purchased at a school-board auction of kitchen equipment. The workbench combines drawers on full-extension slides with panels that hold hooks for hot pads, rolling pins and cutting boards; a recess for trays and cooling racks; a built-in towel bar and open bookshelves. Mary Lee, a sculptor, made the hanging pot rack by welding scrap steel bars to a pair of end supports from an antique English laundry drying device. (Workbench designed by Nancy Hiller and built by Daniel O'Grady for NR Hiller Design.)

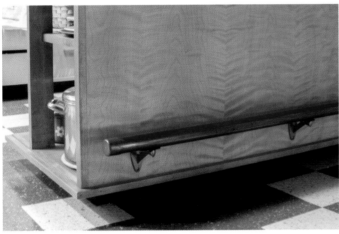

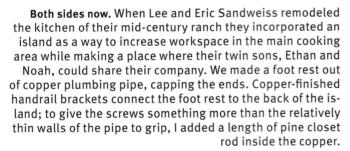

Both sides now. When Lee and Eric Sandweiss remodeled the kitchen of their mid-century ranch they incorporated an island as a way to increase workspace in the main cooking area while making a place where their twin sons, Ethan and Noah, could share their company. We made a foot rest out of copper plumbing pipe, capping the ends. Copper-finished handrail brackets connect the foot rest to the back of the island; to give the screws something more than the relatively thin walls of the pipe to grip, I added a length of pine closet rod inside the copper.

Drawers without faces on the working side of the island, which faces the stove and sink, make it easy for Lee and Eric to see their contents.

Good fences. In the kitchen of Fritz Lieber and Donald Maxwell, a peninsula keeps guests from interfering with cooks, while allowing everyone to share the same basic space. The base cabinet has an integral finished end panel, its left stile mitered lengthwise for a seamless joint with the back. Open shelves with hidden lighting add useful and attractive detail to the back, while a door at the far left provides storage.

On the cook's side of the cabinet the kick space is partially recessed, with face frame stiles extending to the floor. The end and back, which are not working areas, have flush kicks.
SPECTRUM CREATIVE GROUP

Storage & workspace. Ann Marie Thomson and Jim Calli wanted a worktable for their kitchen that would fit the aesthetic of the existing cabinets while enhancing their storage and prep space. The overhang on the public side gives Jim a place to pull up a chair while Ann Marie chops and mixes. (She's the cook. He is grateful.) I made the table in cherry.

The small room just off the kitchen was designed for guests who want to hang out with the cook; it keeps them far enough away for Ann Marie to work without being crowded.

SPECTRUM CREATIVE GROUP

Industrial inspiration. Audim Culver and Ivy Siosi of Siosi Design + Build based their Ama Island on a salvaged heat shrink-packaging machine that they adapted as an island in their own kitchen. The top is edge-grain ambrosia maple butcher block with a waterfall edge and food-safe finish; the base is powder-coated 12-gauge steel.

SIOSI DESIGN + BUILD

Isle royale. The centerpiece of Sherry Holliday and Eric Mitter's kitchen is a 102" by 40" island with a sink, dishwasher, bookcase, sitting area and plenty of workspace on the honed granite counter.

Double-duty dining table. Our last house had no separate dining room, so when I reworked the kitchen I took out the huge island that invited piles of clutter and replaced it with an informal cherry table. Two drawers in the apron on the side facing the sink held silverware and knives. I finished the top with three coats of oil-based polyurethane followed by paste wax, which makes a seriously durable finish. (Contrary to widespread opinion, when polyurethane is applied in thin coats with an appropriate brush it doesn't look like plastic.) To keep the top from being scratched and dented we put a clean dish towel under a wooden board for chopping, mixing or pulping persimmons.

SPECTRUM CREATIVE GROUP

Choreographed heights. When kitchen designer Johnny Grey and his wife, Becca, turned a former garage into their kitchen, they incorporated an island with different heights and counter materials appropriate to each area. A lower section with a granite counter is an ideal place to use a mortar and pestle or tall appliance such as a food processor. The working side of the island incorporates a cooktop with a ceiling-mounted exhaust hood; a maple chopping block is next to the stove, with storage below.

BENEDICT GREY PHOTOGRAPHY

Techniques
Build a Simple Island

Including the countertop overhangs, this island would be 102" long by about 40" deep. To keep the cost down, I planned it as an assemblage of basic cabinets that would be screwed to the floor, then pulled together with a back and end panel. In other circumstances I would have made the back and end with solid frame-and-panel construction, mitering the corners for a neat appearance. But plain-sawn red oak beadboard was a far more cost-effective option in this case. I suggested we run it horizontally to avoid any 1980s country associations.

I made the sink base-cum-drawer base and a separate bookcase in my shop. The clients picked them up, along with the beadboard, counter support brackets and other parts, then took them home to finish. Here are the steps I took to put everything together.

1. Determine the location

I measured the distance from the nearest adjacent wall to the centerline of the middle window, then measured that distance out from the same wall at the approximate location for the island, then marked the spot with masking tape. The architect had specified a distance of 48" between the edges of the counter that will go on the main wall of built-ins and the counter on the island. The cabinets that would go on the stove wall would be 24" deep, so allowing for a 1" overhang, that meant I needed to measure out from the rear wall 25" + 48" + 1" for the overhang of the island counter, to determine the position of the sink cabinet's front. I marked that, too, on the floor with tape.

2. Mark and drill holes for plumbing pipes

Next I marked the centerline of the drain pipe in the cabinet's depth (i.e., front to back), basing my calculations on the position where the front of the cabinet would land. (See Step 1.)

Chuck a hole saw in your drill. The diameter of the hole should be slightly larger than that of the pipe. It's best to avoid making the hole too large, as mice and other pests can squeeze through and gain entry to the cabinet's interior.

Ready, set, go. *The builder had stubbed in the supply lines and the drain pipe so the drain would be centered on the window. I marked the centerline of the sink base on the cabinet floor using a framing square.*

On target. *If you look closely you'll see the spot where the long line intersects with the short horizontal line, marking the center of the hole for the drain pipe.*

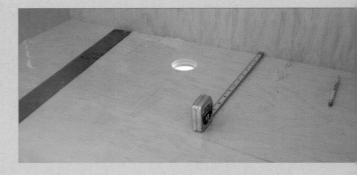

On to the supplies. *Because the drain in this kitchen was going to come up through the floor (and not through a wall behind the sink base), I was able to use the center of the drain as a reference to locate holes for the supply lines.*

Make room for supply lines. *After drilling for the drain, I used a smaller hole saw for the supplies. A lighted drill makes this kind of work so much easier.*

Parallel lines. *Pay attention to any lines in the floor, whether those of floorboards, grout lines between tile or patterns in sheet flooring.*

Through the side. *Sometimes the best way to affix a cabinet is simply to run a screw through the side and into the floor, as in this case.*

Tip: Put a scrap of plywood beneath the cabinet in case your drill bit goes a little too enthusiastically through the cabinet floor.

Next I measured from the center of the drain pipe to the center of the cold supply line and marked that spot on the cabinet floor. I repeated this step with the hot supply line, then drilled both holes, using a hole saw of the appropriate diameter.

3. Set the sink base

Sherry and I lifted the sink base over the plumbing lines and asked the tile setter to come and guide the cabinet into place, since we couldn't see over the top of the sides into the cabinet. Depending on the kind of pipe, it's important to avoid bending or hitting water supply lines, because they can break.

Once we had set the sink base over the pipes, I measured the distance from the cabinet's back edge to the nearest floorboard joint, making sure the cabinet was parallel with the floor. Few things look worse than a cabinet that's markedly out of alignment with the joints between floorboards or tile.

I drilled and countersank a couple of holes through each end of the base cabinet to attach it to the floor. The end visible above would be covered by the bookshelf unit. The other end would be hidden by the dishwasher.

4. Add the next cabinet(s)

Clamp adjacent cabinets in place to hold them securely while you drill and insert screws. Again, to keep the cost of this job as low as possible, I simply screwed through the back of the bookcase into the end of the sink base. As you can see below, I built the drawer base into the same unit as the sink, to conserve materials; the drawer base is between the sink and the bookcase.

To hide the joint between the sink base and the bookcase, and mark the transition from the working part of the island to the more leisurely end that will greet people coming in from the porch, I had a piece of simple rectangular trim milled. I cut it to length and fastened it with brads.

5. Dishwasher panel

In an ideal world there would be a wall or another cabinet to hide the dishwasher, but in this case I had

Building blocks. *Once the sink base was in, I clamped and screwed the other elements of the island to it.*

Easy transition. *I milled square trim to hide the joint between the sink base and the bookcase next to it. On the back of the island I applied a similar-looking trim that I rabbeted to accept the horizontal tongue and groove boards; the trim also does a nice job of concealing those boards' ends.*

Hidden dishwasher. *To make a quick and simple enclosure, I fastened a matching panel to the floor with L brackets, then cut rails to hold the upper end of the panel equidistant from the sink base.*

Parallel lines, again. *A framing square ensures that the dishwasher panel is square to the flooring.*

planned to install a panel. I had added a piece of face frame material to the front edge of the panel to make it look like part of the island instead of an afterthought.

Measure the width of the dishwasher and mark it on the floor. In this case I measured 24" from the protruding edge of the face frame, which created a cavity more like 24-1/2" wide. (Obviously if you have protruding trim such as this and allow just 24" between the panel and the sink base, the opening will be too small for the dishwasher to fit.)

To make the front of the dishwasher panel in line with the front of the sink base I measured from the nearest flooring joint to the front of each and marked the position on a piece of masking tape.

I used angle brackets to fasten the panel to the floor. Screw the brackets to the panel first, then to the floor.

I measured the distance from the sink base to the dishwasher panel at the floor, NOT at the top of the panel, because I know from experience that corner brackets like these cannot be counted on to hold things square. To the contrary; they tend to pull things inward at less than 90°.

I cut a piece of 2 x 4 to the measurement I had made at floor level, then wedged it into place at the upper back of the dishwasher cavity. To secure it temporarily, I shot in a couple of 2" brads.

Finally, I drilled into the 2 x 4 spacer from the interior of the sink base and inserted a couple of screws.

6. Finish materials tie the parts together

I milled a couple of trim pieces to finish the ends of the beadboard. Each trim piece had a rabbet into which the beadboard would slide; this made for a neat finish, in addition to holding the beadboard tightly against the cabinets. (Remember, there was not a whole lot of solid meat to nail the beadboard onto in this case.)

I cut the first piece of end trim (bottom image, right) to length and fixed it in place with 18-gauge brads. I set the end trim loosely in place at the other end so that I could measure for the length of the beadboard, then cut the beadboard for the back to length and simply laid one piece on top of another, fastening them in place with 22-gauge pins.

Next I cut the beadboard for the dishwasher end panel to length and set it in place. Another rabbeted piece of end trim would conceal the cut-off ends at the front of the dishwasher panel.

Double check. *A straightedge (in this case, a 4-foot level) ensures that the front edge of the panel is in plane with that of the sink base.*

Ready for action. *After confirming that all the parts were where they should be, I attached the panel to the sink base at its top.*

You can't be too careful. *One final check is always a good idea, this time to ensure the panel was plumb.*

Time for trim. *Rabbeted end pieces hide the cut ends of the tongue and groove.*

Rough & ready. *The trim I made to hold the beadboard in place at the dishwasher panel end is rabbeted in one direction and grooved in the other, to hold both sections neatly. I cut the rabbets and groove on the table saw.*

Almost there. *Shims inserted to build out the back of the cabinetry at floor level so that the beadboard would lay flat are still visible here. Final touches will include simple rectangular trim at floor level to conceal these shims and give the beadboard a more finished look.*

7. Support brackets for the counter

My clients had asked the counter supplier whether additional support would be needed for the 12" overhang at the back and dishwasher end of the island. Based on the supplier's recommendation, I made up three very simple brackets that combine speed of assembly (remember: affordability!) with strength and reinforce the house's overall architect-modern take on a barn aesthetic. A Domino tenon joins the vertical and horizontal parts at the rear; the angled brace is glued and held in place with #8 twin-thread screws. I centered the brackets on the beadboard section of the back, drilled through the cabinet backs into the brackets, and inserted #8 twin-thread screws, choosing the longest screws the bracket's thickness would take.

To complete the island I made drawer boxes from 1/2"-thick Baltic birch plywood (affordability!), hung them on Blum Tandem slides and applied drawer faces. While working on the second phase of the kitchen I decided that the slab doors I'd originally proposed for affordability were not nice enough. While building frame-and-panel doors for the upper cabinets on the opposite wall I made replacement doors for the island.

3. Counters & Backsplashes

At its most basic, a counter is a surface on which to gather vessels, utensils and culinary ingredients, then use all of the above to make a meal.

Some surfaces are meant for working on directly. Marble is a traditional surface for rolling short-crust pastry; its coolness helps prevent the development of gluten, which makes pastry tough. End-grain butcher blocks made of hard maple resist absorption, and so have been used for centuries for chopping meat. Edge-grain counters made from hard maple are still found in traditional bakeries today; they are ideal for kneading bread doughs. Some cooks use maple counters to chop on directly, a fine solution as long as you don't mind the resulting cuts and stains. Others protect the wood with a cutting board.

Most counters, though, are best used with cutting boards. Not only do cutting boards protect the counter from damage; they can be taken to the sink for thorough cleaning.

Tile is relatively easy to install yourself and makes a durable counter. Being hard, it will break dropped glasses and dishware; another oft-cited drawback is that grout lines require periodic maintenance. But in some circumstances tile offers design possibilities and durability that can't be rivaled – one example being period-style kitchens for homes that originally had tile counters.

It's important to lay countertop tile on a waterproof base such as cement board or fiber cement board. Dark grout colors will hide dirt and emphasize geometric patterns in white or black and white tile. If you're thinking of using white grout, be aware that although it will get stained, it can usually be whitened again with a spray of bleach.

Wood is warm to the touch and affordable if you're a woodworker who can fabricate counters yourself, thereby saving the cost of labor. It is also ideal for period-style kitchens where original counters may have been old-growth fir, pine or maple. Drawbacks to wood include its permeability; you have to treat it as you would any tabletop, except that this is a top where you'll be working – in other words, it's going to take a lot more wear. Wood counters will scorch if you put a hot pot or pan directly on them. They also have to be installed so

Tiles made by an artist. Alex Zdankowicz made these tiles for the kitchen of Johnny and Becca Grey with fluid surfaces and edges that call to mind works by Antoni Gaudi.
BENEDICT GREY PHOTOGRAPHY

White on white. Dark grout sharpens the character of white mosaic tiles with white edging.

Antique splendor. Original glass tile lines the walls of Linda Handelsman's 1926 kitchen.

that they can move with changes in humidity. Finally, the best species for counters are those with tight grain, such as maple, birch, cherry and mahogany. The open grain of elm or oak will collect food particles.

There are several ways of using wood for a counter – flat boards (like a tabletop), edge-grain boards (often called butcher block) or end-grain blocks. Some are finished; some are not.

Obviously an unfinished wood counter, or one finished with a food-grade oil such as mineral oil, will be more susceptible to stains. You will also need to scrape and scrub it daily to keep it clean. At a bakery where I once worked, all the counters were unfinished maple. At the end of the morning's baking we used a baker's scraper to remove residual flour and dough, first working over the surface dry. After removing most of the build-up we flooded the surface with a rag to soften anything that was left, then worked it over again with a scraper. We finished up by washing the surface with a clean rag soaked in bleach solution, then wiped the counter dry. One advantage of an unfinished top is that it's easy to scrape or sand down to clean material if stains and scratches get too out of hand.

Wood counters in kitchens today are often finished, whether oiled or spray-varnished at the factory, or by the cabinetmaker on the jobsite. The greatest concerns about finished wood are that it can be scorched by a hot pan or damaged by moisture, especially around a sink. If you use wood for a counter with a sink, take special care to seal it well with an appropriate finish on the underside and end grain at the sink cutout, in addition to the top. Seal the joint between the counter and the sink with a waterproof caulk. You'll need to be vigilant about spills and splashes; wipe them up immediately with a non-abrasive cloth, working in the direction of the grain, then dry completely. It's critical to keep water from seeping into the joint between the counter and the sink lip for drop-in sinks; moisture will be absorbed by the end grain and will damage the finish, then eventually cause the wood to rot. In recent years it has become more common to use undermount sinks with hardwood counters; in these cases the best species are oily, such as teak, or white oak, with its vir-

Stacked-pattern glass. In the kitchen she shares with her husband, Bruce Chaffin, Jana Moore specified a backsplash of frosted glass tile laid in a stacked pattern. The peaceful view is accentuated by the absence of electrical switches and receptacles, which are mounted on the undersides of the upper cabinets, hidden from view by the doors and side panels. The counters are soapstone.

A cook's benchtop. Linda Handelsman wanted edge-grain maple butcherblock with an oiled finish for her workbench top, where she kneads dough, rolls pastry and makes popsicles from fresh purée. (The day I was there to photograph the kitchen, she was freezing a blend of watermelon and ginger.) To clean the counter after use, Linda uses a baker's scraper that she has had for 40 years.

Two-tone. This Shaker-inspired cabinet I made for Nancy Hiestand's kitchen around 1997 has hard maple counters finished with oil-based polyurethane.
SPECTRUM CREATIVE GROUP

tually impermeable end grain. With white oak, especially, though, the end grain must be sealed well with finish and dried thoroughly after every use.

Good finishes for wood counters include oil-based polyurethane, spar varnish, Osmo and Waterlox Original tung oil.

A counter made of boards needs to be kept flat while also free to move across its width (or depth, in the case of most counters, i.e. back to front). Table-top fasteners such as Z-clips or figure-8 fasteners are a good means of support; wooden buttons are another. A third option is an oversized hole in a stout block screwed firmly to the cabinet side; insert a fender washer and attach the top with wood screws. This will allow the wood to move with changes in relative humidity. You may be tempted to fasten the counter at the center of its depth and allow it to expand and contract equally toward the back and front. In most cases it's better to fasten it firmly at the back and let it move at the front; just be sure you allow for a large enough overhang.

Wood on wood. The counters in Wharton Esherick's kitchen are solid wood. Esherick made a cutting board insert shaped to fit the cutout for his sink to add prep space.

LAURI HAFVENSTEIN

Salvaged wood. The counter on Lauri Hafvenstein's main kitchen cabinet is made of salvaged heart pine from Goodwin finished with Waterlox Original tung oil.

LAURI HAFVENSTEIN

Techniques
Fit a Wooden Counter into a Tricky Space

The birch counter I made for Nandini Gupta and Rick Harbaugh's peninsula took some systematic thinking to fit. One end had to fit the back wall, notch around a half-wall and the jamb of a cased opening, be cut into an L to fill in a narrow gap next to the stove and have finished overhangs.

We took it one step at a time, assessing the cabinets, walls and trim to determine critical orienting points, then fitted one section at a time to get an accurate read on where we'd cut next.

In this case, the most important edge to start with was the main overhang on the kitchen side. Like the overhang at the peninsula's finished end (in the foreground, below), it needed to be 1 inch.

We placed the counter in position accordingly.

Our next step was to fit the end that would go against the wall (visible at the left side of the image below). Walls are rarely square; in this case the counter fit tightly in the corner, where there was a build-up of drywall mud, but there was a gap of about 3/16" at the front edge. In other cases there could be a concave or convex wall plane; it doesn't matter what the shape is, you just need to scribe the counter to conform to the wall.

Ordinarily this would be simple, but in our case we also had to notch the back of the counter (the side that would overhang into the dining room, providing space for a couple of stools) around the jamb of the cased opening between the rooms.

(The "cased opening" refers to the opening in the wall between the kitchen, at left, and the dining room, at right; the jamb is the vertical section of trim that conceals the framing, and the casing is what's commonly called "door trim," in this case composed of casing with one eased edge, bordered by a piece of trim called a backband.)

It was impossible to gauge accurately where we would need to cut the notch until after we had fitted the trapped end of the counter to the wall. But at the same time, we couldn't push the counter up to the end

Start at the most critical edge. *Mark checked the overhang on the kitchen side, which was the most critical edge to start with, then adjusted the counter's position to ensure a consistent overhang of 1". At this stage it didn't matter how the counter fit everywhere else.*

Cut to fit. *Mark cut the closed end square to the first critical edge with the counter still in place, using a track saw. He set the depth of cut to avoid damage to the cabinet below.*

Extend the line. *Mark used a framing square to mark the position of the partial wall on the counter.*

Note the distance. *Mark used a framing square to measure the distance from the inside corner of the wall (near his left hand) to the front of the jamb, then transferred this distance onto the counter.*

Confirm with a tape. *Here Mark is showing the measurement with a tape measure for clarity. This measurement is the distance from the inside corner of the wall to the starting point of the notch for the jamb. (Although Mark has squared a line across from the overhanging edge to the lengthwise mark, he still needs to confirm the angle. See the next picture.)*

Tricky detail. *The pencil tip is at the edge of the jamb, about 5/8" behind the front face of the vertical casing.*

wall, because doing so would have distorted the scribing of the trapped end. To keep the reference points accurate, we left the counter where it was – i.e., with its kitchen-side edge overhanging by 1" and the end that would go against the back wall almost a foot away from that wall. Even at a foot (or more) away, you can scribe an object to its surroundings; in this case, Mark used a piece of scrap cut to the same length as the biggest gap between the counter's end and the wall.

Next we checked the distance from the inside corner of the trapped end to the front of the jamb, which would be the start of our notch.

Next Mark checked the angle of the jamb to the wall/section of the counter that would fit into the inside corner. Never assume a jamb is square!

I thought it would look extra-sharp if we allowed the counter overhang on the dining room side to wrap around the jamb to the edge of the vertical casing. That meant cutting a U-shaped notch instead of a straight line. Mark made these cuts using an oscillating tool fitted with a saw blade.

As with any situation where perpendicular cabinets form an inside corner, it's crucial to allow enough space for drawers or oven/dishwasher doors to open without running into protruding handles. In this case, the kitchen side of the peninsula would have drawers that needed to bypass the handles of the adjacent stove. The stove had an oven with a drop-down door that would in turn have to clear the protruding drawer pulls. I took all of this into careful account in figuring

Don't assume the trim is square. *Confirm the angle if you want the counter to fit.*

Details make the difference. *Note how the counter overhang is notched around the casing so as to fill in the little gap that would otherwise have been left between the counter end and the vertical casing. I took a little more off the notch around the jamb at the front (i.e. the little tooth-shaped section at the right here) to allow the counter to shrink without splitting. The edge at the front here was still rough from the saw. I cleaned it up when I had the fitted counter back in the shop, prior to finishing.*

Back to the beginning. *The filler strip is the narrow vertical piece between the front of the peninsula cabinet and the stove alcove.*

out how wide to make the filler strip that we installed to the right of the stove, which necessitated the little part of the L in the counter.

To lay this shape out on the counter we measured to the end of the filler strip and transferred that measurement to the top of the counter.

Because Mark had worked with his crew to frame the stove opening and install the cabinets, he knew the opening from the back of the stove recess to the front of the oven-door filler strip was square. (You should never assume such things without checking.) He continued the line at this distance back to the wall and marked it in pencil for me to cut when I brought the counter back to my shop to sand and finish.

If you have a filler strip like this one, don't forget to allow the counter to overhang it at the front by the same distance as the rest of the counter overhangs, in this case 1". It would be terrifyingly easy to cut this L straight across, then realize you'd forgotten to allow for the 1" overhang.

Now all that remained was to cut the dining room side of the counter so that there would be a consistent overhang, then mark and cut the open end (at the left of the image immediately above this column). We marked the end of the peninsula base cabinet on the underside of the counter, squared each mark up onto the top surface of the counter, then added an inch for the overhang and joined the lines. That was a satisfying final cut.

Local limestone. Lee and Eric Sandweiss chose limestone quarried from the county where they live for their kitchen counters. Sealed with paste wax, the counters have developed a warm, soft patina over 14 years. Limestone is softer than many stone varieties, so it's vulnerable to scratches and nicks. Happily, this softness means it's easy to blend minor damage into the surrounding surface with sandpaper.

Stone & Stone Composites

Natural stone and stone composites can make extraordinarily durable counters. Although some, such as marble, are relatively porous and liable to stains, denser varieties such as granite, along with composites containing quartz, will resist almost any damage by staining. Being heat-proof, most stone can take a hot pan or baking sheet straight from the stove.

One potential drawback of stone is that, as with tile, most varieties are hard enough to shatter glassware and dishes dropped by slick fingers. On the other hand, soft varieties such as limestone and pale grey soapstone may leave your glassware intact and be dented or chipped themselves. (We have experienced this with our pale grey soapstone counter.) So before you commit to buying a slab, ask questions and ideally perform some experiments.

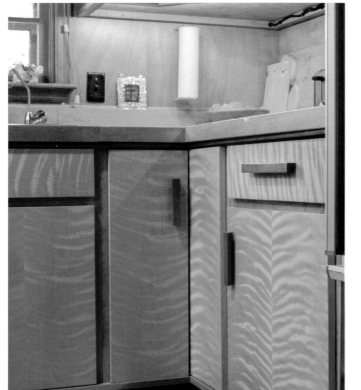

Terrazzo-look composite & glass. For her counters Christine Matheu chose DuPont Zodiaq with patterns that call to mind mid-century terrazzo. She specified back-painted glass as a luminous protective surface for the wall behind her stove and main preparation area.

SPECTRUM CREATIVE GROUP

Wooden backsplash. Lee and Eric Sandweiss wanted to keep their kitchen's original veneered wall panels instead of installing backsplash tile. The veneer bore numerous battle scars from being in use for more than 50 years, but restoring it took just a light sanding followed by three coats of oil-based wiping polyurethane.

Stainless steel. When Lynette Breton redid the kitchen of her 1960 house, she based her cabinets' design on an old metal cabinet she had seen in a garage at a boat-launching site nearby. She wanted a large stainless steel apron sink that would be extra deep for washing produce from the garden. Although she searched the inventory of used restaurant equipment suppliers, she couldn't find the combination of sink, drainboard and backsplash (which had to be low enough to work with the window sill over her sink), so she ordered a custom counter and sink made to her specifications by Elkay (elkay.com). She ordered it through a kitchen and bath showroom in Portland, Maine.

What appear to be tiles are window quilts. The material came from On Board Fabrics in Boothbay Harbor, Maine; Lynette had them made by a friend who sews. The red transistor AM radio came from a flea market. When she bought it, it wouldn't work because it required a kind of battery that's no longer made. Her engineer neighbor, Duncan Wood, retrofitted it to work with contemporary batteries.

MARGARET STEVENS-BECKSVOORT

Metal

Metal is another material suitable for counters. Around the turn of the 20th century it was common to cover wooden counters with zinc, wrapping the sheet metal around the edges. In the 1930s and '40s an alloy of two-thirds nickel and one-third copper called Monel was a popular choice for counters with integral sinks; Monel was not a sheet of metal covering a substrate, but (according to the Whitehead company, which manufactured counters with integrated sinks) a solid surface resistant to heat, chemicals and dents.[9] However, by the 1950s stainless steel had become the go-to for metal counters.

Copper and stainless steel are the most common metals used today. Copper, chosen primarily for its warm color, is susceptible to discoloration caused by reaction with chemicals such as acids. Stainless steel has long been used in commercial and industrial applications such as restaurant and hospital kitchens.

Linoleum

Genuine linoleum, made from linseed oil, resins, cork and pigment on a burlap backing, was invented in 1863. After it was replaced by vinyl sheet flooring in the 20th century, its revival was precipitated by interest in ecologically benign building products.

Although most people think of linoleum as a material for floors, it was often used for counters; the garret I rented during my second year in grad school had its original blue-grey linoleum floor and counters, along with a great-looking '40s fridge that required weekly defrosting and a carnival-esque stove with controls that lit up in colors from green through yellow, orange and red as you turned the knobs to increase the heat. I became a big fan of linoleum as soon as it reappeared on the market.

Advantages of linoleum as a material for kitchen counters include its retro appeal (it's available in a great range of colors and patterns), its eco-friendliness and – if you're a woodworker – its accessibility. While linoleum costs considerably more than lami-

Linoleum inspiration. For a few years beginning in 2003, I made linoleum-topped tables based on an original kitchen table I inherited from a rental in Missoula, Montana. The bases were made to be painted. When Daniel O'Grady came to work with me, he perfected the trimming and edging of the tops and earned extra income by driving tables to buyers around the Midwest.
SPECTRUM CREATIVE GROUP

nate, if you're making your own counters you don't have to pay for someone else's labor. On the other hand, linoleum requires more care in use than many other counter materials. You have to be careful not to cut it by dropping sharp objects onto its surface. You cannot cut directly on it. You need to wipe up spilled liquids promptly. It isn't heat-resistant. And any exposed edges must be finished with a wood lipping or metal.

For more about linoleum's history and a good dose of design inspiration, check out the late Jane Powell's book "Linoleum" (Gibbs-Smith, 2003).

Techniques
Make a Retro-Style Linoleum Countertop

Materials you will need:

1. Linoleum

There are two brands widely available in the United States: Forbo Marmoleum and Armstrong Marmorette.

2. Substrate

For fixed counters and tabletops I have always used high-quality veneer-core plywood. Some jobs call for 3/4"-thick material, others for thicker stock. When I need more thickness, I build it up by gluing secondary layers to a top layer of 3/4" material. If you do this, be sure to use a waterproof glue and apply it uniformly, then clamp thoroughly to ensure that the joints at the edges of the counter are well adhered.

When determining the thickness of the material, take into account the look you're after, the amount of support you're able to provide (for example, intermediate rails across the width of a long table frame, where the top could otherwise sag), and the widths of the edging material that are actually available.

3. Edging

Whereas contemporary laminates such as Formica and Wilsonart are hard enough to be used as edging, linoleum is not. Aside from the material's resilience (which in this respect translates to softness), it has a burlap backing, so if you tried to cut and butt join it on an edge, the burlap would show. There's no reason why you can't use solid wood as an edging, if wood suits your aesthetic. Traditionally, linoleum is edged with metal. My go-to source is Eagle Mouldings (eagle-aluminum.com). For 3/4" counters or tabletops I use Eagle Mouldings part #E-7364. The combination of substrate plus linoleum will sometimes come to just a tad more or less than the available edging. In such cases you can leave the slimmest hair of plywood edge bare at the bottom, trimming it back to keep it from being visible and from catching water or suffering from wear. If the moulding's a little too wide, let it overhang at the bottom; just make sure it can't catch on anything, or else it may get damaged.

Linoleum at home. *Linoleum counters are simple to make with a few DIY tools, as long as you're patient and careful about the details.*

Scribe the substrate. *Lay your pattern material in position against the wall and note the size of the largest gap. Here, the pattern fits tightly into the corner at left, but a gap grows to almost 1/4" wide at the right side of the shot. Cut a piece of thin scrap (or a contractor's shim) to the thickness of the gap at its biggest point.*

Shim simplicity. *Use a section of a builder's shim to trace the shape of the wall onto the pattern. The shim is the same thickness as the largest part of the gap; what I'm doing is extending that same distance across the surface of the pattern so that when I plane down to that line, the pattern will fit tightly against the wall for its entire length.*

Trim to fit. *After scribing, the pattern should fit tightly against the wall.*

Buttered up. *Spread the adhesive evenly using a trowel based on the manufacturer's specifications.*

The most critical point is the top edge where the moulding meets the linoleum; it should ideally be flush, but if it's not perfectly flush, it's better to have it come up a hair over the edge rather than fall under it, because the moulding is what protects the counter's edge. That said, if it protrudes more than a hair above the linoleum surface, it's far more prone to being dented or even ripped off.

A number of profiles are available, some of them clean enough to create an effect that's more modern than retro.

4. Adhesive and spreader

It's best to use the specific adhesive and spreading tool recommended by the manufacturer of the linoleum you are using.

5. Roller

A rubber roller with a long handle will allow you to exert the necessary pressure to lay the linoleum down on the adhesive-covered substrate.

6. Notching tool

If you plan to have round corners, you'll need to notch the edging. If you don't want to buy a special tool (such as the Crain 870 vinyl notcher), you can notch with a hacksaw; you just have to be careful not to distort the face.

7. Router, flush-timming bit and slot cutter

You'll use the pattern-cutting bit to trim the substrate to conform to the surrounding walls, then trim the linoleum to fit flush with the substrate. Because this last procedure dulls edges and makes a big, sticky mess, I recommend that you invest in two pattern-cutting bits – one for the plywood, the other for the linoleum. Make sure that the slot cutter you buy has a blade the correct width for the thickness of the toothed section of the moulding that will fit into the slot.

8. Hacksaw with a fine blade for cutting the metal edging

9. Drill, bits and countersink

10. #6 or #8 oval head slotted aluminum or nickel-plated screws

11. The usual measuring and safety equipment: tape measure, pencil, utility knife, straightedge, eye and ear protection, dust mask

Be sure you take into account any desired overhangs at the front or end of a cabinet run, in addition to radiused corners, and be sure you note the farthest points in all cases (such as areas along the length of a wall where the wall dips in), to make sure you don't cut your material too small.

I strongly recommend making a scrap piece at least 18" x 6" or so in size and performing all the following steps on it so that you can test your setups. An accurate test piece is especially important when it comes to routing the slot for the metal edging.

Start by cutting and scribing the substrate. Make a pattern for any parts that need to be scribed. You can make a pattern from 1/4" or thicker scrap.

Cut and shape your pattern with hand tools, checking the fit against the walls as necessary. When the pattern fits well, clamp it to your counter substrate and rout using a pattern-cutting bit. Check the fit.

Cut the linoleum roughly to size with a utility knife. Turning the material upside down allows you to score the backing. Then turn it right-side up and fold it over a table or bench edge to break it along the score line. Leave a little extra on every side for trimming.

Apply the adhesive and wait until the parts are ready to put together, as directed by the manufacturer. It helps greatly to have another pair of hands when setting large pieces of linoleum because it's important to avoid trapping air that would form bubbles and keep the linoleum from lying flat.

Ideally, you should start by laying the linoleum down at one end, allowing it to overhang just a little all around, then ease it in place along its length, rolling as you go to work out any air. If you don't have a helper, you can lay strips of wood across the surface of the substrate to keep the linoleum from touching it until you're ready; just remove each strip of wood as you get to it, rolling the sections as you lay them in place.

Roll the entire surface, starting in the center and working toward the edges to force out air. Finally, roll the edges carefully to make sure they're well sealed.

Leave the adhesive to dry for at least the minimum time specified by the manufacturer.

Trim off any excess more than 1/8" with a utility knife, taking care to avoid cutting into the substrate or marring the edges of your workpiece.

Turn the workpiece over and rout the linoleum flush with a pattern-cutting bit. Alternatively, you can use a

Heavy pressure. *Roll as hard as you can, especially near the edges, to ensure a good bond.*

Close to the edge. *Trim upside-down so you can see the edge of the substrate. Stay away from the corners.*

Router magic. *Use a router with a flush-trim bit to cut the linoleum perfectly even with the substrate edges.*

Aim for even. *The top of the edging should be flush with the top of the linoleum. If you have to err in one direction, it's better to make it a hair too high; in this case you run the risk of bending the edge when sweeping crumbs or wiping spills off the counter, but if you're careful, you can live with it. If you make the top edge too low, you'll leave a little bit of the linoleum edge uncovered, which can cause far more problems.*

Careful set-up. *When setting the depth for the slot, be sure the collet nut won't rub against the top corner of the linoleum, which would mar it.*

Tap, tap. *Start at one end and tap gently but firmly with a rubber mallet to avoid distorting the profile. Work your way along the piece; don't jump around, or you may ruin the fit and cause kinks.*

bottom-bearing flush-trim bit with the workpiece right side up if you prefer. Just be sure you don't hold the router at an angle and cut into the linoleum.

Clean up the sticky mess.

To rout the slot, set your router's depth so that the top edge of the metal edging will be perfectly flush with the top surface of the linoleum or just a hair above it. This is where the linoleum-covered scrap piece really comes into its own. It may take a few tries.

When you have it right, rout the slot for the metal edging.

Now it's time to apply the edging. Cut the edging just a little over-long. If you don't have any curves to negotiate, you're set. Clamp the workpiece in a vise and start at one end, tapping the edging into the slot. I use a rubber mallet.

I like to use a few judiciously placed screws to help keep the edging firmly in place. I measure the positions for the holes carefully, then drill and countersink to fit an oval-head screw, lining up the slots.

Square corners are sharp, especially with metal edging. If you have small children or are making a top for a confined space, you should probably not have sharp corners. On the other hand, square corners are the easiest to pull off; simply miter the material and apply it.

Once you've made the miter cuts, remove the burr with a fine file and check the fit. When the fit is good, cut the other end to length and install. Start at the mitered end. It's helpful to run in a screw somewhere near the corner (about an inch from the corner on each piece of metal edging works well) to keep the miter tight while you tap the rest of the piece home. Alternatively, you can miter the edging on a powered miter saw or table saw, using a fine-tooth blade. Just be aware that if you have a SawStop, aluminum will activate the safety feature. (Please don't ask how I know this.)

Rounded corners are far less likely to bruise hips, but bending the edging material is a challenge.

Begin by cutting the radius on your workpiece. I like to do this at the bare substrate stage, using a 1/4" or 1/2" plywood pattern and a pattern-cutting router bit; that way I can trim the linoleum to the necessary radius at the same time as I'm trimming it along the rest of the workpiece.

Measure for miter. *Measure as you would for any edging. Mark the miter with a soft pencil and cut with a hacksaw in a miter box.*

Radiused corners. *To bend the aluminum edging around a radius, you have to notch the tongue.*

After cutting the radius, form the slot along the entire length of the workpiece.

Now comes the slightly tricky part. The section of moulding that will go around the radiused corner needs to have its barbed tongue notched in order to bend. The first step here is to mark the area that needs to be notched. Lay your length of metal edging roughly in place on your workpiece to determine where the radius will fall along its length. If you have just one curve, you can measure from one end of the edging.

Be sure to go a little past the actual radius; it's better to notch a bit more than to notch too little. Mark the metal edging at this point, as in the image above.

Now you can measure the distance of the section that will be bent by simply using a tape. I start at the 1" mark for accuracy.

Transfer the measurement onto the tongue of the metal edging.

You can notch the tongue with a special notching tool, though the tool is not inexpensive. It takes a good bit of hand strength to notch the thicker parts of the

Ready to bend. *The metal edging is just barely inserted into the slot so that I can mark the approximate location where the radius starts. It's a good idea to go a little farther away from the radius than strictly necessary, to make sure you notch enough of the tongue to let the moulding bend smoothly around the curve. You can see the pencil mark I made to mark one end of the radiused section here.*

Flexible measurement. *Use a flexible tape measure to determine the approximate length of edging that will have to be notched.*

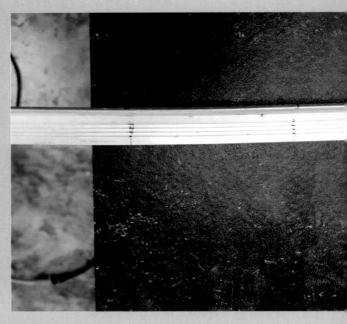

Quick reference. *Simple pencil marks at the ends of the radius are helpful.*

Jaws of steel. *A specialty notching tool makes short work of notching, but if you'd rather not invest in one, you can cut the notches with a hacksaw.*

Rigid no more. *With the tongue notched, the aluminum edging will easily bend around the radius.*

metal, so I usually start small and nibble my way up.

Alternatively, you can cut notches with a hacksaw. The important thing is to notch the material sufficiently so that it can bend. Work carefully, or you may kink the metal.

Once you have notched the area for the radius, begin applying the metal edging at one end and gently ease it around the curve, working in one direction and making sure you've got it fully inserted and tight to the radius before you move forward. You can use a rubber mallet to gently bend the top of the edging inward to hug the curve.

Boomerang revisited. Lynette Breton used Wilsonart's retro-style "Boomerang" pattern for her counters and open shelves. She finished the counters with aluminum edge from Eagle Mouldings (eagle-aluminum.com), but instead of edging the shelves, she left the core of the laminate exposed, adding a subtle bit of sharp horizontal emphasis.
MARGARET STEVENS-BECKSVOORT

Laminates

Laminates such as Formica and Wilsonart dominated the market for counters in the mid- to late-20th century. They are affordable and practical and come in a vast array of patterns and colors. If you're going for a retro look in a kitchen that would originally have had a laminate counter, you can do no better. Just be careful about period details such as edge treatments; true mid-century counters generally had a square edge, which was superseded by a rolled upper edge that kept spilled liquids from flowing onto the cabinet fronts below.

Plywood substrates used on mid-century counters were made with adhesives that are no longer used. They were far more water-resistant than the particleboard and other substrates most commonly used today. This makes it even more important to seal joints (such as those between the countertop and

backsplash) well. Otherwise water can quickly cause the substrate to swell and break the joint with the laminate.

Whatever counter and backsplash material you use, be sure to seal the joint between these parts at the wall to keep spilled liquids, flour and other substances from working their way into the seams and causing possible damage to the cabinets or wall.

Linoleum tile. This checkered floor is made with linoleum tile.

4. Ceilings & Floors

As with any room where people work on their feet for long periods, think about your feet and joints when selecting a kitchen floor material. Wood is comfortable underfoot, kind to dropped dishes and can be finished in a variety of ways, but it is more vulnerable to damage by floods from malfunctioning dishwashers or fridge-defrosting leaks.

Porcelain, ceramic and cement tile, along with solid cement, are durable and can be made waterproof with finish, but they are hard on joints, as well as dropped dishes.

Resilient floor coverings such as sheet vinyl, vinyl composition tile (VCT), genuine linoleum and cork share many of wood's virtues. Sheet goods and tiles (whether linoleum or VCT) come in a mouthwatering variety of patterns and colors that can be combined to make custom patterns.

Pretty in paint. Don't overlook painted wood, with or without added decoration. Carol Parks had her kitchen subfloor painted in a quilt pattern. Painting by Richard Jenkins, Bloomington, Ind.

SPECTRUM CREATIVE GROUP

Converging checkerboards. Like many kitchens that date to the mid-20th century, this one in the home of Lee and Eric Sandweiss has a resilient tile floor. Similar in appearance to today's vinyl composition tile but notable for its smaller size, the floor is extremely durable in addition to being period-perfect (and in this case, original). The ceiling, too, is original, an Artmstrong tile faced with textured cedar.

SPECTRUM CREATIVE GROUP

An artist's choice. The floor in Wharton Esherick's kitchen is vinyl. Esherick used two treatments for the ceiling — at this end of the kitchen it's plaster with black cement paint. At the other end, he left the rafters exposed and painted them green.

LAURI HAFVENSTEIN

Put a cork in it . Bruce Chaffin and Jana Moore love their floor of floating cork floor panels that click together and are protected with a water-based finish. Not only is it resilient underfoot; "it hides the right amount of dirt," Bruce says. "Some floors are incriminating," he adds. "This one isn't."

Fully exposed. One way to increase a ceiling's loft: expose its structure. Here the rafters and undersides of the subfloor above have been painted to resemble whitewash.

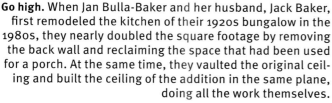

Go high. When Jan Bulla-Baker and her husband, Jack Baker, first remodeled the kitchen of their 1920s bungalow in the 1980s, they nearly doubled the square footage by removing the back wall and reclaiming the space that had been used for a porch. At the same time, they vaulted the original ceiling and built the ceiling of the addition in the same plane, doing all the work themselves.

Jan, a professional cook, ran a business called The Chocolate Factory in the early 1980s. She closed the business but kept the neon sign.

To vent the exhaust hood integrated into their microwave to the exterior, Jack simply ran ductwork up the wall. Why hide it in an era when the no-nonsense industrial look of "professional" stoves is sought after even by those who never cook – especially considering that this is the kitchen of a bona fide professional?

Fit for king or queen. Taking their cues from an antique catalog of 1940s Armstrong linoleum floor patterns, Jenni Wilkinson and her partner took cheap vinyl composition tile (VCT – the kind available at home centers all across the country) to a whole new level, creating a bold red border around their green floor and inlaying a pinwheel medallion on the tiny landing at the top of their basement staircase.

Shadow & light. Lighting on the interior of this cabinet in the home of Lee and Eric Sandweiss makes for nice ambient glow in the evening behind fluted-glass doors. Under-cabinet lights are invaluable for working in a kitchen with a single central light fixture in the ceiling.

Builder's special. Mark retrofitted two of the cabinets in our kitchen with inexpensive undercabinet lights.

5. Lighting

It should go without saying that lighting is an important part of kitchen design, not just for working but for atmosphere. Natural light from windows or skylights is a blessing. If you lack natural light and can't install a skylight, it's worth considering whether the architecture of your home will allow for a sun tunnel such as those made by Velux and Solatube. A sun tunnel will provide an astonishing amount of light during the day and even on moonlit nights.

Aside from natural light, you should have some kind of general lighting from the ceiling. Lights installed in a recess beneath upper cabinets make work a pleasure, especially for aging eyes. Don't overlook types of light fixtures less commonly seen in kitchens, such as pendants and sconces, or creative placement such as lights inside cabinets or shelves.

Finally, always check the manufacturer's specs to make sure you don't create a fire hazard; some lights get hot enough to melt chocolate.

Mix & match. The owner of this kitchen in a 1930 Tudor Revival used antique Art Deco ceiling fixtures and an English Arts & Crafts pendant over the sink.

Inner glow. Kitchen designer Johnny Grey designed illuminated shelves made from an off-white Corian "box" with LED lights inside.

BENEDICT GREY PHOTOGRAPHY

Light on the horizon. Bruce Chaffin and Jana Moore installed Edge Lighting's Soft Strip lighting over their cabinets for a luminous glow.

Light from several sources. Contrary to prevailing dogma, you can get plenty of illumination without installing recessed can lights in the ceiling. This is especially important in old houses, where can lights inject a glaringly contemporary look. In the kitchen of Carol and Roger Parks, a central ceiling pendant is the primary lighting, with additional illumination from a two-lamp fixture over the sink. Task lighting in the recess below the upper cabinets' floors brightens the work surfaces and the exhaust hood lights the stove. Rope lights inside the glazed upper cabinets provide ambient lighting at night when the primary fixtures are switched off.
SPECTRUM CREATIVE GROUP

Interior illumination. One of artist Wharton Esherick's practical idiosyncrasies was his habit of putting lights inside desks and cabinets. The lights in this base cabinet switch on when the doors are opened.
LAURI HAFVENSTEIN

In the box. Christine Matheu designed open shelves between her kitchen and adjacent dining space with integrated lighting in the lower section. The small lights illuminate the bar and are a lovely source of light at night when the main fixtures are not in use. The lower shelf is made of two plywood layers with solid maple edges; the lights and wiring run through a hollow area between the layers, then down through the floor via the shallow maple chase affixed to the wall. Ben Sturbaum of Golden Hands Construction installed the shelves and made the cut-outs for the lighting.
SPECTRUM CREATIVE GROUP

Brighter mornings. Inexpensive strings of holiday lights make dark winter mornings cheerful. They're also festive for dinner.

Sconces over suds. A pair of rewired antique sconces light the sink area in the kitchen of Lauri Hafvenstein's 1917 house.
LAURI HAFVENSTEIN

6. Venting

When I was in high school, one of the classrooms was in a third-floor room that had originally been a servants' dormitory, reached via a narrow dog-leg stairway that always smelled of stale cooked onions. Some cooking smells are delightful; one of my favorites is onions and garlic sizzling in olive oil. But let the smell of cooking onions permeate your curtains and wallpaper, and the remaining sulfur compounds will be far less appealing. Frying anything will disperse atomized fat infused with mushrooms or pork throughout your kitchen and sometimes farther afield. The lingering scent of baking fish or boiling brassicas will turn even the stoutest stomach.

The conventional solution is ventilation. An open window may do the trick, though without a cross breeze it may simply concentrate smells in your kitchen. Mechanical vents are the standard today; some municipalities require them by code. They come in two primary varieties: those that draw air through a filter, then recirculate it into the room and those that exhaust the air outdoors. The last are most effective.

If you don't mind seeing a hood, there's a world of products to choose from. Besides effective venting, bear sound level in mind. Competent HVAC professionals will stress that the sound of an exhaust vent is related to more than the unit's motor; it also varies according to duct material and size, the location of the motor relative to the cooking area and the material to which the unit is mounted.

If you prefer your vent to be invisible, there are several options, a few of which I've included here.

Focal point. Instead of trying to hide their hood, which is visible from the front door of their house, Jenni Wilkinson and her partner made it a feature with surface-mounted ductwork that goes straight up the wall and through the roof.

Ceiling mount. For his own kitchen, Johnny Grey designed an exhaust vent that incorporates an integral rack for hanging utensils.
BENEDICT GREY PHOTOGRAPHY

Ductwork hidden by cabinets. The owners of this kitchen wanted a hood that would exhaust to the exterior but didn't want a bulkhead, so their contractor, Michael Martin, fabricated ductwork that runs through the upper cabinets and out through the closest wall.
SPECTRUM CREATIVE GROUP

Screen time. When David Berman installed his restored Glenwood stove, he wanted to add an exhaust vent but didn't want to see it. He used a commercial exhaust fan, venting it through the flue that originally channeled coal smoke up to the chimney. He hid the ugly mechanical parts in a box he built from Southern yellow pine with a screen hand-cut in a Voysey pattern.

Big bends. Jane Powell, author of "Bungalow Kitchens," was in the midst of restoring the kitchen of her 1905 home, the Matteson House in Oakland, California, when she died. The 1940s O'Keefe and Merritt stove here was a temporary stand-in for a 1930s Spark with which she planned to replace it. The rounded hood is made from plywood sides with a curved front made from metal lath. The plywood and metal are plastered and house a modern exhaust insert.
SPECTRUM CREATIVE GROUP

At recess. Nandini Gupta and Rick Harbaugh wanted serious venting without an obvious hood. Their stove, hood and the upper cabinet to the right take advantage of a recess in the wall that was designed to house the original cookstove in their home. The contractor, Mark Longacre Construction, installed a custom hood insert by Best and we integrated it with the surrounding cabinetry.

Remote blower. Jane Goodman wanted high-performance venting over her stove but also wanted a clean look in keeping with her 1912 house. A remote blower mounted on the exterior wall did the trick. Ductwork runs through the wall behind the stove into a pantry closet, then outdoors. A cast metal grille ordinarily used for HVAC registers provides period-inspired disguise; the grille is lined with filter material to trap grease and keep large particles from being sucked into the powerful fan.

A fan of the forest. In the kitchen of his former home, architect Kris Floyd built a custom surround for an exhaust vent out of 2 x 4s and drywall, and hired artist Veda Stanfield, a neighbor, to paint the housing with a mural.

SPECTRUM CREATIVE GROUP

7. Pantries

Pantries were integral to most 19th-century kitchens. Separate rooms, usually with a window, they were fitted with open shelves for storing canned goods and staples. Advertisements for Hoosier cabinets in the early 20th century capitalized on the cabinets' consolidation of storage and prep space and claimed that women could conserve valuable energy for more enjoyable pursuits by saving (literal) steps.

Today a pantry is something of a luxury, a space beyond the kitchen, often hidden by a door, for overflow storage and things you don't want to see, such as recyclables.

Pantry-cum-mudroom. Mark and his crew added a pantry/mud room onto our kitchen. With 2x6 construction, the pantry gives us increased insulation and deep window sills for house plants, along with space to store recyclables and room for serving platters, decorative tins, cookie cutters, an industrial-size mixing bowl for bread and ugly folders of recipes. The antique Hoosier cabinet is from the turn of the 20th century and came from my mother, who found it in a junk shop in the 1960s.

Instead of a full-size door, we fitted the doorway with a gate I made from curly maple, which allows us to keep our dog out of the kitchen when necessary while still filling the room with light from the pantry windows, as well as a greater sense of space. The hinges are salvaged full-size architectural butts.

Pantry plenty. David Berman of Trustworth Studios has not one, but two pantries (left and above) just off the kitchen of his 1910 house. The rooms, still fitted with their original cabinetry in Southern yellow pine, provide invaluable auxiliary storage and preparation space.

Surviving centenarian. Open shelves make this pantry in the kitchen of a multi-residential building in Chicago ideal for storing things that wouldn't look at home in a period kitchen, such as a microwave. With a window for light and fresh air on fine days, it's also a pleasant auxiliary workspace. The homeowners, Tasha Vorderstrasse and Brian Muhs, added an old woodworking bench for storage and counter space; it's a great place to press homemade pasta.
SPECTRUM CREATIVE GROUP

An artful larder. Johnny and Becca Grey added this small pantry to their kitchen; it provides extra storage space and allowed them to add a small south-facing window.
BENEDICT GREY PHOTOGRAPHY

Add paint & new doors. The previous homeowner had cherry cabinets installed in the hallway between the kitchen and living room. The cabinets were solidly built and perfectly usable; the section at the left has adjustable shelves, while the larger section on the right has pull-out trays. So instead of replacing the cabinets I suggested removing the full-overlay doors and retrofitting the face frames with inset frame and panel doors hung on butt hinges to match those in the kitchen.

Some may consider it criminal to paint over cherry, but the clients, Nandini Gupta and Rick Harbaugh, wanted these cabinets to match the others. The new doors are made of hard maple, painted. I sanded, primed and brushed the face frames with oil-based paint.

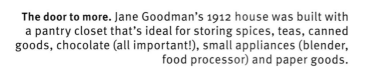

The door to more. Jane Goodman's 1912 house was built with a pantry closet that's ideal for storing spices, teas, canned goods, chocolate (all important!), small appliances (blender, food processor) and paper goods.

Systematic stacking. Lauri Hafvenstein stores herbs and spices in matching jars on a tiered rack for easy viewing. The alphabetized jars are labeled with the names of their contents and the purchase date for freshness.
LAURI HAFVENSTEIN

8. Spices

Practical spice storage comes in different forms but always takes ease of access and identification into account. Unless you run a professional kitchen that goes through cups of saffron and gallons of oregano per month, you should generally buy spices in small-enough quantities to use up while fresh. This typically means small jars or tins – just the kind of receptacle that tends to get lost when stored in a conventional upper cabinet 12" deep. It's no fun having to dig out 14 jars of other herbs and spices to find the basil at the very back. The best storage for such items is one jar deep, or two at most.

It's also useful to be able to identify spices and herbs at a glance. Clear labels are helpful in differentiating between marjoram and oregano, or caraway and black cumin seed.

If you have to store herbs and spices in a deeper cabinet, take a tip from Lauri Hafvenstein (see above) and use stepped shelves. Better yet, follow her example in noting the purchase date, to ensure your seasonings are fresh, and arrange the containers in alphabetical order.

Back of the door. Gary and Linda Anderson store large containers of spices in a simple rack mounted on the inside face of a pantry door.

Global capacity. No typical spice cabinet would be up to the task of storing the array of international seasonings Carol Parks uses in her cooking. "When I was a little girl, I was more interested in archeology than dolls," she told me. "I always wanted to see the world. I've been fortunate enough to see some of those places from my childhood fantasies: India, Hong Kong, Korea, Rio and, of course, Europe. Like most people who live in Texas," where Carol and her husband, Roger, moved when Roger retired, "we are able to visit Mexico easily and to sample an abundance of Mexican food."

Instead of a static panel to conceal the open side of the fridge, we built a tall, shallow cabinet that holds spice jars or small cans of food, one item deep. I used Soldier Blue milk paint for the cabinet. Carol wanted the back painted red for a zing worthy of the cabinet's piquant and aromatic contents. (The cabinet as seen here holds herbs and spices of the house's current owners, who kindly allowed me to have their kitchen photographed for this book.)
SPECTRUM CREATIVE GROUP

Medicine cabinet inspiration. The design of the spice cabinet in our kitchen is based on an antique medicine cabinet. The door is crudely pocket-screwed together. (I just wanted it to be done.) Glass shelves take up minimal vertical space and are easy to clean. The finish is milk paint.

Hole in the wall. This client had me use an antique leaded glass door to make a spice cabinet. The shallow cabinet insert is recessed into the wall; its face frame matches the glass frame as closely as possible. Salvaged butterfly hinges and a tiny knob complete the picture.

Small change, big impact. Gary and Linda Anderson added hooks to the bulkhead beside the hood in their '40s kitchen. The cluster of pans adds the look of serious cooking as well as a vertical element.

Hanging from the rafters. Artist Wharton Esherick stored pots and pans on his kitchen's exposed rafters, which he painted green.

LAURI HAFVENSTEIN

9. Pot Racks (& Exposed Storage for Pots & Pans)

Pots and pans can take up a lot of space. They're also heavy – at least, those made of cast iron or thick stainless steel. One convenient way to store them while keeping them close at hand is to hang them on a pot rack, a mode of storage with the added benefit of enhancing the aesthetic of a kitchen that's truly used.

If you're considering incorporating a pot rack in your kitchen, plan for safety – make sure pots and heavy pans are easy to remove without danger of them falling on your head, your cat or your beautifully tiled floor. You should also keep in mind that any openly stored cookware you use infrequently is likely to need occasional cleaning, as it will gather dust.

Rackus maximus. Bert Gilbert, a general contractor and sculptor, made this 30" x 48" pot rack for the kitchen of the home he shares with his wife, Amy Dyken. The main structure is steel bar; the hooks are made from electrical panel grounding wire.

Still working. Knowing that they would be without a stove while they waited for their antique Wedgewood to be restored, Tasha Vorderstrasse and Brian Muhs cooked on this vintage two-burner electric hotplate they found for sale online. It goes so well with their backsplash tile that they've kept it in plain view.

SPECTRUM CREATIVE GROUP

10. Small Appliances

Will there ever be an end to the development of small kitchen appliances, every generation of them marketed as new and better than the last? The toaster, mixer, blender and electric kettle are classics, along with the old-fashioned coffee percolator or automatic drip. Today we have countertop coffee machines featuring a disposable plastic container with every cup. There are cappuccino machines that start by roasting and grinding the beans and see the process through to steaming the milk. Step away from the world of caffeine and you're into other dimensions of "must-have" appliances – the juicer, automatic bread maker, toaster oven, slow cooker, air-popcorn maker, rice cooker and food processor. More recently we've been graced with the spiralizer and air fryer.

A few decades ago, kitchen designers responded to the overpopulation of counters by these and oth-

Coffee behind closed doors. Denise Gaul designed her cabinets with compartments where she could store small appliances and keep them plugged in, ready to use.
DENISE GAUL

er appliances by devising the "appliance garage," a counter-level compartment within an upper cabinet that allowed users simply to slide appliances inside when they were not in use, then pull down a door. Appliance garages have largely fallen out of favor – partly because most kitchens have too many appliances to fit within them.

Today's reigning minimalist aesthetic encourages tidiness. Small appliances can be put away in base cabinet pull-outs or drawers. They can be stored in pantries. Some of us have even gone so far as to give away those we don't use regularly. The trick is to avoid replacing them.

Some small appliances are so aesthetically pleasing that they deserve a place on the counter. The classic KitchenAid mixer is one. Others, such as some models of microwave oven, are designed to be built-in. Here are some examples of small appliances both hidden and in open view.

Ready when you are. Lauri Hafvenstein uses her Vitamix blender every day. The motor is heavy, so she wanted a drawer where she could leave it plugged in for use. She only has to remove the carafe for cleaning.
LAURI HAFVENSTEIN

Check the pantry. A floor-to-ceiling cabinet just to the left of the coffee station is fitted with adjustable shelves that store dry goods and small appliances – a blender, food processor, toaster and the like. The only appliances left out are the espresso maker and coffee grinder in the kitchen of Bruce Chaffin and Jana Moore.

PHOTO OF INTERIOR: JANA MOORE

Bring them to you. I retrofitted a cabinet in our kitchen with two pull-outs on Blum Tandem slides for convenient, easily accessible storage of pots and small appliances.

11. Full-size Appliances

There's a universe of appliances available today. Even though this is a book about kitchens, I'm not going to touch on the functional side of this world, which is constantly changing – not just with such improvements to cooking as induction stoves and convection ovens, but now also with an increasing variety of so-called smart components. Instead, I'll keep this section short and focus on visual design.

Many of my clients keep their existing appliances when they remodel the kitchen. Even if they redo the floor and replace the cabinets and counters, I find they're generally loath to replace the dishwasher, stove and fridge unless the appliances are beyond repair. It's certainly harder to get my work published

Glenwood splendor. A serious baker who often cooks for guests, David Berman treasures his restored 1928 Glenwood Super Capacity range.

in magazines when there's a white dishwasher from 2016 in a kitchen with a stove designed to resemble one from 1900 and a fridge that's a dead ringer for one from the mid-1950s. That said, these are not my kitchens, but my clients'; they are spending their money, not mine, and in most cases their reason for keeping the old appliances is simply to avoid the rampant wastefulness of our time, so I'm not about to complain.

On the other hand, some people would prefer not

Hidden in plain view. Denise Gaul and Alice Collins kept their existing dishwasher, which was manufactured to accept a decorative panel. When she redid the kitchen in 2018, Denise applied a panel veneered in quartersawn teak to match the rest of the cabinets.

DENISE GAUL

Focal point. Rick Harbaugh and Nandini Gupta cook on a Lacanche range. Along with the British company AGA, American brand Viking and French brand La Cornue, Lacanche manufactures ranges that are eye-catching and produced to high standards.

Fridge with feet. Lauri Hafvenstein found this antique Frigidaire, in great cosmetic condition, and had its working parts repaired. She has to defrost it regularly but considers it totally worth the effort in exchange for having such a beautiful appliance in her 1917 kitchen.

LAURI HAFVENSTEIN

to see a modern refrigerator in the midst of their turn-of-the-century cabinets. One way to make appliances disappear is to put them in a nearby room, such as a pantry or mud room just off the kitchen. Some of my clients have a small antique fridge and perhaps a restored stove but keep their modern appliances for heavy-duty use, such as holiday cooking for friends and extended family. A basement is ideal for this, as long as you can run the necessary gas line or electrical service to that location. The same goes

for a pair of clients who had us install a pair of integrated refrigeration drawers and one freezer drawer in a section of built-in cabinets in the kitchen; with two small boys, they decided to keep their full-size fridge in the basement.

Another way to make an appliance disappear is by applying a decorative panel. Some appliances are made with unfinished faces to accept a custom panel. This can be an ingenious way to make a brand-new fridge look like an early-20th-century icebox.

Often mistaken for the real thing. Big Chill is one of several companies that manufacture retro-style appliances. The main detail that gives away the true age of their mid-century fridge is the stationary handle; many antique handles were hinged and worked as latches to open or shut the door.

Like a rock. Tasha Vorderstrasse and Brian Muhs cook on a restored Wedgewood stove.
SPECTRUM CREATIVE GROUP

Another take on full-size appliances is to choose those designed for the look you're after. A growing number of manufacturers are making stoves and fridges with a view to design. So-called professional ranges fall into this category. Other remodelers bite the bullet and buy a genuine professional range. Professional appliances, especially from the mid-20th century, were generally built to last. In the late 1960s my mother bought a used Vulcan range that had come out of a restaurant kitchen. I wouldn't be

surprised if it were still going strong.

Failing these measures, if you want to make your appliances look a little less prosaic, you may be able to change out one or more elements such as handles or control knobs.

Restored antique appliances have striking looks; some stoves, especially some mid-century models, will out-cook and out-bake their contemporary counterparts.

12. Trash

Sometimes I feel like cabinetmakers have become the doctors of the cutting-edge hardware world. We're visited by hardware company salespersons and bombarded with literature about new products that will open doors, close drawers, lift lids, hide appliances and make exhaust vents invisible. Our clients see these wonders in their neighbors' kitchens or advertised in magazines and want them.

My basic attitude toward such gizmos is the equivalent of the sign my doctor used to have on her office door: Pharmaceutical Representatives Not Welcome. In my kitchen, the cabinet doors hang on surface-mounted butterfly hinges and we toss our trash into a freestanding can beneath the sink. I like simple.

Things are different when I'm discussing hardware with clients. It is, after all, their kitchen. There's a spectrum of ways to store trash until you're ready to take it outside, beginning with a three-tined fork in the road: Would you like a freestanding trash can, an unassuming bin beneath the sink or a dedicated trash cabinet?

If you opt for one of the first pair, you're done. Just put the receptacle in your kitchen and get cook-

A touch of trash. The trash cabinet (to the left of the sink here) opens hands-free with a slight push, thanks to a Blum Tip-On with Blumotion unit. Alternatively, you can open the door with the pull.

ing. Choose the latter and you've launched the cabinetmaker's equivalent of an automated answering system: Enter your account number followed by the pound sign. Press 1 for customer service. Now press 2 for residential or 3 for commercial. Etc. How will the cabinet open? Will it have a door on hinges or be made like a drawer? Will tossing that tea bag wrapper mean reaching into the cabinet, or will the trash receptacle slide out to meet you?

For pull-outs, you can either buy a unit or build one. If you're going to build it, will the design allow for bottom-mounted runners (such as Blum Tandem slides) or will it need to be side-mounted higher up to counteract the stress on the door if the pull is at the top?

Are you willing to use a knob or drawer pull, or do you want the unit to open hands-free? If the former, great; just install it. If the latter, there are several further options, from a foot-operated pedal that pushes the unit open to an electric servo drive.

Ride the rails. The drawer rails on the original cabinet at right are original and support the runners on which the drawers still slide. The drawer rails on the new cabinetry at left are only decorative; the drawers are mounted on Blum Tandem slides, but without the drawer rails between them, the added cabinets would look glaringly modern.

PHOTO: SPECTRUM CREATIVE GROUP

13. Frameless versus Face Frame

Traditionally kitchen cabinets in the United States have been constructed of a basic solid-wood carcase with an added face frame. The face frame adds significant rigidity and counters racking. It also allows for rich design opportunities as the widths of rails and stiles may be varied according to particular historic styles.

If you build carcases with sheet goods, whether particleboard (common in the 1980s), MDF or veneer-core plywood, a solid-wood face frame is even more important as a means to counter racking and protect the cabinets' front edges. While some plywood is arguably dense enough to use without a solid edge – Baltic birch is the best example – it is still more likely to be damaged if left exposed than is a solid face frame.

Frameless cabinets have become more common since the early 1980s. They are certainly faster to build, and the absence of protruding face frame parts simplifies the installation of side-mounted hardware such as drawer slides. The front edges of a cabinet are largely protected from direct damage by impact and spilled liquids by full-overlay doors and drawer faces, which are typical for this type of construction. However, the edges should still

Best of both worlds. The clean, rounded lines of mid-century metal cabinets and fridges inspired Lynette Breton's cabinet design. True to her inspiration, Lynette mixed face frames with frameless intersections between certain elements such as where doors or drawers come together.

Lynette made the doors and drawers from solid quartersawn maple, finished with milk paint in a custom blend (part Mustard and part Snow White, both from the Old Fashioned Milk Paint Company [milkpaint.com]), topcoated with Osmo Polyx Oil. She has found the finish surprisingly durable for vertical surfaces in her kitchen.
MARGARET STEVENS-BECKSVOORT

be finished, whether with solid lippings or veneer trimmed flush.

If you're going for a traditional or period-specific look, think about intermediate drawer rails, even if they're not functional. These face frame rails traditionally supported the wooden runners on which drawers slid in and out of the cabinet. If you're working in a style that would historically have had intermediate drawer rails you should use them, even if they are only decorative; otherwise the absence of these rails will be a dead giveaway that you don't know what you're doing when it comes to historic style.

14. Kicks

There are two main treatments for the part of built-in cabinetry that meets the floor: a recessed toe-kick or a continuation of the face frame's bottom rail to the floor. I call this last a flush kick. Flush kicks take a little getting used to for those accustomed to their recessed counterparts, but there's no substitute for an authentic look in many turn-of-the-century kitchens. The other consideration with flush kicks is that you'll have to scribe them to the floor for a clean look (see page 50) or hide any gaps with shoe moulding.

Whether your kick will be recessed or flush, your feet will thank you for taking them into account in your planning. If you wear shoes in the house, put them on and perform the following experiment. If you have a policy of no shoes in the house, do the experiment in your sock feet.

Modified kick. A second way to make a recessed kick look less modern is to extend the face frames at each side of each base unit to the floor and recess the area between them. You can modify this treatment by adding decorative brackets or cut-outs to make feet.

UNIVERSAL MILLWORK CATALOG

If you've never worked in a kitchen with a flush kick, mock one up by shimming a block of wood or a short length of 2x4 into the recess under a sink cabinet so that the face of the block or 2x4 is flush with the plane of the cabinet's face frame. Stand at the sink as you would when washing dishes and see how it feels. The first time I worked in a kitchen with flush kicks it took a couple of days to get used to; initially I felt like I had to make a point of turning my feet slightly to one side. But once I got used to it I stopped being aware that there was no recess. The overhang of the counter, which is usually be-

On tiptoe. Among the first things Carol Parks said she wanted when we met to discuss her kitchen in 2005 were "feet." These are made by adding a triangular piece in the corner between the bottom rail and stile. When the glue is dry, I cut out the shape.
PHOTO: SPECTRUM CREATIVE GROUP

More like furniture. The cabinets in the kitchen of Nandini Gupta and Rick Harbaugh have stiles that go down to the floor with recessed toe kicks between them.

tween 1" and 1-1/2" beyond the face of the cabinet, creates its own partial recess, even with a flush kick.

To measure for a custom recess, stand at the sink and have a friend get down on the floor with a tape measure. Have the friend measure how far the front of your shoes extends into the space beneath the cabinet. Then measure how high your shoe comes at the highest point. (Unless you are an elf with upturned toes, the highest point should be at the ankle end, not the toe end, of your foot.) This will give you the minimum depth and height for the recess.

Keep in mind that the kick will typically be added after the cabinets have been installed, so be sure to factor its thickness (typically 3/4") into the recess you build into your base cabinets. The same goes for the vertical space: It's a minimum of the distance you should have under the front of the cabinet. If your cabinet is frameless, this will translate to the

underside of the cabinet's bottom. If the cabinet has a face frame that hangs down a bit below the underside of the bottom, as is typical, factor this in when figuring the height of your recessed cutout.

There are several ways to make a recessed kick look less modern. One was widely used in the early 1930s: The recess is continuous along the entire series of built-in cabinets, but at each end of the run the face frame stile comes down to the floor.

A third option for kicks is an applied baseboard. This is a look drawn from public rooms such as built-ins in living rooms, dressing rooms and residential libraries and is not traditional to kitchens. It also has the arguable drawback of decreasing toe-space even more than does a flush kick. If you want to add baseboard to your kitchen cabinets, go for it. You can scribe them to the floor as necessary using the technique outlined on page 50.

15. Hinges

Hinges are more than a means of hanging doors. They contribute significantly to a kitchen's look. In principle you can use any type of hinge for kitchen cabinet doors, but this section will focus on those that are most common.

Butt hinges

Doors on traditional kitchen cabinets were inset and typically hung on butt or butterfly hinges. Let's start with the former. Butt hinges come in several varieties. There are extruded brass butts (known in Britain as solid drawn brass butts) with fixed pins and loose-pin butts that allow you to separate a door from its cabinet by simply removing the pin, leaving the hinge leaves in place. All traditional butt hinges are made to be mortised into the edge of the face frame (if there is one) and door, though in British cabinetry it is not uncommon to find them let only into the door; in these cases the cabinet leaf is simply screwed to the face frame stile.

Alternatively, you can use salvaged architectural hinges that were originally made for use with full-size house doors. Yes, they're over-sized for most kitchen cabinets, but there are times when this kind of exaggerated scale packs a stylistic punch that no conventionally sized hardware can.

Another kind of butt is the adjustable, no-mortise hinge. This hinge is designed to resemble a traditional butt, with or without decorative finials, but is screwed to the surface of the door and face frame, the idea being that it is far quicker to install and requires fewer tools and lesser skill. The drawback, at least in my opinion, is that these hinges are a poor imitation of real butts; they look under-scaled. And to any craftsperson, they suggest an easy way out. That said, they do offer a relatively decent traditional butt hinge look and can make a set of cabinets significantly more affordable when the client or homeowner is on a tight budget.

Two kinds of butt hinge. An extruded butt with a fixed pin, right, and a butt hinge with loose pin, left.

Easier going. Loose-pin butt hinges are easier to use, in many circumstances, because they allow you to remove a door without removing the entire hinge. One leaf stays on the door, the other on the cabinet, while you take the door to your bench (or outside, if you're working on a jobsite) to plane off an extra 1/32".

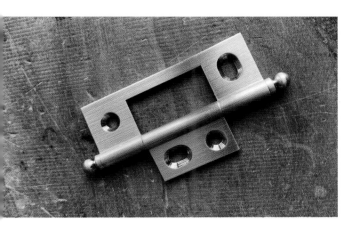

Easy way out. Many cabinetmakers use adjustable surface-mounted butt hinges to save on labor.

Butterfly hinges

In the early 20th century, as companies turned out large numbers of cabinets, it became clear that inset doors came with their own built-in problems, the greatest being that they require a bit of skill to install well. On any cabinetry supplied with doors already hung – Hoosier cabinets are an ideal example – the tendency of doors to bind when cabinets were delivered to real-world locations became an even more pressing issue; the cabinets were sold with the claim that they were readily affordable and ready to use. So it was not surprising to me, as a cabinetmaker, to find in the course of my research on Hoosier cabinets that the largest manufacturer of these kitchen furnishings pretty quickly switched to half-inset (also known as half-overlay) doors. They marketed this as an improvement on the grounds that the resulting lip would keep dust from getting into the cabinet through the gaps in traditional inset doors.

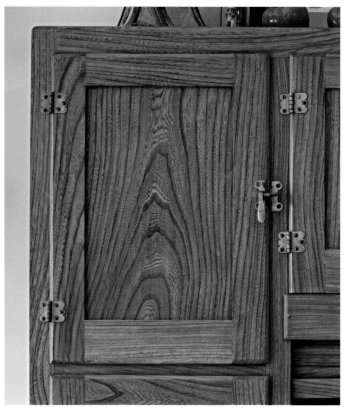

Fill the gap. A half-inset door on a reproduction Hoosier cabinet.
SPECTRUM CREATIVE GROUP

Salvaged butterfly. Lauri Hafvenstein gathered together a collection of salvaged butterfly hinges with similar patina for use in her newly built cabinets.

LAURI HAFVENSTEIN

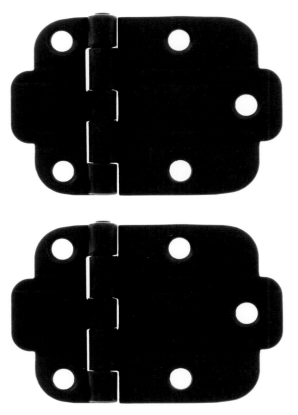

Deco detail. These streamline-style hinges are a Deco-era classic, though historically they were most often plated with chrome.

PHOTO COURTESY OF HOUSE OF ANTIQUE HARDWARE

Surface treatment. A fold-back hinge on a cabinet I made for our former kitchen, based loosely on details from Hoosier cabinets. The hinges came from Kennedy Hardware (kennedyhardware.com).

SPECTRUM CREATIVE GROUP

Butterfly hinges have been used since the 19th century, if not before, and were widely used into the 1930s. Their popularity comes and goes with changes in decorating fashions. For a decade or so in the early 2000s there was a wide range of designs and finishes available, but ever since mid-century modern became the new "it girl" and gave "old-house" styles the boot, those of us who appreciate early 20th-century architecture have been reduced to choosing from a few reproduction designs offered by reputable manufacturers. One solution to this diminished variety is to look for antique hinges at salvage yards, antique shops and online.

A variant on the older-pattern butterfly hinge is the offset butterfly hinge, designed for use with half-inset doors. And there are other variants on this one, some Art Deco-inspired, others the fold-back hinges used on certain Hoosier-type cabinets.

3/8" Inset Hinges

From the mid- through late-20th century another type of hinge was widely used for kitchen doors. The "3/8" inset" hinge came (and is still available) in a few patterns, the most distinctive being a sort-of bullet/streamline design. This type of hinge is available in free- or self-closing forms. It is extremely simple to install, with one caveat: You must allow enough space in the rabbet around the door's perimeter to account for the distance by which the hinge will push the hinge stile away from the face frame. The only circumstances in which I would recommend using these hinges today are when replacing a broken hinge or adding new doors to an existing kitchen full of cabinets hung on them or, of course, if you are recreating a period-authentic kitchen in a movie set or a house that originally had them.

European Hinges

European hinges were designed for use with European-style cabinets, also known as frameless cabinets. Underlying this system of cabinet building and installation is a desire to maximize efficiency by standardizing components based on 35mm (approximately 1-3/8") increments.

European hinges come in a vast variety, each designed to work in a different application. Even so, most consist of just two basic parts – a hinge and a mounting plate.

To make a simple matter slightly less so, European hinges also come in a variety specifically designed for use on cabinets with face frames; these have an integral mounting plate. But you don't have to use this "face frame" hinge to use European hinges on cabinets with face frames; you can just as well use the two-part variety, provided that you choose the correct combination of hinge and mounting plate for your application.

Depending on which combination of hinge and mounting plate you use, these hinges can work with doors that are inset, half-inset or full overlay. And there are even more variations! A full-overlay door may overlay the cabinet face by 1/4" or 1-1/4", depending on the mounting plate you use. Doors can open 95° or as much as 165°. They can be free closing (these do not hold themselves closed but require

Cabinets for everyman. Many mass-produced kitchen cabinets in the 1940s and '50s had doors on half-inset hinges such as this one, still produced today.

A no-show hinge. To keep his cabinets as clean-lined as possible, Bruce Chaffin used hidden European hinges. The doors open and close by means of touch latches.

Just the ticket. Lynette Breton found the best solution for her full-overlay doors is the XXI surface mount concealed hinge.

MARGARET STEVENS-BECKSVOORT

a catch) or self-closing. Some are even available with a soft-close feature that shuts the door for you once you give it a gentle push. (Aside from their undeniable coolness, these are useful for keeping children from slamming their fingers in cabinets.)

Despite the huge variety, all of these hinges have the same pattern for drilling the hinge cup mortise in the door: a hole drilled to the depth of the cup (about 1/2") with a 35mm Forstner bit.

There are two good reasons to choose European hinges in select applications. First, being invisible when a door is closed, they offer a clean look. If not seeing the hinges is important to your design, these may be your guys. Second, they offer adjustability in three planes, which makes fitting any kind of door — inset, half-inset or full overlay — ridiculously simple compared to using traditional butt hinges.

Specialty hinges

If knife hinges are your thing, there's no reason why you can't use those or any other type of hinge less commonly used for kitchen cabinets. In some applications where none of the conventional options will work, you just have to go looking for a special hinge.

16. A Few Extras

No book titled "Kitchen Think" would be complete without a variety of miscellaneous objects the inspiration for that title connotes. Here's a smattering of suggestions for details that are practical and fun.

Spoon rack. Jason Thigpen made this rack to store a variety of handmade spoons. The pegs for the spoons are made of white oak shaped by hand with a block plane, then installed using the tapered mortise-and-tenon tooling from Lee Valley. The 3/8" tapered tenon tool is used in this case and the pegs are angled upwards by about 5° to help the spoons stay on. (Jason says that if he built another spoon rack in the future, he would probably increase that to about 10°.) The base of the spoon rack is pecan harvested from a dead tree Jason felled just outside of his family's yard. The spoon rack is mounted by means of keyhole slots in the back.

JASON THIGPEN, TEXAS HERITAGE WOODWORKS

Adaptation of an adaptation. Megan Fitzpatrick built this tiger maple plate rack based on adaptations to an original design by Johnny Grey that had been developed by Nancy Hiller and Kelly Mehler in the course of planning the kitchen Kelly shares with his wife, Teri. It's made to fit Megan's dinnerware; the depth and central shelf heights accommodate her various plates, and the racks are removable, which makes the unit flexible for other uses. The top shelves in the two side sections are adjustable.
AL PARRISH, COURTESY OF ACTIVE INTEREST MEDIA

Homage to my first employer. In our former kitchen, I built a plate rack inspired by the kitchen dressers I made for Roy Griffiths at Crosskeys Joinery in the early 1980s. This one is made in cypress. The built-in cabinets are ash with salvaged hardware. The counter is green-black soapstone.
SPECTRUM CREATIVE GROUP

Possibly the world's most influential plate rack. Johnny Grey designed this plate rack for the kitchen in his family's home. The sides are cherry, but the rails and dowels are teak. If you're planning to use a plate rack for its historical purpose, to drain dishes, it's important to use a water-resistant species for all parts that will regularly get wet.
BENEDICT GREY PHOTOGRAPHY

Utensil rack & knife holder. Jenni Wilkinson mounted a tool bar over her stove to keep cooking utensils handy.

Second sink. If you have enough room, a second sink can be very handy. These clients added a small second sink between the main part of their kitchen and the dining room.
SPECTRUM CREATIVE GROUP

Wine column. My clients and I planned this wall of cabinetry around an awkward structural element. Along with the fridge and microwave, it houses a trash pullout. With just a few inches of width to spare, the clients suggested incorporating a set of shelves for wine.
SPECTRUM CREATIVE GROUP

Pet feeding station. Instead of buying a generic feeding station for her dog, Beau, Lynette Breton made one that goes with her kitchen. She laminated two layers of 1/2" Baltic birch plywood for the substrate, then glued the same Wilsonart Boomerang laminate she used for her counters to the top and underside for stability, using a vacuum press with Titebond glue. The chrome tubing was left over from a custom towel rack commission; she made the station with three legs, adding white cane-tip protectors found at her local hardware store.

The shape of the top was inspired by the boomerang pattern on the laminate.

MARGARET STEVENS-BECKSVOORT

No dull edges. The MagBlok by Benchcrafted holds knives safely with a powerful magnet concealed behind wood. Unlike commercial magnetic holders, which have metal on their faces, the MagBlok won't dull a sharp edge when hastily removed.

FATHER JOHN ABRAHAM

Pull-out cutting board. True to her mid-century inspiration, Lynette Breton incorporated a pull-out cutting board in her cabinets. The board is made of maple with a breadboard front; curved edges overlap the cabinet face.
MARGARET STEVENS-BECKSVOORT

Road food. Narayan Nayar, an avid cook and woodworker, wanted to equip his travel trailer's galley with some nice cooking knives for an extended road trip. He wanted the knives to be readily accessible, in addition to well-protected. He designed this knife tray, which sits on runners at the top of a drawer, along the lines of the drawers in which he stores his lathe tools. Knives are separated by two holders — one that secures the handle and one the blade. The tray is bottomless to prevent the accumulation of detritus; this feature also keeps the contents below the tray visible. The tray is made from a leftover beech countertop sink cutout and holds the four knives he wanted to have for 100 days on the road: paring, boning/fillet, 7" santoku and bread.
NARAYAN NAYAR

Plate Rack

Aim for realistic conditions. I set one of the plate rack's sides up against a wall so that I'll be mindful of the actual width available. It's easy to forget that in most cases there will be a wall behind the rack, which will prevent dishes from going back as far as you might be tempted to imagine. The rails that will hold the dowels must be spaced close enough together to keep dishes from falling through, but far enough apart to let the curve of the plates etc. fall down into the space between them, which will hold them in place.

Traditionally, plate racks were built for drying plates and other dishware; as such, they were mounted over a drainboard that sloped down toward the sink. In the age of dishwashers, drying racks are less necessary in most kitchens, but many people still incorporate a plate rack in their plans because these pieces are so versatile and attractive. The king of the plate rack realm is Johnny Grey, whose plate racks (and pot racks) are so diverse in their conception and materials that they really deserve an entire book to themselves.

Plate racks are also an exercise in balance and geometry. You can build one based on proportions you find lovely, taking a few critical measurements such as the outside diameter of your dinner plates and the depth of your soup bowls into account, only to find that the plate rolls right out of the rack onto the counter and shatters, or the bowl won't fit through the supports. For best results, you should design a plate rack to store the particular pieces of dishware that will go in it.

There are several ways of supporting dishes.

The plate rack offered as a project here has what I call the "prison bar" method of support. There are dowels, which may be square or round, wood or metal, at both front and back. The dishes fit between them. The width between the dowels has to be enough to let the plate pass through, but not so wide that the plates lean back very much, as excessive leaning translates to wasted space.

It's also important to space the dowels close enough from front to back to support dishes or plates of specific diameters. Too much space and your small plates may end up between the front and back rows of dowels, without any vertical support, so they fall over. On the other hand, you need enough space between the front and back dowels to allow the curve of the dishes to fall down a bit into that cavity; this will keep the plates etc. from simply falling forward out of the plate rack and onto the counter. (Crash.)

A versatile plate rack. *I designed this plate rack for a class I taught at the Lost Art Press storefront. It's made from solid maple with hand-cut joinery and can be finished clear, stained or painted. Not only is it a good exercise in hand-cut dovetails and exposed tenons, it's also surprisingly capacious. As with most designs, you can modify it to suit your needs and available space.*

Height matters. *Once you have the spacing of the front and back rails basically figured out, move on to the vertical supports. Begin by measuring the width you're likely to need for different bowls or plates. Remember, the edge of a soup bowl is just one part of its depth; you need the entire distance, from the underside of the bowl to the topmost edge of the lip. The best way to measure this depth is to lay the dish on a benchtop, set a straightedge across the top of the dish and measure the distance from the top of the dish to the straightedge.*

Also, remember that this is the space you'll need between the dowels or rods, not the distance from the center of one hole to that of its neighbor.

Drill holes in the front and back rails; a Forstner bit in a drill press will aid precise alignment and give you flat-bottomed holes of consistent depth. Set the dowels or rods in place and try the dishes.

Try all the dishes. *Don't just experiment with one size of dish, unless it's the only one you plan to store. Try different dishes until you hit on a distance between the front and back rails that will support all of those you plan to store.*

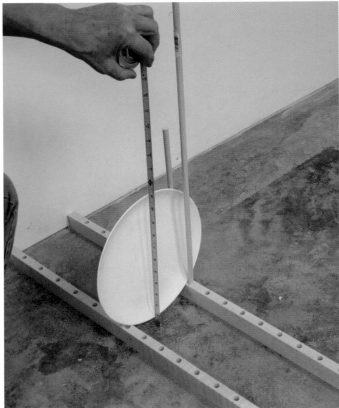

In and out. *Don't confuse the measurement taken when the plate is in place – i.e., resting below the top edges of the dowel support rails – with the actual height you need. If you put a shelf at this height, your plates will not fit in. It seems obvious once you see it illustrated, but it's easy to overlook in practice.*

Easy access. *A plate rack with diagonally oriented supports offers ready purchase to the hand. This one, in the home of Cheryl and Patrick Munson, was made in walnut by Hewins Cabinets.*

CHERYL MUNSON

Once I have a basic aesthetic in mind, I mock up the support components using waste material and experiment with the plates and other objects the plate rack is going to hold until I have these critical dimensions figured out.

The vertical distance is generally less critical, other than that you probably don't want to make it any larger than necessary, to avoid wasting space. That said, be sure you allow enough height for the plates to be put in and taken out.

Some plate racks, such as this one (right) that I call the New Century, only have vertical supports at the back, with horizontal supports below. This type of support allows you to space the vertical supports more closely together, because the full depth of the dishware doesn't need to fit through supports at the front.

Others have vertical supports at the back and diagonally placed supports that go from a higher point at the back to the low point at the front.

Historic inspiration. *I designed this plate rack with Edwardian design in mind. The back framework is inspired by the wagon-work framing often used by Ernest Gimson and Sidney Barnsley, best known for their Arts & Crafts furniture in the Cotswold School of design; the curve at the top is inspired by a 1905 dresser made by Ambrose Heal of Heal & Son. The circular bosses at the sides evoke the billowing sleeves of Edwardian ladies' dresses.*

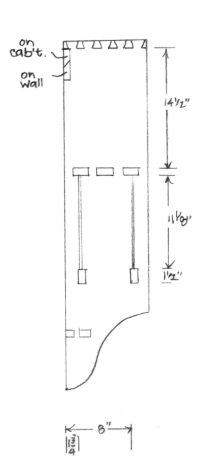

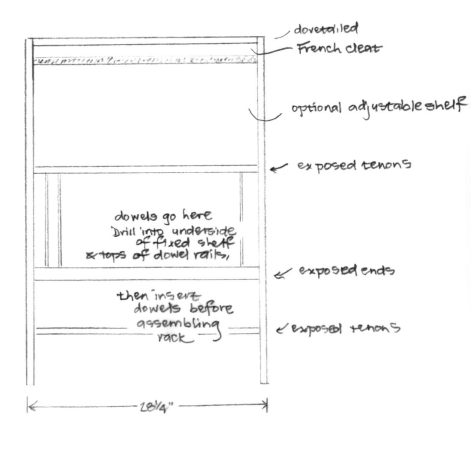

on cab't.

on wall

14½"

11⅛"

1½"

8"

⅓ ¾

dovetailed French cleat

optional adjustable shelf

exposed tenons

dowels go here
Drill into underside
of fixed shelf
& tops of dowel rails,

then insert
dowels before
assembling
rack

exposed ends

exposed tenons

28¼"

Build a Plate Rack

Start by determining the basic spacing you'll need between the components discussed above.

Shape the bottom ends of the sides. I cut the basic shape out with a jigsaw or band saw, then use a template to rout it with a pattern-cutting bit.

Lay out the joinery. Set a cutting gauge to just a hair more than the thickness of the stock and mark this on the tops of the sides, as well as the ends of all the fixed horizontal parts (top, fixed shelves and dowel support rails).

Cut the dovetail joints at the top, then move onto mortises.

Chop the mortises, then lay out the tenons.

When all the basic joints are cut, lay out the holes for the adjustable shelf supports and drill them.

Lay out the holes for the dowels or rods on the dowel support rails, then transfer them to the underside of the large fixed shelf.

Drill the holes with a Forstner bit. Note: Make the holes about 1/16" deeper than necessary to give you some vertical play. The value of this will become clear when you are putting the parts together.

To assemble the plate rack, start by inserting the dowels (or rods) into the holes on the underside of the fixed shelf. It's easiest if you lay the shelf upside-down on the bench. Next, set the dowel rails onto the dowels. It's trickier than it sounds to get them aligned.

When this assembly – shelf, dowel support rails and dowels – is put together, carefully turn it over. Spread glue on the parts for one side – the dovetails and all the tenons (I started with the left side of the plate rack) – and put those parts together on the bench. Be very careful not to dislodge the dowels.

Now spread glue on the other parts and lay the second side in place. Tap it all together with a mallet, then clamp and check for square.

When the glue is dry, sand as necessary, then apply the crown.

Instant duplication. *A plywood template makes it quick and easy to finesse the shape.*

Laying out. *Use a cutting gauge to mark the thickness of parts across the grain of the sides, top and shelves.*

Different grain direction, different marking gauge. *Use different marking gauges to lay out the front-to-back edges of the mortises.*

6
Make a Partial Change

*Sometimes a kitchen's bones are fine but the room
could do with some changes in look or function.
Here are several examples with advice on techniques.*

NO Nail

One room or two? French doors between the kitchen and living room allow the kitchen to be closed off while remaining in view from outside, and vice versa. I love the interplay between the two spaces.

Window shelf. A shallow shelf over our kitchen window holds pieces of early 20th-century pottery.

Case Study 6.1

The Cobbler's Kitchen

When I moved into my house in 2005, it was a shell. Sure, there were windows, exterior doors, finished drywall and a working toilet (not to be taken for granted), but there were no light fixtures, interior doors or trim. Apart from the bathroom, laundry room and kitchen, where I hastily laid down plywood and covered it with vinyl composition tile, the floors consisted of raw oriented strand board (OSB). And you can bet there were no cabinets or other built-ins.

Before. The colorful vinyl composition tile floor worked fine with this small enamel-topped table, which probably dates to the 1940s.

Over the next two years, sometimes with help from my then-employee, Daniel O'Grady, I put down hickory floorboards, installed baseboards and trim for windows and doors, built a handrail for the steps and basic carcases with cypress faces for the kitchen. As an experiment, I made counters out of linoleum with a retro metal edge. In time I paid Daniel to make doors and drawers for the cabinets. I finished the main cabinets with a dark reddish-brown concoction – my kitchen is a lab where I experiment before offering new products and design ideas to clients. At last I had a recognizable kitchen.

For a few years during the Great Recession I rented the house to others; I had moved in with Mark. Not long after we sold his house in 2016 and moved to mine – now ours – I built a hayrake table for my book on English Arts & Crafts furniture. The table was a keeper. But as soon as we put it in the kitchen I knew some changes would have to be made. The funky floor pattern, which I loved, was an insult to the restrained Cotswold School-style table. The dark-stained cabinets looked out of place. It was time to upgrade from retro chic to something more grown-up.

I pulled out the cabinets and stripped the cypress to bare wood, which I refinished with oil-based polyurethane. Mark and his employee, John Dehner, laid a hickory floor and our neighbor, John Hewett, sanded and finished it. We added pale grey soapstone counters and an undermount sink.

Glazed end. The upper cabinet beside the window has a glazed door, so I glazed the end of the cabinet as well, to allow light from the window to diffuse through the cabinet. I love seeing dishware behind glass; a glazed side just enhances the view. Note that if you glaze the side of a cabinet, the ends of the shelves should be trimmed to match the front edges, as they will be visible.

Finished end panel (bottom right of the photo). This end of the base cabinetry is visible, so to elevate the design from hardscrabble utilitarian I made a panel in solid cypress that matches the cabinet doors. Note that the rails and stiles are scaled up from those of the doors and the front stile is narrower than the back by the thickness of the face frame so that they appear to be the same width.

Removable cabinet (as seen to the left of the stove here). We don't need a dishwasher, but I designed the cabinets so that a future homeowner can install one with minimal disruption. The crude cabinet is a basic plywood box on casters. Two pull-out trays hold bakeware. I built the cabinet in cypress to match the rest but styled it with different details and hardware (the bin pulls are salvaged) so there would be a logic to its distinctness.

Eat-in kitchen. The house has no separate dining room, so the kitchen table serves as an auxiliary prep surface as well as for dining. I finished the top with three coats of oil-based polyurethane, applied thinly, for excellent durability. For further protection from scratches and dents, I made a large tabletop worksurface out of cherry with felt pads on the underside. It's not a cutting board, but a place on which to put the cutting board – or mixing bowl, or persimmon mill – to keep the work from damaging the table.

Freestanding versus built-in. A mobile cabinet made of welded steel and glass holds glassware with bowls on the open shelves below. A small laundry room is just off the kitchen; a quickly stripped exterior door keeps the washing machine from being in direct view. Simple painted shelves with a mish-mash of early 20th-century planters and vases make a colorful sight through the glass at the top of the door.

Pantry for extra space. An antique Hoosier cabinet my mother bought from a junk shop in the 1960s is an attractive place to store overflow from the kitchen.

Spacious Susan? When I originally built the cabinets, I installed a half-round Susan in the corner at the left of the stove, mainly to test the fixture's usefulness for potential future clients. By the time I stripped the cabinets I was ready to dispense with the ugly plastic-shelved fixture, which I replaced with drawers designed to hold every item I'd previously kept in the (cough) space-saving storage device.

Unmatched cabinets. I wanted the kitchen to show its pieced-together history. The upper to the left of the sink is a different design from the main built-ins and is finished in milk paint. The cabinets as seen in these photographs are still not completely finished; after stripping them I hastily rehung the doors with just a minimum of screws. Every door needs final adjustment. It will happen, someday. In the meantime, as always, I put my best attention into work for clients.

Trompe l'oeil. What appears to be a cabinet with five drawers in our kitchen really just has two. The compound faces hide low-sided pullouts on full-extension runners, an excellent way to store large items such as pasta pots, food processors, blenders and so forth. The drawer faces have swollen so much this summer that I need to trim them. But this is my kitchen, and I have more important work to do.

Hidden microwave. I prefer not to have our microwave on a counter, so I built a cabinet that would accommodate it along with dishware, pantry goods and cookbooks. The microwave is plugged into an outlet in the wall at the back.

Sources & Service Providers

- General contractor: Mark Longacre Construction (marklongacre.com)
- Cabinets: NR Hiller Design
- Floor sanding and finishing: John Hewett, Bloomington, Ind.
- Counters: Quality Surfaces Inc. (qualitysurfaces.com)
- Backsplash tile work: Rusty Robertson, Bloomington, Ind.
- Backsplash tile: American Olean (americanolean.com)
- Main ceiling pendant: Rejuvenation (rejuvenation.com)
- Sconce over stove: Schoolhouse Electric (schoolhouse.com)
- Sink: Kohler (kohler.com)
- Faucet: Delta (deltafaucet.com)
- Pendant over sink: salvaged
- Hinges and latches on main cabinets: Rejuvenation (rejuvenation.com)
- Red knobs for stove: Wilson Elements (wilsonelements.net)
- Fridge: Big Chill (bigchill.com)
- Wall clock: Antique
- Dish towel: Vincent Desjardins (vincentdesjardins.com)
- Milk paint: The Old-Fashioned Milk Paint Company (milkpaint.com) and The Real Milk Paint Company (realmilkpaint.com)
- Painting: Frank Haydu
- Framed enamel still-life: Karl Drerup (karldrerup.com)

Techniques
Convert a Two-Door Cabinet To a Cabinet with Drawers

Through much of the 20th century it was conventional for base cabinets in kitchens to have doors with shelves inside – usually one fixed shelf about half-way up, projecting between one-half and two-thirds of the way toward the cabinet front. The shelves' partial depth allowed users to see more of the contents on the cabinet's floor. Those familiar with such cabinets can attest to their impracticality. They are an invitation to stack contents high, so when you need a griddle or wok you have to get on the floor and perform an archaeological excavation, pulling out everything you don't want in order to reach what you do, only to shove the lot back inside to clear the counter so you can cook. And who has not experienced the frustration of a plastic storage container avalanche?

For a few years a transitional mode of storage reigned, with pull-out trays hidden behind base cabinet doors. The trays were typically mounted on runners that extended about three-quarters of their length, allowing you access to most of the trays' contents without getting on your knees. But you still had to open the cabinet doors to pull out the trays. Not only did this system require wasted motion; in many cases it also wasted space, necessitating extra room on each side of the trays to allow them to bypass the thickness of the opened doors.

Enter the latest solution for base cabinet storage: the good old-fashioned drawer. A sturdy drawer on full-extension slides gives you access to the cabinet's contents with a simple pull of the handles. As one of my customers put it, "It brings the contents of the cabinet to you, instead of you having to go into the cabinet and scrounge around for them."

It's relatively easy to convert a cabinet from doors to drawers. You just have to mind the specifications of the hardware you're using, as well as allow for how your cabinets are made. Here are some points to bear in mind and a step-by-step example.

Are the doors inset, half-inset or full-overlay? Your answers will have implications for how you plan, build

Easy access. *A convenient way to store pots and small appliances is in large pull-out trays designed to look like drawers.*

and install the drawers.

Which type of slide hardware will you be using?

Follow the manufacturer's instructions regarding the position of the drawer slides. For instance, Blum Tandem slides may be mounted to the cabinet side; alternatively, you can mount them to the face frame and cabinet back, by means of a bracket. If your cabinet has a face frame that protrudes into the door opening relative to the cabinet sides, as in the example, you also have the option of shimming the slides out so that the drawers will bypass the face frame.

Here's how I converted a two-door cabinet with pull-out trays to a drawer cabinet in our kitchen. To save time and materials I reused the existing trays, modifying them as necessary to work with the new slide hardware. Had I built new drawers, I could have gained a little extra space at each side, but instead I kept the existing spacers that had shimmed out the trays so they would bypass the doors. This is our kitchen, so the work is less refined than what I would put into a customer's house, and I compromised in ways just to get the job done.

With the cabinet width sorted out, I turned to the location of the slides relative to the front of the cabinet. Tandem slides need to be mounted 4mm behind the plane of the drawer face. In this case, the faces would be inset, so that meant adding 4mm to the thickness of the applied drawer face. Tandem slides also have specific requirements regarding the depth of the drawer. Their lengths vary by 75mm (or 3") increments. Fortunately my tray-drawers were 21" from front to back, ideal for the 21" Tandem.

After trimming the drawers, I applied the Tandem locking devices and drilled the holes at the back for the tilt mechanisms.

Next I built the faces. These faces are more complicated than most, because they are designed to look like multiple drawers, a sleight of hand I often employ to get desirable proportions. You could make faces out of plywood with solid edges if you're going to paint the cabinets, or you could build frame-and-panel faces (like doors, but placed horizontally). I wanted the look of a chest of drawers, so I made drawer faces to match the proportions of those at the right of this cabinet, gluing them to false drawer rails. I cut a tiny rabbet into the drawer rail to mimic the look of the space that would be around a drawer face if the rail were real. For the vertical divider between the two top drawer faces, I used biscuits to line up the parts but only applied glue part of the way up, to allow the faces to expand and contract.

Aside from finessing the fit of all the parts, the last step for low-sided drawers with tall faces is to fabricate a support system that will keep the drawer face flat and square to the drawer while allowing the drawer face to move with changes in humidity. My crude solution in this case was a pair of angled struts joined at the top by a horizontal rail. Oversize holes in the horizontal rail are fitted with pan head screws run through washers, to let the drawer face expand and contract.

Before. *The cabinet originally had two pull-out trays behind a pair of doors.*

Adaptive reuse. *I changed out the slides for Blum Tandem hardware. Because I wanted to reuse the existing trays as low-sided drawers I had to modify the width of the cabinet interior in order for the new hardware to work. I did this by adding a thin strip of wood, as you can see at the left.*

Critical dimensions. *To alter the distance between the underside of the bottom and lower edges of the front and sides, either trim on a table saw, using the rip fence, or add strips as necessary.*

Techniques
Three Ways to Mount Drawers

1. Wooden Slides

Traditionally, drawers have slid on wooden runners: strips of wood tenoned into horizontal rails at the face of a cabinet. In casework where a drawer will not be guided by the cabinet's sides – for example, when the cabinet has a face frame that protrudes into the drawer opening – the runners are fitted with guides to keep the drawers from sliding left or right and binding as they're closed.

Wooden runners have several qualities to recommend them:

• They work wonderfully when drawers are well-fitted. When it comes to fine furniture, they're the gold standard, not least because it takes finesse to make a drawer fit snugly while not so tightly that it's a challenge to open and close.

• Their only cost is your labor.

• The drawer front is the finished face.

• They let your drawer sides and joinery shine without intrusion by metal hardware.

At the same time, wooden drawer slides are less than ideal in some respects:

• They don't allow for full extension. Once you pull the drawer out to a certain point, it will sag and can fall out of its opening.

• A well-fitted drawer can stick in humid weather where humidity fluctuates significantly.

For decades, cabinetmakers have had access to mechanical slides, the features of which have improved steadily. Today there's a variety of options offered by manufacturers such as Blum, Accuride, Salice, Knape & Vogt and more. I cover just a couple here.

Mechanical slides have a few advantages over traditional wooden runners, even if they lack the cachet that comes with a piston-fit drawer. They're quiet, smooth-running and allow you to pull a drawer out fully without danger of it tipping its contents all over the floor, or worse, falling out and being damaged.

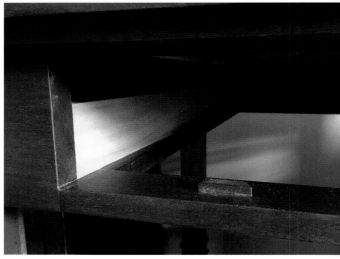

Age-old elegance. *A traditional dovetailed drawer that slides on wooden runners in a table made by Kent Perelman. The guides at each side are precisely in line with the opening and perpendicular to the table's face. The runner itself is just wide enough to accommodate the thickness of the drawer side. The table is fitted with traditional wooden drawer stops that go immediately behind the face. The runners and side guides have been waxed to promote smooth movement.*

An earlier generation of full-extension hardware. *A drawer in a simple set of kitchen cabinets fitted with Accuride side-mounted ball bearing slides. This kitchen uses Accuride model 3832. One part of the slide is screwed to the interior of the cabinet; the other, visible here, to the drawer. The slides telescope to allow for full extension, which makes a drawer's contents completely accessible.*

2. Side-mounted Ball Bearing Slides

Side-mount ball bearing slides, such as those made by Accuride, are affordable, dependable and hard-wearing. They come with a huge variety of optional features, among them a detent (helpful in cases where you want to use whatever is on the pull-out surface, such as a keyboard, without the drawer or tray closing when you touch it); extra-heavy load capacity; specialty slides for file drawers, lateral files, and so forth. Other advantages include:

• They're extremely easy to install in casework. You can put them almost anywhere you want, mounting the support to the cabinet side or using mounting plates to attach the hardware to the cabinet's front and back.

• They only impose one constraint on the dimensions of your drawer – the width of the drawer must be at or just a hair under the precise width between the slides once they've been installed. Beyond this, you can use these slides on drawers that are deeper (from front to back) or shallower than the slides, depending on your application.

• It doesn't matter how your drawer bottom fits into the drawer, i.e. whether it's flush at the bottom surface, fitted in slips, or slid into grooves in the drawer front and sides.

• While this flexibility may not sound so impressive in principle, it can be a life-saver in rare circumstances where you need the combination of affordable price, full extension and flexibility in drawer construction that such hardware allows.

These slides allow the drawer to be removed simply by disengaging a lever. To replace the drawer, slide it carefully into position – if you don't align the parts perfectly, you can damage the slides – then push until you hear a "click." Now pull the drawer out and close it fully to check the fit.

Before you install set screws, the slides are adjustable up and down in addition to forward and backward, thanks to slots on both parts – the part that goes on the drawer and the part that goes in the cabinet. Some models also have screwdriver-adjustable cams.

As for drawbacks, side-mounted ball bearing slides are not completely silent; there's a metal-on-metal sound when the arms of the slides are closing or opening, but it's minor. These slides also take up some width. This space varies somewhat, depending on the model; most require 1/2" on each side. As a result, in most applications, you need to cover the front of the drawer with an applied face. This face can be inset, as shown here, half overlay or full overlay.

When choosing these or other mechanical slides, read the specs and installation instructions to make sure the slides are compatible with your design.

My least favorite feature of these slides is their visibility. Although they come in different finishes (many lines are available in white, black and stainless, in addition to zinc), they do detract from the pristine beauty of a nicely finished drawer side – at least, when the drawer is open. When the drawer is closed, the slides are invisible.

The bee's knees – with exceptions. *A drawer on Blum Tandem undermount slides, which are invisible other than a little lever just behind the drawer face (not visible in this photo). While Blum Tandem drawer slides work well in many applications, there are times when ball-bearing (or other) slides are the best choice for the job.*

3. Self-closing Undermount Slides

Since about the turn of the millennium, cabinetmakers have had access to a type of slide that combines full extension and smooth, silent operation with almost complete invisibility. The Blum Tandem is the most widely known version, but as soon as other manufacturers saw how popular the new design was with cabinet manufacturers and their customers, they began devising their own variations on the theme.

Not only are these slides silent, smooth-running, full extension and invisible, when fitted with the right locking devices (available from the same suppliers as the slides themselves), they offer a new dimension in adjustability over previous kinds of drawer slide hardware. You can move the drawer face up or down, forward or backward, tilt it to make it flush with the face frame and move it from side to side – a boon when you're dealing with inset drawer faces in particular. These features come with some strict requirements:

• There are precise dimensional requirements: Drawers must be just the right width and depth (front to back) to fit specific slides. These and other specifications are laid out in a handy instruction guide published by hardware manufacturers.

• There needs to be a 1/2" recess beneath the drawer bottom so that the sides and front will conceal the runners.

• You need to drill a couple of holes at the back of the drawer for the tilt mechanism.

• Because the position of the slide hardware is fixed in relation to the drawer sides (it has to go below the drawer bottom), you need to be more precise in positioning the hardware inside the cabinet than you do with side-mounted ball bearing hardware. You must also leave more clearance in height than with side-mounted hardware, which can eat up space, depending on other elements of a cabinet's design.

As with the side-mounted slides, there will be a bit of space on either side of the drawer with undermount hardware. This space works out to about 5/16" on each side. An applied drawer face hides the gaps.

Hidden ingenuity. *Here's a 12" Blum Tandem undermount slide in the closed position. The slide incorporates a frame for attachment to your cabinet; built into this frame is a full-extension runner with parts that allow for tilting the drawer to fine-tune the fit. The smaller piece is a locking device. (This is an older example. New locking devices are wider and allow for horizontal adjustment.) The locking device is screwed to the underside of the drawer, then clicks into place on the slide when the drawer is inserted.*

Further exposed. *Here the slide is partially extended to show some of the mechanical parts. Blum Tandem slides incorporate a soft-close feature; when you give the opened drawer a push, it closes most of the way, then at about 1-1/2" from full closure this mechanism comes into play, pulling the drawer home. The soft-close feature has two advantages: First, it closes the drawer for you. Second, it keeps the spring from snapping the drawer back forcefully, which would pose a risk to children's fingers.*

A Quick Guide to Sizing Drawer Parts When Using Blum Tandem Slides

1. Choose your slide model and length

Note: The following instructions are for Blum Tandem 563 slides. The drawer width requirements are slightly different from those for model 569.

The slides come in 3" increments, starting at 9" and running up to 30", but the most commonly used length is 21", because it's the size that works with standard 24"-deep base cabinets. Why not use a 24"-long slide? A standard 24"-deep cabinet won't accommodate it. The slide lengths are nominal, not actual; they refer to the depth of the drawer you'll build, not the length of the slide. The slides themselves are a little longer than their nominal size, to accommodate the adjustment features.

2. Decide the thickness of your drawer box parts

The thickness of your drawer parts will affect the length of the drawer's front and back, so it's a good idea to decide this element early on. My preferred thickness for most applications is 1/2", because it looks finer than, say 5/8" or 3/4". That said, if you're starting with 4/4 stock and are just going to be turning the unneeded thickness into chips, you may prefer to keep your parts thicker to save material and time. For this exercise, I'll use 1/2" as the thickness.

3. Determine the other dimensions of your parts

If you're using Blum Tandem slides, you'll need to apply a face to the drawer front to conceal the spaces around the drawer box. The face can be inset, half- or full-overlay. Here, I stick to the drawer box, separate from the face.

You need to consider three primary dimensions in determining the size of your drawer: width, depth (front to back; in this case, the depth of the drawer corresponds to the length of the slide) and height.

*A. Drawer depth from front to back
(i.e., length of sides)*

For this exercise, we're going with a standard 21" (nominal) drawer slide. Because I'm going to build the drawer with through dovetails, my sides will be the full (nominal) length of the drawer slide: 21".

The same would apply were I putting the drawer together with biscuits; the sides would need to come all the way to the front of the drawer box, with the front and back fitting between, for maximum strength (i.e., to resist coming apart when pulled forward).

If you plan to use half-blind dovetails such as those produced by many router jigs, you will need to subtract the amount of wood left at the front and back from the overall length of the slide to determine your drawer sides' length.

Translating instructions to real life. *This large drawer for storage containers has relatively high sides to keep the containers and their lids from spilling over the edges. The width between the face frame stiles is what the slide instructions call the "opening width." Because of the way Blum Tandem slides are engineered, there will be a little gap between the outside of the drawer (at left and right) and the edges of the face frame.*

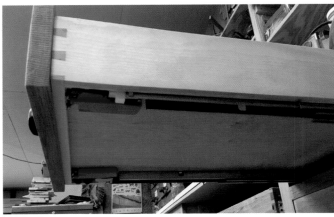

Seen from below. *This drawer is made with dovetails and has an applied face.*

B. Height

Because the runners are designed to sit between the drawer sides and are 1/2" high, the height of your drawer will need to factor in this 1/2" below the drawer bottom plus the thickness of the bottom, plus however much vertical clearance you need for the contents you plan to store in the drawer. Let's say you're building a drawer for a food processor, a blender and a few other small kitchen appliances. The first question: Can you take the appliance apart to reduce the height you'll require?

Now add your net height requirement plus the drawer bottom thickness plus the 1/2" required by the slides to get the net vertical dimension. *Note that the drawer sides don't have to come up to the top of the contents. For many applications, it's more convenient to have lower drawer sides, as they make moving bulky objects in and out of a drawer easier. For appliance drawers, I often make the sides, front, and back just high enough to keep the contents from sliding out – in this case, 4". But the net vertical dimension is still determined by the height required by the contents.

You'll need at least 9/16" below the drawer sides and 1/4" above them, i.e. a total of 13/16" in additional height, to determine your minimum vertical opening.

Let's say I'm going to use a 1/2"-thick bottom for this drawer because these appliances and the others I'm going to store in it are relatively heavy. This means I need: 10" plus 1/2" (drawer bottom thickness) plus 1/2" (slide requirement) equals my net vertical dimension, i.e. 11".

Now I'll add the 13/16" of space for clearance below and above to yield the minimum vertical opening: 11-13/16".

If I'm putting this drawer at the bottom of a three-drawer stack in a cabinet with a traditional face frame and drawer rails, this means the distance between the bottom cabinet rail (i.e., the top edge of the bottom face frame member) and the first drawer rail (i.e., the lower edge of the bottom-most drawer rail) must be at least 11-13/16". Of course, I can make this distance larger if I have space and aesthetics demand it, but I cannot make it smaller.

You need to go through the calculations above to lay out the vertical components of your cabinet (unless you just want to space your drawers based on how the faces will look, rather than trying to plan for particular objects that need to be stored). Once you've done that, if you decide it would be most convenient for your drawer box to be just 4" high (even though the space

it will fit into will be at least 11-13/16" high), go for it. That's the dimension I'm going to use here.

So now we know that our sides will be 4" x 21".

C. Width

The width of your drawer box's front and back will be determined by (a) the type of joinery you plan to use, (b) the thickness of your drawer parts and (c) the width of the opening.

For example, if you're making your drawer with biscuits, the front and back will fit between the sides. If you're making your drawer with dovetails, the front and back will run the full width of the drawer.

The width of the opening is the width between the cabinet sides, or, if you're using a face frame, between the face frame stiles. *Note: If your face frame stiles protrude into the carcase, you will either need to shim out the sides by the amount of that protrusion so that the drawer slides will sit flush with the inside edge of the face frame or use a rear mounting bracket.

What matters ultimately in determining the width of your drawer box is, to quote the Blum installation instructions: "Inside drawer width must equal opening width minus 42mm (1-21/32") for TANDEM to align and function optimally."

If you're using biscuit joinery, this makes it easy to figure how long the front and back need to be, because the length of the front and back is precisely equal to the "inside drawer width." Say your drawer opening (the opening between the face frame stiles) is 15". Your "inside drawer width" will be:

Drawer opening of 15: minus 1-21/32" equals 13-11/32".

If you're using dovetails, the calculation takes an additional step:

Drawer opening of 15" minus 1-21/32" equals the inside drawer width of 13-11/32", as above. Now you need to add the length for the pins, which will be the same as your drawer sides' thickness. So if the sides are 1/2" thick, the whole calculation will be:

Drawer opening of 15" minus 1-21/32" plus (2 x 1/2") equals 14-11/32". Because 21/32" is just a hair over 5/8", and because, as I mentioned above, I'm using

Alternative attachment. *Rear mounting brackets allow for installation in cabinets with face frame stiles that protrude into the carcase. In this case, the drawer slide is screwed to the cabinet at the front, then slotted into the rear mounting bracket which is screwed to the back of the cabinet.*

drawer sides that are 1/2" thick, I can take a shortcut and simply subtract 5/8" from the opening width in calculating how long my drawer box front and back should be.

Here's my finished cutting list, based on 1/2"-thick stock for a drawer box 4" high made with through dovetails:

Sides: 2 @ 1/2" x 4" x 21"
Front and back: 2 @ 1/2" x 4" x 14-3/8".

I will cut my parts to length and do the joinery with the back at the same width as the front, then rip it to fit over the drawer bottom after I've cut the grooves in the front and sides.

The Blum Media Center at blum.com has installation guides for all hardware. Look for "runners" then go to the Blum Tandem sections (https://www.blum.com/us/en/02/90/). Always make sure that you're following the instructions for the specific model you are using.

Two Jigs to Install Blum Tandem Drawer Slides

As with most innovative hardware, there's a range of accessories you can buy to ease installation. When I first started using Blum Tandem slides, I bought both of the jigs available at the time: one for drilling the hole at the back of the drawer, the other for the front corners, where the locking devices fit. Before long the locking device design had gone through not one, but two phases of improvement; as a result, one of the jig's holes has become obsolete. I no longer use it.

Each passing year seems to bring new jigs for installing this hardware to market. I've come up with my own system, which works well and allows for some variations in slide installation depending on whether the drawer faces are inset, half overlay or full overlay.

The first is a quick depth-setting jig for the slides. For full overlay drawers, the slides should be mounted 4mm, or just over 1/8", behind the front of the face frame.

For cabinets with drawer faces fully inset, make your jig the thickness of the drawer face (typically 3/4") plus the recommended 4mm, i.e. approximately 7/8". For faces that are "half-overlay" (i.e., faces that are rabbeted around the edge so that only 3/8" of the thick-

Get to work. *Here's the depth-setting jig in action: Simply hold it against the face frame at the side of the cabinet so that the slide is inset by the desired amount (in this illustration, where the drawer faces were full overlay, the slides were inset 4mm).*

Shop-made jig. *My high-tech depth-setting jig: a piece of scrap the thickness of whatever inset I need, plus the 4mm the hardware manufacturer recommends.*

ness is proud of the face frame, with the remaining face thickness inset), your jig will be 3/8" plus 4mm, or approximately 1/2".

The kitchen in these images (opposite) has half-overlay drawer and doors, so I made a depth-setting jig 13mm thick, or just over 1/2".

Before screwing the drawer slides in place, I make up another quick jig to support the drawer slide and hold it square to the face while I screw it in place. This works like a charm provided that your cabinet floor is square to the face. "Jig" may be a little fancy for this bit of apparatus; it's really just a piece of scrap wood or plywood cut to length so that when the bottom of the piece is standing on the cabinet floor, its top comes just above the drawer rail. It will work equally well if your cabinet doesn't have drawer rails; just cut your support piece long enough so that when your slide sits on top of it, it's where it needs to be.

Step One

Start with the top slides in each cabinet. These will use the longest piece of plywood scrap. It's best to use the widest piece you have available, for maximum consistency in the height from front to back. If you don't have a piece at least 8" wide, use two – one toward the front, one toward the back. In the picture at top, the slide is resting on the scrap and set to the necessary depth (behind the face frame) using a jig like the one at left, but made with a setback of 13mm. (I'm not showing the setback jig, because it would obscure the front of the slide.) When I'm installing these, I rest the drawer slide on the support "jig" (i.e., plywood scrap) and push it to depth using my depth-setting jig. You can hold both the depth-setting jig and the front end of the slide to keep it from falling with one hand; the other hand holds the drill, then screws the slide in place.

At this stage it's best to attach each slide through the elongated screw holes – one toward the front, one toward the back – to give yourself a bit of depth adjustment. Once you have the drawers in place you can finish up with set screws.

Step Two

After you've installed the top slide on each side of the cabinet, you can either re-use the scrap slide supports in any other cabinets with drawers at the same height, or cut them down for the next drawer, as shown in the next picture. The slides should be just above the face frame rail, if there is one. The height isn't all that critical; just keep in mind that the front of the slide needs to be above the rail, not below it, in order for the hardware to work (duh!). Also, the higher you mount the slide in the cabinet, the less vertical space you'll have available for the contents of the drawer.

You can keep cutting your slide support scraps to whatever length you need as you get lower down in the cabinet. You won't need them for the bottom drawer in most cases, as the slides can just sit on the cabinet floor. In this case, just set the slide depth using the depth-setting jig, then insert the screws.

From the top. *With this method the top slide goes in first. This way, you can reuse the plywood support for the drawers below; just cut it to the appropriate length as you go.*

Move on down. *Here the second slide is being screwed in place.*

The height of the slide is not super critical. *It just needs to be at or slightly above the drawer rail, if there is one.*

Not for dummies. Refacing cabinets to the standard of this pantry in the former kitchen of my clients Karl Sturbaum and Judith Rice is an art. Karl and Judy had a vision for the room that would mix veneered panels with aluminum and glass.

Trim to fit. Although using sharp handplanes on MDF is not my idea of a good time, I used a couple of planes to trim the mitered ends to fit. As with any onsite installation, you shouldn't expect the work area (in this case, the island cabinetry) to be perfectly level, square or plumb.

Case Study 6.2

Refacing at the High End

There's a widespread sense that refacing existing cabinets is a slapdash way to make poorly built cabinets look new. But not all cabinets are poorly built. Refacing some or all of them, while repairing or replacing parts that no longer work well, can be a viable way to transform a kitchen's style while avoiding the waste of sending perfectly usable cabinets to the landfill.

The kitchen, before: dark, monotonous and put together with little consideration for practical use. The island dominated the open-plan room. A pair of pre-hung hollow-core doors with fiberboard skins formed a closet with a ton of wasted space.

Refacing is not always less costly than replacing. If you buy stock cabinets at a home store you can probably spend less than it costs to pay a professional to do a quality refacing job, though if you're replacing sturdy cabinets with home-store versions, you may find yourself looking to upgrade those in a few years, considering how poorly many of them are made.

The kind of cabinet refacing I occasionally do entails technical challenges, too, which makes it satisfying as a subset of the cabinetmaker's craft. When you're changing a kitchen from full overlay doors with rounded edges and large gaps between them to one with tight margins and continuous grain across long banks of units, you have your work cut out for you.

When Karl Sturbaum and Judith Rice moved into their home it had a whale-sized island that dominated the combined space housing their dining and living areas as well as the kitchen. The island was made from a collection of base cabinets that incorporated a dishwasher, microwave and sink in a ponderous neo-classical style, the whole thing painted black. The vast granite counter curved outward, encroaching on the traffic area between the room's related spaces and making it appear even larger than it was.

They didn't object to the island in principle; it added a lot of worksurface to the kitchen, as well as a good place for friends or relatives to pull up a stool. But they wanted to streamline its dimensions and bring its aesthetic into line with their contemporary take on modern design. Because I had refaced their previous cabinets, transforming them from 1980s rustic hickory to a clean 21st-century look with horizontally laid teak composite architectural panels, they asked if I would do something similar with the island.

Lining it up. This cabinet (shown in full on the previous spread) began as part of a kitchen filled with dark, full-overlay hickory doors and drawer faces. The two-thirds of the pantry on the right were the original cabinet; I added the section on the left, as Karl and Judy requested. The panels are faced with teak composite veneer run horizontally.

Retrofitting the old pantry with aluminum-framed glass doors was relatively simple; fabricating a cabinet side and doors in the teak composite and fitting everything so the grain lined up was less so. To face the door edges so the grain would be continuous from the door faces, over the edges and across the side, I cut the door blanks a little oversize, ripped off the section between them and the cabinet side, then ripped the veneer off the 13/16"-wide off-cut. I glued the veneer to the edges of the doors with wood glue, cauls and clamps. The vertical front edge of the side panel is faced with hickory veneer, which I used on all the door and drawer face edges that didn't have to show continuous horizontal grain at cabinet sides.

The other challenge was to tie the old pantry into the new section to create a cohesive look by making a single recessed toe kick and a thin piece of trim that carried around the top at ceiling level (see page 204), all Karl and Judy's idea.

Karl had already come up with a plan. He would have the company that had supplied the granite counter trim it to his specifications, then re-install it on the island. He hoped they would saw it to size in place, but they would not. They charged a hefty fee to remove it, then take it to their facility for cutting. There was no guarantee the stone would not break in transit or while being cut; Karl and Judy would have to pay the fee even if they never saw the counter again. There would also be a fee to deliver and install the resized counter. After serious consideration and some research into what it would cost to

Exposed. Karl had removed the original end panels down to a skin of construction-grade plywood that would provide a surface for brads and screws.

Clean & contemporary. The refaced island is a workhorse for meal preparation and clean-up, in addition to seating three people comfortably.

Two-person job. Mark and I installed the panels together. It was not a one-person job; the back panel was almost 3' high by just over 8' long, and faced with very expensive veneer. For accuracy, we waited to measure and cut out openings for receptacles and switches until the time of installation. To prevent tear-out we scored our lines with a utility knife, then cut with a jigsaw. I have learned from experience that the vibration of a jigsaw base can bruise or scratch finished material, so I now protect the area where I'll be cutting with layers of wide blue tape.

Space at the floor. Karl had specified a small gap at the floor to keep the panels from soaking up water or other liquids from spills. We shimmed the panels and scribed them to fit the plywood skin. The corners on the working side of the kitchen are mitered; we glued and pinned them for a good fit.

replace the original counter, they concluded that the fees were worth paying.

The re-sized stone counter would have a smaller overhang requiring minimal support. This allowed Karl to sketch a design with extended end panels and a back panel between them. He and Judy chose a dyed eucalyptus veneer laid up by Heitink Veneers of Bloomington, Ind. They wanted to preserve the pale grey color, so after cutting the panels to size, edging them as necessary (with eucalyptus veneer trimmed from panel scraps, then adhered to the edges with Titebond II, cauls and clamps), I finished them with Osmo Natural, which contains a small amount of white pigment to keep pale woods light.

In addition to the island, Karl made significant changes to the cabinets in the rest of the kitchen, doing most of the work himself. The replacement doors with aluminum frames and glass are from Maplecraft USA.

On the edge. I edged the panels with scraps of eucalyptus veneer ripped off the MDF substrate with a Forrest Duraline High A/T table saw blade.

Close tolerances. The minimal overhangs Karl specced made for a stressful installation. After we had the microwave re-installed, I turned to the doors and false drawer faces concealing tip-out holders for small items such as sponges.

Better without the sink. *This job would have been vastly easier without the sink, but because of my relatively inflexible work schedule, it had already been re-installed in the newly sized top. To ensure that I drilled the holes for the sink-front tip-outs in the right positions I made a plywood template, stuck it to the old false drawer faces with double-sided tape, then removed the old faces. I drilled all the way through the fronts of the old faces, into the plywood templates, marked the templates to make sure I didn't mix them up (or turn them upside-down) and used them to drill the holes in the new faces.*

Utterly transformed. This massive island started out with a very different look.

Service Providers & Sources
- General contractor: Karl Sturbaum and Judith Rice
- Retrofitting cabinets with glass doors, building corner shelves etc.: Karl Sturbaum and Larry Bender
- Cabinet refacing: NR Hiller Design and Mark Longacre Construction
- Veneered panels: Heitink Veneers
- Finish: Osmo
- Aluminum and glass doors: Maplecraft USA
- Stove and microwave: JennAir
- Hood: Electrolux

Dramatic transformation. Beneath the solid cherry face frames, doors and drawer fronts lies a set of frameless white laminate cabinets most likely installed in the 1980s.

SPECTRUM CREATIVE GROUP

Case Study 6.3

Another Method of Refacing

Occasionally you may encounter a situation in which you're asked to reface a kitchen of frameless cabinets made of melamine-coated particleboard. Why would anyone want to keep such cabinets, you wonder. I know…but once in a blue moon, it happens. In this instance, working with the client's aesthetic, I made solid cherry face frames, doors and drawer faces, along with end panels for the island and appliance housings. Dick Stumpner of Stumpner's Building Service affixed them to the existing cabinets with glue and pocket screws.

Shelf paper. Knowing she wanted most of the upper cabinets to be open, Jenni searched for colorful shelf paper that would complement the kitchen's funky vibe.

Case Study 6.4

Add to Existing Cabinets

Jenni Wilkinson and her partner bought their 1953 bungalow in 2001. The kitchen was a dark, cramped room at the middle of the house. A wall hid the kitchen from the entryway and dining room, as was typical when the house was built. On the bright side, the kitchen still had its original built-in cabinets. "Of course you'll want to get rid of those," remarked their architect, who was also a friend, on seeing the room for the first time. Jenni laughed.

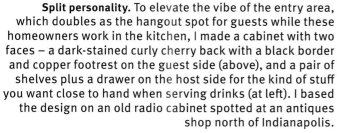

Split personality. To elevate the vibe of the entry area, which doubles as the hangout spot for guests while these homeowners work in the kitchen, I made a cabinet with two faces – a dark-stained curly cherry back with a black border and copper footrest on the guest side (above), and a pair of shelves plus a drawer on the host side for the kind of stuff you want close to hand when serving drinks (at left). I based the design on an old radio cabinet spotted at an antiques shop north of Indianapolis.

Grandma's kitchen. With a bit of TLC from Jenni, a new counter and new sink, the original cabinets function well. The window over the sink now looks through a laundry room to the trees outside.

Handy pans. Jenni came up with the design of this pan holder after seeing the hooks from Cooks Standard on the internet. The simple open box incorporates vertical storage for cutting boards, small trays and lids. Not visible here is the brass back Jenni fabricated for this narrow section of wall where a doorway had originally opened to a hallway; she used an old piece of sheet brass that had lined the edge of an architectural door – a bit of architectural salvage she'd been carting around since the early 1980s.

New cabinets patterned on old. I built the cabinets to the left of the stove to the same basic specs as the original ones, with door stiles and rails sized to the same widths, the same radius around their edges, and salvaged hinges and door pulls. Behind this retro façade, the carcases are made from easily cleaned prefinished maple veneer-core ply and full-extension, self-closing drawer slides. The gaps below the upper and lower drawers result from the faux drawer rail between the bottom drawers and those above them; to gain the necessary vertical space for storing the large items my clients wanted to have in these locations, I had to make the rail part of the bottom drawer face.

As someone who had lived in old houses her entire adult life, with a grandfather who worked as a carpenter, she grew up with a love for reuse and restoration. The old cabinets were one of her favorite things about their new home.

Over the next several years they remodeled their home extensively, inside and out, finishing with the kitchen. They vaulted the ceiling to give the room a more spacious feeling and added two north-facing skylights, as well as an opening in the wall to the living room, which faces south. They removed the wall between the kitchen and the entryway to the house, opening up the kitchen, because they love to entertain. Jenni restored the original cabinets on the sink wall and had a small section of base cabinets built to match to the left of the stove; they also added upper cabinets, some salvaged and others made to order.

One of the kitchen's most notable features is the floor, which Jenni and her partner laid themselves, basing the colors and border pattern on vintage examples. For an extra flourish they made a pinwheel medallion in the tiny hallway between the kitchen and rooms at the back of the house.

Artful flooring. Vinyl composition tile (VCT) need not be boring. With careful layout and a sharp utility knife, the homeowners turned these durable and affordable 12" tiles into a floor that's fun as well as practical.

Tricky business. Two drawer faces and an intermediate rail combine to make one drawer with extra vertical capacity for large pots.

Service Providers & Sources

- General contractor: Jenni Wilkinson
- Cabinetmaker: NR Hiller Design
- Tile: Handcrafted Tile Inc., Phoenix, Az. (hctile.net)
- Tile setter: Tom Stocker, Bloomington, Ind.
- Vinyl composition tile: Armstrong (armstrongflooring.com)
- Additional salvaged upper cabinets: Habitat ReStore (monroecountyhabitat.org)
- Retro metal counter edge stock: Eagle American (eagle-aluminum.com)
- Laminate counters: Laminated Tops (laminatedtops.com); Wilsonart, Maroochy Brush #4745-60 (wilsonart.com)
- Stove: Capital, Santa Fe Springs, Calif. (capital-cooking.com)
- Hood: Spagna Vetro from Euro-Kitchen Inc., Hayward, Calif. (euro-kitchen.com)

Sink. A frieze of chefs cast in plaster, then painted, turns the old bulkhead into an aesthetic virtue. Gary painted the cabinets black and taupe and replaced the original hardware with custom-fabricated chromed pulls. For extra pizazz he added fretwork chromed panels over the dummy drawer faces below the sink. The sink wall was originally an exterior wall with a window in the recessed area.

Busy bakers. A close-up of the gloss-painted plaster bakers shows their 3-D detail.

Case Study 6.5

More is More

Gary and Linda Anderson had to move quickly when they bought their house in 1985. Their former home had sold faster than expected and they'd agreed to vacate it sooner than would have been convenient. With limited time to get the new place ready, their first order of business was to paint everything beige to cover up the ubiquitous pink and mint green. Loathe to undertake a full-blown kitchen remodel, they decided to work with what they had – the Celotex-paneled ceiling, 1940s cabinets and bulkheads.

Refacing cabinets. Gary and Linda Anderson transformed the look of their 1940s plywood cabinets with paint and new hardware. In keeping with their black, red and off-white Art Deco-inspired color scheme, they painted the upper cabinets pale and added a stenciled motif in the corners. The base cabinets are black. They replaced the original door and drawer pulls with custom chromed pulls that Gary made.

Over the next few years they transformed the room with paint, tile, new hardware and a flair for campy Art Deco style.

"During the 1930s, to help the economy recover from the Depression, everything got redesigned to look faster, sleeker, modern," says Gary, a retired sign maker with skills in woodworking, metal, sandblasting and lettering by hand. "As a nation, we were moving forward. Industrial designers paid attention to everything – toasters, cars. It didn't matter how unimportant an object was. It got designed." The couple took this ethic to heart, choosing every element of their kitchen, right down to the chip clips, for its contribution not just to function, but to the overall style.

Entry view. Unless you really look hard, you won't notice that this black cabinet end panel is a dishwasher door. With limited potential locations where they might add a dishwasher, Gary and Linda decided the best place was smack in the middle of the entryway from the living room to the kitchen. Knowing that the dishwasher would be the first thing visible, Gary effectively made it disappear, blending it into the surrounding black base cabinets. Slick bar stool seating and the roadhouse-style sign Gary made for Linda distract the eye from the prosaic appliance.

Corner bar. A small red cabinet from Target creates a bar that makes a corner pop.

Subtle division. Etched glass sidelights made by Gary frame the opening into the kitchen from a sunken sitting room added to the house in 1965.

All together now. Color-coordinated tools and appliances of Streamline design give the kitchen its fun retro character.

A bit of fun. To break up a large area of stainless steel, Gary had a silhouette of the kitchen guy, as he calls him, cut out of diamond plate and attached it to the back of the hood.

Service Providers & Sources
- Design and remodeling: Gary and Linda Anderson
- Backsplash tile: Lowe's (lowes.com)
- Floor tile: Dura-ceramic floor tiles from Color Tile (carpetspluscolortile.com)
- Counter materials: Formica solid surface (formica. com)

Hoosier originals. With its original wall of built-in cabinetry, the 1926 kitchen is an extraordinary example of historic style.

Before. The baker's work-bench was designed to store many of the items that were formerly stacked on and under this table.

Case Study 6.6

A Breakfast Nook Puzzle

The kitchen in Linda Handelsman's 1926 bungalow is a rare gem. Over the almost 100 years since her home's construction, this room has seen very few changes. The layout is original – a central work area with a pantry closet, breakfast nook and ante room leading to the basement and backyard. The cabinets on the east wall are also original; made by the Hoosier Manufacturing Company of Newcastle, Ind., they still have their flour bin and sifter. Glass wall tile in greenish-grey and off-white lines all three of the kitchen areas, completing a nearly extant historical space.

Temps perdu. The built-ins still have their flour bin and sifter. The flour bin is in a zinc-lined tip-out with the sifter in the door compartment below. Linda stores miscellaneous items in the sifter compartment but says the bin is in effect useless. Even so, she hasn't altered it because she appreciates how special it is to have this kind of original working part in a kitchen that's nearly a century old.

There's just one problem: a 1920s kitchen is not so practical for most 21st-century cooks.

Linda is a serious baker whose specialty is artisan cakes and pastries. Her Chocolate Cloud Cake and Dutch Almond Cookies are powerful draws to potluck dinners; she occasionally donates these and other confections for sale at auctions benefiting area arts foundations. The single wall of counter space, almost a third of it taken up by the sink, was just not enough for her work.

She also found the kitchen's layout something of a quandary. The stove is visible from the dining room. It would originally have been hidden by a swinging door, but the door had been removed and it's convenient to leave it off. Protruding from the west wall, the stove creates a mild obstruction to the visual and traffic flow between the dining room, kitchen and backyard. At the back of the room, valuable square footage was broken up into a pair of small spaces, a breakfast nook and pantry, both original to the house. Friends suggested she remove the wall between them and enlarge the kitchen-proper, but she thought that taking out this wall of glass tile made by the Nurre Mirror Plate Company and losing the arched doorway that was a major feature of the room's charm would be a kind of crime.

Linda lived with the kitchen for five years, paying attention to how she used the space, before she decided which changes she wanted to make. The breakfast nook also proved a good place to store oversized items such as her KitchenAid mixer and Instant Pot, but without cabinets designed to accommodate those and other items, many of them large, she ended up with piles of clutter.

Linda decided that one way to make the breakfast room work better for her was to add a workbench. I based the design of the workbench on her original cabinets, which have inset doors on butt hinges and surface-mounted latches. The previous homeowners had painted the original built-ins in two-tone off-white. I had the colors matched as closely as possible at one of our locally owned paint stores.

We installed glass knobs fastened by a removable nut and bolt. We also added pull-out shelves to the original cabinets' door bases. Eventually she will replace the laminate counter.

Puzzle pieces. The kitchen still has its original breakfast nook and back pantry, small spaces that were tempting to incorporate into the kitchen proper by removing the intermediate wall. Instead, Linda turned the breakfast nook into a room designed for context-sensitive storage with a baker's workbench. The fridge is in the rear pantry/mud room. A small enamel-topped table provides workspace next to the stove. Linda plans to replace the stove with one that's more attractive; the open doorway between kitchen and dining room means the stove is always in view.

Baker's workbench. Linda and I worked together to customize the details and dimensions of the workbench parts so the piece would give her maximum usefulness and pleasure. The top is edge-grain maple butcherblock with a factory-oiled finish. I built the base in two sections for ease of delivery. The workbench is painted in a two-tone scheme matched as close as possible to the rest of the cabinets.

Service Providers & Sources
- Workbench: NR Hiller Design
- Maple counter: Boos (johnboos.com)
- Bin pulls, hinges and latch: Rejuvenation (rejuvenation.com)
- Glass knobs: House of Antique Hardware (houseofantiquehardware.com)
- Paint: Benjamin Moore Satin Impervo oil-based paint from Bloomington Paint and Wallpaper (bloomingtonpaintandwallpaper.com)
- Wall tile: vintage

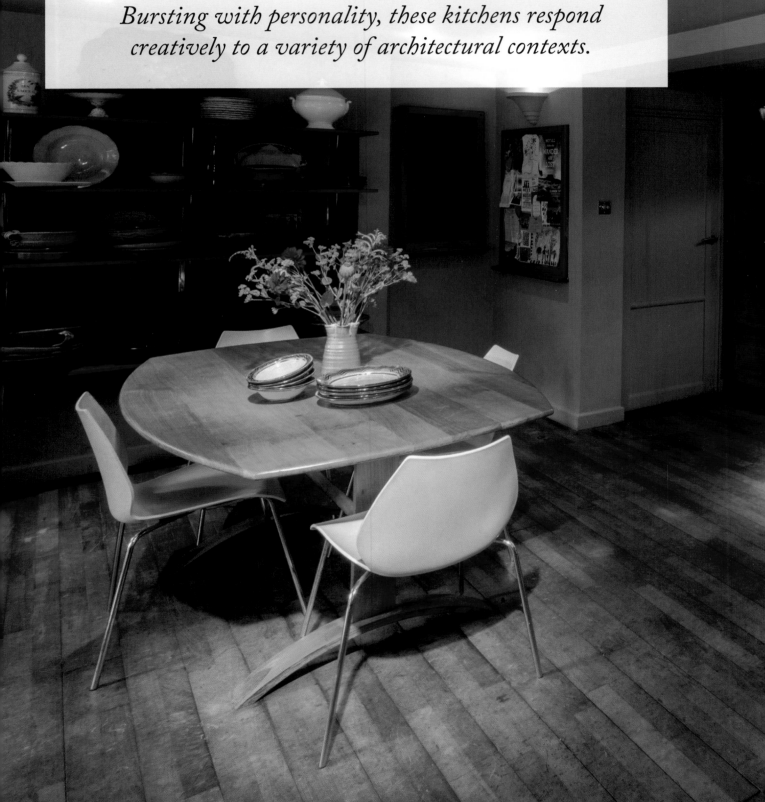

7
A Varied Portfolio

Bursting with personality, these kitchens respond creatively to a variety of architectural contexts.

Room for everyone. Johnny and Becca Grey have welcomed their children into the kitchen since they were little. Encompassing areas for dining, reading, studying or simply enjoying the garden view, the kitchen is furnished with a mix of freestanding and built-in pieces, some of them old and others new.

BENEDICT GREY PHOTOGRAPHY

Old & new. One of Johnny's innovations was to add antiques to purpose-made kitchen furniture, a good way to give a kitchen the feel of a room for living, not just work. Early on, this idea met with resistance from cabinet companies. "All kitchen companies want to do is sell their cabinets," he complains. "They're ruthlessly commercial." The dresser in the Greys' kitchen was the first antique Johnny bought for himself. It was made around 1760; the back planks have marks from being pit-sawn. The design is unusual in that the piece has no back legs but was made to rest against the wall — very practical as a means to prevent the legs from rotting with regular exposure to water when the floor was washed.

BENEDICT GREY PHOTOGRAPHY

The Original Sociable Kitchen

Kitchen designer Johnny Grey first came to my notice in the early 1990s when furniture maker Tom Replogle showed me his copy of Grey's first book, "The Art of Kitchen Design." I immediately went out and bought my own copy, which I devoured. I especially appreciated the historical survey by means of which Johnny argued that the kitchen-as-isolated-workroom was a modern anomaly. Instead, he wrote, the kitchen has historically been a room used by the whole family for more than just cooking – and should be so, again, in our time.

As befits a room where family members don't just prepare meals, but also read, draw, study, listen to music, have conversations and weave flowers into bouquets, the kitchen should be furnished with a view to beauty and comfort no less than handiness and hygiene. I was also fascinated to learn that Elizabeth David, a widely respected author on food and cooking, whose books featured large in my mother's kitchen during the 1970s, was his aunt; he had grown up visiting her kitchen.

Years later, *Fine Homebuilding* magazine hired me to write a Q&A about Johnny. We set up a talk by phone, and I was relieved to find him deliciously funny and down to earth. That impression was confirmed when my husband and I visited him and his family last spring. It's not every day you're invited by one of your design heroes to have dinner with him and his wife, Becca, then stay the night. After momentarily thinking I couldn't possibly say yes, I told myself that this was too rare and warm an invitation to decline. Walking into their house, I felt instantly at home – which shouldn't really have come as a surprise, considering that I'd spent years studying images of their kitchen in Johnny's book. But now the room was alive, with dachshunds Richard and Margot lying by the fire and Ken, an enormous retriever puppy, begging for after-dinner scraps. Here were Johnny and Becca's daughter Gus, who's training to be an architect, and her fiancé, Henry, a doctor. Having read so much about "the sociable kitchen," there we were, in Johnny and Becca's prototype.

Johnny grew up in the austerity of post-war London, one of five children born to a father who was a physician and a mother he calls "a bit of a romantic." After his mother persuaded her husband to buy a rundown two-bedroom cottage in Sussex, they acquired an old gypsy wagon to use as a third bedroom. The wagon's roof leaked, and Dr. Grey's children were introduced to woodworking by the frequent need for repairs, leading them all to become amateur woodworkers, and Johnny to furniture making.

While studying architecture at the Architectural Association in the 1970s, Johnny was exposed to leading thinkers of the day such as Ivan Illich, Buckminster Fuller, Christopher Alexander and Lyall Watson. He ran an antiques business on the side, which gave him valuable grounding in dates and styles and influenced him as a designer.

He claims he got into kitchens by accident. "I disliked the corporate world and loathed the business of my hours being 'owned' by other people. Because of my bohemian background in Sussex, I felt I couldn't handle a job where I wouldn't be making anything. The thing about kitchens is that you can do a bit of everything: design, making, meeting the clients, doing something new and creative."

After setting up as a designer-maker in 1976, Johnny sold his concept for the Unfitted Kitchen to the kitchen cabinet company Smallbone in 1986. He has worked for clients around the world since then. In 1990, he and Becca moved to a house in rural Hampshire. Originally built in the 1960s for Ann Moorsom, who had worked with garden designer Gertrude Jekyll, the simple house was conceived as a place to enjoy solitude in quiet, green surroundings and has an enviable view across England's pastoral South Downs.

Shortly after moving in, they completely reworked the kitchen. Johnny was 40; it was the first time he'd had a chance to make a kitchen for himself, and he did it on a meager budget. The plan: take a low-ceilinged garage at the back of the house and open it up to the front room, creating a large space for cooking, eating and living. They added French doors leading out to the garden, which brought that breathtaking view over the Downs into the heart of the house.

Johnny's publisher, Cassell, put his family's kitchen on the cover of his first book, "The Art of Kitchen Design." The book proved hugely influential. Although plenty of Americans may never have heard the name Johnny Grey, they've been furnishing their kitchens with echoes of his ideas since the late 1980s. For one, the notion that the kitchen should be the focal point of the home has become accepted wisdom. Less happily, so has the penchant for mixing cabinet depths and heights, and combining natural wood cabinets with those that are painted; so widespread are these tropes today that they've become trite – never more so than in cases where mass manufacturers who appreciate the visual appeal but lack the requisite restraint mix these elements willy-nilly, simply for the sake of breaking up a finish or a plane. And then there's his influence on hardware:

For about a decade beginning in the mid-1990s, you could buy stainless steel arc drawer pulls inspired by those seen on the cover of his book – one based on a ship's cleat, the other a pair of curved wires. Pointing out that his pulls were often mounted over a concave section in the face of a door or drawer, he says he likes being "invited, both physically and visually, into using a piece of furniture"; the concave back also helps keep clothes from being snagged on the end of a cleat-style pull. Another of his pulls that remain influential to this day is what he calls the suitcase handle; today you can see these all over the internet in wood and leather.

Although Johnny's influence on how I approach kitchen design may not be obvious (and there are certainly matters on which we disagree), his historically informed perspective and championing of the kitchen as a room for living have played an enormous part been in how I think about kitchens. It's an honor to be allowed to include his family's kitchen in this book.

Island view. This island was Johnny's first experiment with what he calls soft geometry. "People move around a kitchen a bit like water flows over a rocky river bed," he wrote in "The Art of Kitchen Design." "Human beings do not walk around corners by following a precise right angle…. The concept of soft geometry recognizes the principle that of the hundreds of mini-journeys that are made in the kitchen everyday, many would benefit from furniture designed using curved or soft shapes which enhance the ease of movement in the room."[10]

The green bar stool (see the opening spread of this chapter) was an Italian design from the 1980s. Aside from its looks, its best feature is its easily adjustable height. A footrest is also essential; it's irksome to sit with your feet dangling in space. Johnny considers his greatest innovation on the island the low-level counter for children to use. The lower counter is also perfect for using tall machines such as a food processor or toaster. "Why would you put a toaster next to your eye-brows?" he asks. The area by the stove is also lower, not only to make using long-handled utensils more convenient, but to keep the cook's face from being burned by boiling water or splashed frying fat. (Each section of the island has its own counter – granite for the low section, cherry for the high, which is not a work surface. Around the stove is stainless steel.)
BENEDICT GREY PHOTOGRAPHY

A new level. Cornish granite makes a practical counter for a toaster and other small appliances.

BENEDICT GREY PHOTOGRAPHY

Colorful corner. Small annexes such as pantries don't have to be boring. Becca's sister, Lucy Turner, painted this tiny corner, transforming it into a thoroughly inviting space.

BENEDICT GREY PHOTOGRAPHY

Service Providers & Sources

- Kitchen design and general contracting: Johnny Grey (johnnygrey.com)
- Cabinetmaking: Jonathan Morriss
- Decorative painting: Lucy Turner
- Tiles: Alex Zdankowicz (alexzdankowicz.co.uk))
- Metalwork legs by window seat: Paul Jobst (pauljobst.com)

Wooded view. The shelf to the left of the window is made from Cornish granite, the same material used on the island's lowest counter. The drainboard is naturally water-resistant teak, now 30 years old; Johnny refinishes it periodically with a decking oil made by Osmo. The fireclay sink is by Shaw's; it's large enough for big pots and baking sheets and has plenty of depth, which minimizes splashing.

The inlays on various cabinet elements break up flat expanses of veneer and evoke associations with traditional craftsmanship. They're also flush, which makes doors and drawer faces easy to clean.
BENEDICT GREY PHOTOGRAPHY

Not square. Esherick built curved cabinets under the south-facing window. The counters are solid wood with a polyurethane finish and hammered copper sink. He built the oven for open-flame cooking but also incorporated a conventional gas stove. (The stove here is not original.) The floor, which is original, is vinyl.
LAURI HAFVENSTEIN

Swing-out storage. Instead of mounting the drawers in this curved corner cabinet on slides, Esherick made them pivot on hinges.

LAURI HAFVENSTEIN

Case Study 7.2

Kitchen as Working Sculpture

Wharton Esherick, a sculptor considered by many of his contemporaries as the dean of American craftsmen, built a studio in 1926 and remodeled the structure 14 years later to turn it into his home. In 1965 he began planning an addition that would house a larger kitchen within a structure inspired by the form of a silo, to honor the agricultural history of his rural Pennsylvania location.

The story behind the kitchen, the design of which was integrated with a dining room and deck, is recounted in the biography, "Wharton Esherick: The Journey of a Creative Mind," by Mansfield Bascom. "On summer evenings," Bascom wrote, "Wharton would sit on a bench outside his kitchen door, in the shade of the big oak, enjoying the breeze that funneled between the studio and the shop and thinking how much more enjoyable life would be to have a deck off the dining room." He went on to describe how Esherick blended his desire for a congenial place to sit outside in the company of friends with inspiration from farm buildings in the surrounding countryside and boardwalks on the coast. On the piers supporting the deck he smoothed "the plum-colored stucco finish, slightly flattening one

Tree-top dining. The kitchen opens onto the dining room, which is also furnished with pieces Esherick built. In addition to the furniture, he made the puzzle-like floor, finished the walls with wood and fabricated the light fixtures. The doorway goes out to a deck overlooking the forest.
LAURI HAFVENSTEIN

Novel drawers. The other end of the kitchen has a pair of curved cabinets, upper and lower, also with a solid-wood counter. Instead of pulling out as regular drawers do, these pivot on hinges. Note that the doors have finger holes instead of added pulls. The painting is by Esherick's grandson, David, when he was a child.

LAURI HAFVENSTEIN

Forest inspiration. Considering that Esherick's home and studio are in the forest, it's fitting that these post-mounted shelves call shelf mushrooms to mind. The shelves inside the base cabinets are painted green to match the ceiling.
LAURI HAFVENSTEIN

Inside scoop. The sink cabinet does not have a floor. Esherick added wooden straps to form slots for lid storage, and as with the other cabinets, he installed interior lighting.
LAURI HAFVENSTEIN

side to leave an edge, such as the kind produced by generations of cattle rubbing their sides." He had the silo, built of stuccoed concrete block, finished with "a large abstract fresco of autumnal colors that matched the surrounding woods" and put a wood-burning oven in the kitchen so he could broil steak while cooking vegetables on the stove. The window in the west wall allowed Esherick to watch the sun set from the kitchen.

Integrated chopping. Esherick made a cutting board to fit the perimeter of his hammered copper sink, adding a chopping surface handily located for disposing of waste.
LAURI HAFVENSTEIN

Enjoy the view. When your kitchen utensils are beautifully handcrafted artifacts in their own right, not mere means to an end, there is every reason to have them on display.
LAURI HAFVENSTEIN

Main work area. The short leg of the L-shaped main preparation area has storage for cutlery, baking pans, wood cutting boards and cookbooks. The sink is at the right, beneath a north-facing window.

Light switch. An antique light switch rewired to modern code is a subtle touch.

Case Study 7.3

Inspired by Voysey

The 1930 Tudor Revival that's home to this kitchen had many handsome original architectural features when its current owner, Betsi Grabe, bought the place in 2002. Unfortunately, the kitchen was not one of them. Instead, the room had boring cabinets with plywood doors and drawers, all painted a tummy-troubling shade of green. A shiny marble-tiled floor was equally out of place in the larger architectural context, which includes divided-light metal casement windows, textured plaster and distinctive trim.

Cornered. This inside corner has an L-shaped cabinet with two doors – one primary, the other secondary. A pie-cut Susan occupies most of the interior, but the wider leg, at right, had enough room left over for a separate section with vertical storage for baking sheets and trays.

Hardware. In place of regular door hardware, we used salvaged steeple-tip architectural butt hinges provided by the homeowner and an oversized casement latch.

Betsi hired my company in 2006. Once we had a plan, she demolished the entire kitchen herself and started from scratch, making the most of what original fabric remained – ceiling joists, subfloors, plastered walls.

Today the room's floor is the old pine subfloor, sanded and refinished; where a wall once stood between the main part of the kitchen and a breakfast nook, she decided to embrace the differing floorboard directions instead of considering them a detraction. To give the room a more spacious and earthy feel, she tore out the ceiling, cleaned the joists and underside of the upstairs subfloor, then had all of the ceiling timbers finished to resemble whitewash.

Daniel O'Grady was the main cabinetmaker on this job. He built cabinets with quartersawn oak faces inspired by those at The Homestead, a 1905 English country house designed by architect C.F.A. Voysey. The inset doors are hung on hand-wrought strap hinges and opened by means of hand-turned pulls; the boards are attached to braces with Tremont wrought-head nails. Our client wanted the wood to look less than perfectly surfaced (it would not be seemly to use the actual word she used to describe the look she was after), so Daniel planed the occasional board against the grain. Just right.

A glazed cabinet for dishware and another that holds spices are made with salvaged hinges – steeple-tipped butts and butterfly hinges, respectively. Tiled counters and backsplashes, antique lighting and reproduction appliances complete the picture.

Service Providers & Sources

- Cabinets: NR Hiller Design; primary cabinetmaker Daniel O'Grady
- Tile setter: Tom Stocker, Bloomington, Ind.
- Electrician: John Houff, Homeowner Service (homeownerserviceelectric.com)
- Stove: Heartland Appliances (heartlandapp.com)
- Fridge: Big Chill (bigchill.com)
- Taps: Barber Wilsons & Co. (barberwilsons.com)
- Strap hinges: Horton Brasses (horton-brasses.com)

Back door view. Looking toward the back of the house, the fridge is at the left. An antique dresser provides freestanding storage.

Shoji screen inspiration. The original window over the sink offered a stark view of the neighboring house's brick wall, so Bruce and Jana replaced it with luminous glass block. The soapstone counter and undermount sink make clean-up easy, and when the cook's hands are dirty, the faucet turns on and off by touch – no need to use the handle.

Silverware storage. Bruce added adjustable dividers to the silverware drawer to keep the contents organized. He left the core of the plywood exposed, sanding and finishing it to make an interesting feature when drawers are open.

Case Study 7.4

East-Coast Pacific

The neat brick façade of Bruce Chaffin and Jana Moore's 1878 row house in Philadelphia opens onto an eclectic interior filled with artwork, antiques and a collection of colorful shawls and scarves, most of them knitted by Jana. This contrast between minimalist exterior and interior abundance is reversed at the back of the house, where Jana's prize-winning container garden, a masterful composition of textures, proportions and color, is the focal point of a serene, minimalist kitchen.

The kitchen you see here stands in dramatic contrast to its appearance in 2003 when Jana bought the house – 1980s white melamine-coated particleboard cabinets, worn laminate counters and a filthy vinyl floor. The cabinets gradually fell apart ("in a way that could not be fixed," adds Bruce). When the handle of the faucet broke off (literally), they improvised with Vise-Grips for a year and a half.

The clean lines owe as much to Bruce's planning as to the couple's tidy habits. When Bruce designed the cabinets, he gave a lot of thought to what he and Jana wanted – and did not want – to see. And when he built them, he incorporated some ingenious storage devices that make it easy to keep the counters clear of clutter. Wondering where the receptacles are? Don't worry; they're here, per code; they're just concealed beneath the upper cabinets. The absence of surface-mounted hardware also contributes to the clear view; doors and drawers operate by means of touch latches and slides.

To bridge the 7' between the banks of cabinets and make a place for casual meals, Bruce built a table with an apple wood slab top. A pair of matching stools offer seating that's easily stowed beneath. Natural materials – cork flooring, bamboo cabinet faces and soapstone counters – age gracefully, and the long horizontal lines lead the eye outward to the garden.

Follow the lines. When building the stools to go with the table, Bruce cut the seats from the same slab so their grain would line up when they're stowed beneath the table.

A graceful approach to old-house challenges. Leveling feet concealed by recessed toe kicks made it relatively easy to deal with an uneven floor. Aware that the ceiling was equally out of whack, Bruce decided to stop the upper cabinets a few inches below and installed Edge Lighting's Soft Strip lighting on the cabinets' tops. While it's not "practical," strictly speaking – the illumination is superfluous to requirements and doesn't qualify as task lighting – the glow enhances the luminous character of the room.

Use every inch. Instead of leaving the sink base largely empty, Bruce built storage drawers that fit around the pipes.

Minimize stacking. Rather than stacking drawer contents high, Bruce installed secondary pullout trays in drawers. This one holds the lids of the pots and pans below.

Pops of color. Jana painted the cabinet backs orange for user delight.

Service Providers & Sources

- Architect: Joseph Brin
- General contractor: Louie DiCicco Construction, Philadelphia, Penn.
- Cabinet design and building: Bruce Chaffin
- Lighting over and under cabinets: Soft Strip by Edge Lighting (lightology.com)
- Sink: Kohler K-5409, 29" with 16-gauge stainless steel (kohler.com)
- Faucet: Delta Trinsic Touch20 (deltafaucet.com)
- Stone supplier: Bucks County Soapstone (bcsoapstone.com)
- Bamboo plywood: Cali Bamboo (calibamboo.com)
- Cork flooring: Duro Design (duro-design.com)
- Tile backsplash: Alys Edwards (alysedwards.com); the "Man About You" collection; "Peak My Interest" color; with matching grout
- Tile setter: Louie DiCicco Construction

The point of it all. The garden is the focal point of the room — no surprise, considering that Jana has won multiple awards, among them the 2018 blue ribbon from the Pennsylvania Horticultural Society in the container garden category.
JANA MOORE

A lovely place to wash dishes. Bert and Amy chose soapstone counters and a soapstone sink for their hardworking farmhouse kitchen. The nicks from wear make the counters look perfectly at home in the 150-year-old house. The cabinets have recessed toe kicks and angled feet.

Always smiling. One of Amy's sisters gave her this pestle, which gets regular use for grinding spices.

Case Study 7.5

At Home on the Land

Bert Gilbert and Amy Dyken, who operate Gilbert Construction, based near Bloomington, Ind., lived in their 150-year-old I-house for about 20 years before redoing the kitchen – plenty of time to think about how they wanted the new kitchen to work.

Pivotal character. The house's original chimney (there's a fireplace in the living room just through the door) provides a wonderfully textured focal point with large sandstone blocks marked by tools and more than a century of wear.

Bert and Amy installed maple floorboards salvaged from an Indiana University gym. East-facing windows at the north end of the kitchen and in the adjoining front hallway make this antique oak table an inviting place for meals.

When they bought the house in 1987, the kitchen was a handyman special created by a previous homeowner in the early 1960s. A gold-flecked sheet faux-tile backsplash hung over varnished birch plywood cabinets coated so thickly with grease that Bert and Amy had to scrape it off with a putty knife before they could wash the cabinet faces. The water supply for the kitchen sink had only recently been converted from a cistern-fed hand pump on the counter to a single-handle faucet fed from the spring by an electric pump.

Even though Bert and Amy didn't care for the former kitchen's style, they respected the effort their predecessor had put into it. He hadn't just built the cabinets himself; he'd done so in a primitive shed across the road. Eventually, however, they were ready for a higher-functioning kitchen. The 32"-high counters with their mere 13" of vertical workspace would have to go, along with the 7' ceiling – 18" of which was occupied by useless bulkheads.

Bert and Amy designed the new cabinets based on an original built-in, specifying inset doors with square-pegged tenons, hung on butt hinges. The cabinets have solid cherry faces with prefinished plywood interiors. Uppers are 13" deep for extra capacity and extend up to the ceiling; instead of scribing the crown moulding to the dramatic irregularities of the old joists over the fridge, they filled that area in with drywall. Although Bert and Amy did most of the design work, cabinet designer Michelle Hewins, who runs Hewins Cabinets with her husband, Mark, made invaluable suggestions for tweaking details with a view to keeping options open for replacement appliances down the line.

Open storage as decorative as it is practical.
Open shelves store jars of beans, grains
and spices over a prep sink conveniently
located near the stove. Bert and Amy
mounted an antique coffee grinder on the
cabinet at left over the sink; they use it
occasionally for decaf. Bert and Amy found
the scoops hanging on the opposite cabinet in the kitchen, apparently shop class
projects from years gone by. Bert found the
antique holophane pendant, one of three
in the kitchen, partially buried beneath the
dirt behind a shed across the road.

Sources & Service Providers
• Design and general contracting: Gilbert
Construction Inc.

• Cabinetmakers: Hewins Cabinets, Solsberry, Ind.

• Holophane pendants: salvaged

• Floor: salvaged

Some like it hot. A hot sauce caddy by woodworker Dave
Diegel, a close friend, adds a colorful touch.

Stove detail. The cook's side of the peninsula stores pots and pans in drawers without faces for optimal accessibility. Drawers to the right of the stove hold potholders, spices and cooking utensils. The open area beneath the counter offers a place to work while sitting on a stool.
SPECTRUM CREATIVE GROUP

Salvaged parts. Fritz and Don planned their kitchen remodel around the treasure trove of architectural salvage from a family home that was demolished. Oversized hinges and knobs lend an Alice-in-Wonderland playfulness to the serious masculine cabinets and counters of dark quartersawn oak and honed granite.
SPECTRUM CREATIVE GROUP

Case Study 7.6

Industrial Rustic

Homeowners Fritz Lieber and Don Maxwell contacted me in 2004 after hearing from a mutual friend that I like to incorporate salvaged hardware and house parts into my work. Fritz's grandparents' home on the outskirts of Indianapolis had been demolished to make way for suburban expansion, and Fritz had salvaged every scrap he could.

View toward the dining room. My original design for the glazed upper cabinet over the peninsula had the cabinet supported at the wall and by means of a wooden left side that would transfer weight to the counter. General contractor Bert Gilbert, who has a degree in fine arts and is an accomplished sculptor as well as builder, came up with the ingenious suggestion to suspend the outer end from the beam instead. It's a practical solution that has the bonus of making the space feel lighter and more open. The cabinet is hung by threaded rod with washers and nuts; the rod runs vertically through the cabinet behind the corner frame stiles, and the nuts beneath are hidden behind the recess below the floor.

The upper peninsula cabinet is glazed on three sides to allow the unrestricted diffusion of light, preserving maximum openness between the cook's area and the area for guests. The dimensions of the leaded-glass panel determined the basic dimensions of the cabinet. In planning the doors, I factored in the large protruding stove hood a few inches away.

At the far wall, Fritz and Don wanted to incorporate a bar sink and wine fridge with a small drawer for bar tools. We added an upper cabinet to store glasses — another opportunity to use a leaded-glass panel. The large cabinet at the left is a pantry fitted with doors, hinges and knobs from Fritz's family's house.
SPECTRUM CREATIVE GROUP

Sink view. The cook's end of the kitchen is arranged in a classic work triangle with the large farmhouse sink below a three-section window. Windows to the east and west in addition to a skylight and clear-finished maple floor make this kitchen an invitingly bright space even on the greyest winter days. Bert suggested the recessed niche in the wall as a place for decorative objects. The sink base has legs to suggest that it's a freestanding piece of kitchen furniture along the lines of a Hoosier cabinet.

The Italian smoked glass subway tiles also came from Fritz's family's house. Bert and his crew painstakingly removed old mastic from the tiles' backs before fitting them in their new home.

SPECTRUM CREATIVE GROUP

At our first meeting I asked whether the clients really wanted to take out the original painted steel cabinets. They were certain; they appreciated the cabinets' mid-century style but were ready for something different. "Industrial-rustic" was the term they used to describe what they were after. Also important to Fritz and Don was the kitchen's layout. As serious cooks who like to entertain, they wanted to come up with a way to keep friends within conversation distance but out of the main workspace. As we started to think about layout, we came up with a plan for a peninsula that would divide the more public area from the kitchen proper.

The basic footprint of the combined space would remain the same, though a big part of the contractor's job was to build an enclosed screened porch accessible from the kitchen at the front of the house, because it has western exposure. The contractor, Bert Gilbert, suggested vaulting the ceiling and adding a tie-beam for architectural interest as well as structural reinforcement.

In 2004, industrial-rustic was not yet a thing, but I had an idea at least for the industrial part, based

Dual orientation. Cabinets don't always have to face forward. Those at the end of a run may be more useful, not to mention much more fun, if they offer access from two directions. This cabinet houses a microwave behind a retractable flip-up door, a pair of baskets for potatoes and onions, drawers and a deep area behind a door for storing large items. Instead of covering up the static sections with plain cabinet sides, Fritz and Don said they wanted a steel panel for magnets. We also incorporated a panel for push pins. What appear to be two drawers adjacent to the produce baskets are false faces.

SPECTRUM CREATIVE GROUP

Service Providers & Sources

• General contractor: Bert Gilbert, Gilbert Construction (gilbertbuilt.us)

• Cabinet design, construction and installation: NR Hiller Design

• Basket weaving: Linda Boyle Gibson, Bloomington, Ind.

• Stove and hood: DCS (now Fisher & Paykel Professional) (dcsappliances.com)

• Sink: Kallista (kallista.com), purchased through Lee Supply (gotolee.com)

• Faucet: Newport Brass (newportbrass.com)

• Electrician: John Houff, Homeowner Service (homeownerserviceelectric.com)

• Light over sink: Troy Classic, RLM Lighting (troyrlm.com)

• Windows: Pella (pella.com)

• Skylight: Velux (veluxusa.com)

on an old building in town that had recently been adapted for re-use. Bloomington's Frosted Foods Building, near the railroad tracks on the city's west side, was originally a cold-storage plant for meat. The building had been sensitively restored under the direction of Duncan Campbell and Cynthia Brubaker, of Preservation Development Inc., and converted to commercial space for offices and retail. Among its most impressive features were the many divided-light metal windows; one of my favorite details was a windowed wall between the retail anchor space and an adjacent hallway leading to offices at the rear of the building. I suggested that we model the upper section of the peninsula loosely on this theme, incorporating one of the salvaged leaded-glass panels from Fritz's grandparents' house.

Quartersawn white oak with a dark dye and stain would go some way toward expressing the rustic part of the design brief. It is also an appropriately masculine combination. And we would use Fritz's salvaged architectural-scale butt hinges and knobs for the cabinets.

In plain view. Jonathan and Alex agreed to forgo doors and drawer faces in part of the kitchen to keep regularly used items in plain view. This is a working kitchen, a true workroom, and they wanted to honor that concept. A popular idea? Absolutely not; contemporary wisdom holds that most cabinet contents should be hidden from view. But open cabinets work well for them, and we designed the cabinetry so that it could be retrofitted with doors and drawer faces someday, if they or future home-owners decide to add them.

Spooning. A pair of spoons from South Africa with telephone wire-wrapped handles.

Case Study 7.7

An Easygoing Kitchen for a Family of Cooks

Alexandra Morphet and Jonathan Elmer bought their house in 2006, their move prompted by a desire to live in a school district where their children, Nathaniel and Lydia, could study with renowned jazz music educator Janis Stockhouse at Bloomington High School North. The previous homeowner had thoroughly reworked the interior to create a dramatic space for entertaining; for cooking, not so much.

265

Dresser inspiration. When all the walls and doorways had been reconfigured, the room was left with a long empty wall. With approximately 14" between it and the casing of the door to the living room, there was nowhere near enough depth for standard cabinets, but plenty of room to store all sorts of kitchen contents if you think outside the box. I designed a set of built-ins loosely based on the form of a traditional Welsh dresser. The casework is maple with a light stain; the blotchiness is intentional. We were emulating the look of an old piece that had been stripped and refinished. Open areas with adjustable shelves and steel-blue backs display antique plates, art pottery, everyday dishes and glassware, along with a few interesting bits of cookware. They also keep spices, teas, jars of dry goods and cookbooks handy. Large appliances and less attractive supplies are behind the doors and inside drawers on full-extension slides.

The kitchen was shoehorned into an 8'-square corner of the open-plan living room, more like a cappuccino bar than a place for serious cooks to prepare meals. Alex and Jonathan worked with architect Malcolm Woollen to reconfigure the space to create a comfortable living room with a dining area in what had been an enclosed porch. He directed the builders to rebuild a bearing wall that had been removed (with theatrical columns providing support for the upstairs floor during that era of the house's history), to allow for an attractive and practical kitchen.

They wanted to have some of the kitchen cabinetry open; as Alex explained in our first meeting, "I want my children to know where things are and participate in putting them away." Furnishing a kitchen with a good percentage of cabinets that have no doors or drawer faces is about as daring as having your husband wear a skirt (hats off to you kilt-wearers), so by way of assuring Alex that her idea had a good precedent I contacted Jan Bulla-Baker, a former neighbor of mine who runs the Blooming-

ton Cooking School. I'd visited Jan's kitchen several times and loved its welcoming, no-nonsense character.[11] It was an ideal example of a comfortable space designed for cooking – and like Alex and Jonathan's kitchen, it had a sunny garden view. Many professional cooks have kitchens that defy prevailing design dogma. I know pros who happily live without a dishwasher, keep appliances on their counters and have many of their cabinets' contents in plain view. Jan kindly let us visit her kitchen, which provided several points of inspiration for this one.

With their entire house under construction the summer they moved in, Alex and Jonathan had no kitchen for six weeks – a perfect opportunity to cook on the grill. "Even though it wasn't such a great time to visit, my father-in-law visited that summer, from South Africa," remembers Jonathan. "It turned out fine. Like most South Africans, he'd eat chops on the grill every night if he had the chance. But every visitor who ever comes over comments on our beautiful kitchen. And I can still grill if I need to."

Garden view. In choosing their appliances, Jonathan and Alex were more interested in performance and price than having everything match. The cabinets are cherry, with counters in pale green granite; the stone fabricator milled drainboard slots into the section at the right of the sink. An old table base bought at a favorite Bloomington store makes a comfortable place for looking through cookbooks and taking informal meals. The top is finished with distressed milk paint sealed with oil-based polyurethane. We made sturdy benches to match. Alex, a professional couturier, made the cushions.

Drawers under the cooktop. "I'm tired of being on my knees. I want to see what's there," says Jonathan, recalling why he opted for shallow-sided drawers on full-extension runners to house cookware. Directly beneath the cooktop, cookware is readily at hand. A wall-mounted pot rack augments storage.

Forget the corner. Rather than incorporate a storage unit in this inside corner, Jonathan and Alex decided to make the most of the space with open drawers for cookware and adjacent drawers for silverware, cooking utensils, dish towels etc. We had a few inches left after the sink was centered on the window and the stack of drawers and trash pull-out were in place, so we installed a pull-out for condiments and oils.

Open view. Across from the dresser, a section of counter and wall functions as a landing pad; the house's front door is just around the corner. Through the opening is the living room with a fireplace designed by architect Malcolm Woollen. Note that we planned the dresser and door casing to work together; the dresser comes right up to the edge of the casing and the top hat trim is cut flush to utilize every bit of storage and display space and avoid leaving a skinny strip of wall to bedevil future painters.

Service Providers & Sources

• Architect: Malcolm Woollen
• General contractor: Golden Hands Construction Inc. (goldenhandsco.com)
• Countertops: Tremain Tile and Marble, Indianapolis, Ind.
• Cabinetry: NR Hiller Design

This will floor you. Original glass block wall tile and a quilt pattern painted on wood floorboards were the foundation of this kitchen's design, which combines cherry cabinets with others finished in milk paint.
SPECTRUM CREATIVE GROUP

Distinctive doors. I made the doors for the spice cabinet to a different design from those of the rest of the kitchen, adding a vertical profile at the center of each panel, and also used different hardware.
SPECTRUM CREATIVE GROUP

Case Study 7.8

Green on Green

Carol and Roger Parks had lived in their home for 15 years when they decided it was time to do the kitchen in 2005. They'd made some improvements to what was there when they bought the house, a 1927 Colonial Revival just a block from the university campus where Roger taught, but those changes had been relatively minor – paint for the cabinets, a new sink and dishwasher, new Formica counters.

Finished ends. Because this kitchen opens onto public spaces – the dining room and the four-season porch – I wanted the end panels of the main cabinets to be nicer than plain flat slabs. These panels are integral to the cabinets, not applied. They follow the same basic design as the cabinet doors, though the rails and stiles are slightly scaled up in view of the panels' larger size.

SPECTRUM CREATIVE GROUP

Service Providers & Sources

- General contractor: Golden Hands Construction (goldenhandsco.com)

- Painting, including floor: Richard Jenkins, Bloomington, Ind.

- Electrician: Homeowner Services (homeownerserviceelectric.com)

- Cabinets: NR Hiller Design

- Counters: Tremain Tile and Marble, Indianapolis, Ind.

- Milk paint: The Old Fashioned Milk Paint Company (milkpaint.com)

- Cabinet hinges and knobs (main part of kitchen): Rejuvenation (rejuvenation.com)

- Hinges and knobs for spice cabinet: Paxton Hardware (paxtonhardware.com)

- Green glass knobs: available at the time of printing from House of Antique Hardware (houseofantiquehardware.com)

They had also installed an antique retail store counter perpendicular to the south wall to create a peninsula. The counter itself was full of character and added considerable worksurface, but as a cabinet, it wasn't a particularly functional piece. Just as importantly, the arrangement created an additional inside corner, which wasted space. Carol loves to cook, and they were ready to make the kitchen more functional and aesthetically coherent.

This kitchen has three doorways, making it a relatively high traffic area. One door goes to the dining room, one to a back porch and one to a back hall (and on from there to a half-bath in one direction, the basement in the other). We decided to think of the kitchen as a room with two parts: the main workspace and the more fluid traffic zone.

In the kitchen proper there were three primary considerations. First, Carol wanted a more practical layout. She was determined to preserve the room's original glass block wall tiles, which were manufactured locally by the Nurre Mirror Plate Company in the early 20th century, and planned a color scheme around them. Finally, she wanted to keep the floor painted in the quilt pattern she had seen in a magazine, though it would need to be redone.

On hearing that Carol and Roger had put the house on the market pending their relocation to Texas, I worried that the buyers might tear out the kitchen, which is undeniably idiosyncratic with its seafoam painted cabinetry and emerald glass knobs. Carol herself had joked during construction that the layering of greens would likely prompt some of her friends to question the state of her mind. So it came as a huge relief when I contacted the new homeowners several years after they had bought the place, and learned they'd made very few changes to the kitchen.

U-shaped room. The kitchen has a U-shaped layout with the sink centered under the west-facing window and the stove in its original location on the north wall. The layout initially included a small worktable with a maple base, turned legs, a drawer and stone counter, but Carol and Roger took the table when they moved. The ceiling pendant was installed by the new home-owners in place of a ceiling fan.

Carol decided to mix cherry base cabinets with painted uppers and chose recessed toe kicks, painted black, with decorative feet. The upper cabinets are cypress; the milk paint is applied more as a wash than an opaque paint, to leave the cypress grain slightly visible. Note that the end panels of the base cabinets run down to the floor without a recess, for a finished look.
SPECTRUM CREATIVE GROUP

Working fridge recess. The fridge is housed beneath a capacious cabinet that stores large bowls and platters along with trays and cookie sheets. The shallow spice cabinet is meant to look like a freestanding piece brought into the kitchen later on. I would design this area quite differently today.

SPECTRUM CREATIVE GROUP

Milk painted cabinets. For the upper cabinets I mixed Tavern Green with Snow White milk paint, experimenting with proportions until I had the look Carol wanted. While milk paint is a durable coating, it does not resist stains, so in a hardworking area I recommend adding a protective finish. Almost any finish can be used over milk paint; the choice should take into account the look (sheen, whitening or ambering) and level of protection required.

For this kitchen I experimented with water- and oil-based polyurethanes, subjecting each test piece to cruel and unusual punishment – once the finish had cured, I put a dollop of various typical kitchen substances (Indonesian hot pepper sauce, red wine, rubbing alcohol, Dijon mustard, ketchup, vinegar, olive oil, butter, soy sauce, cola) on the surface, left the test piece lying down to encourage the substances to penetrate the finish for worst-case-scenario effect, then wiped them off after a few hours. The oil-based polyurethane proved resistant to any damage. The water-based poly did almost as well; its weak point was the butter. I discussed the results with Carol, who does a lot of baking with butter. In the interest of avoiding buttery fingerprints around her emerald glass knobs, she opted for the oil-based poly.

This introduced another challenge. The water-based poly kept the cool tone of the custom milk paint mix just as Carol wanted it to look, but the oil-based finish made it warmer. I made up more samples with higher proportions of white, covering each with oil-based poly to ensure that they would be accurate representations, before we hit on the final color.

SPECTRUM CREATIVE GROUP

Furniture for the kitchen. For a less rigidly built-in look in a corner of the kitchen with doorways onto other rooms, I designed a freestanding cabinet that holds a microwave and lots of large kitchen items. Carol specified the bun feet.

SPECTRUM CREATIVE GROUP

Subtle ending. To punctuate the working part of the kitchen and make a transition between it and the adjacent dining room, I made the end cabinet extend from the counter to the ceiling. This cabinet is made of cherry, like the base cabinets, and is a few inches deeper than the upper cabinetry next to it. Glazed sides as well as doors and shelves allow light to flood through the cabinet; integral lighting makes the glassware inside sparkle.

SPECTRUM CREATIVE GROUP

Center of the room. Architect James Rosenbarger designed the layout with a 102"-long by 40"-wide island at the center and a single wall of cabinets.

Valley view. The sink in the island is centered on a bank of windows that look out across the hills, a view that's beautiful in all seasons.

Case Study 7.9

Barn-Style House on a Budget

My brief for this kitchen was simple: follow the architect's basic layout, which called for a large island with a short run of cabinets along the back wall, and make the kitchen as affordable as possible.

My clients, Sherry Holliday and Eric Mitter, had owned the property, high on a hill in a rural county in southern Indiana, for 16 years.

277

Architectural echoes. The island counter has a 14" overhang supported by angle brackets that echo those supporting the front porch roof overhang. We decided to finish the island with red oak beadboard run horizontally and finished to match the rest of the cabinets.

Over that time they had spent weekends and vacations working to restore the land, removing invasive plants and re-introducing native grasses and wildflowers following suggestions from a state forester and a wildlife biologist from the Department of Natural Resources. They planted a vegetable garden and an orchard with apple trees, blueberries and figs.

As retirement neared, they decided to make the place their home. The property had a prefabricated house on a foundation with a walk-out basement. Architect James Rosenbarger helped Eric and Sherry understand that the decrepit manufactured house should be demolished, and Jim designed a new house using the existing foundation. They sold their house in town in 2016, and in 2017, they started construction. When visiting the worksite, they slept in a tent set up in the property's old barn.

I suggested that we keep the design of the cabinets simple, relating key elements to the barn-like aesthetic of the house. Plain-sawn red oak with full-overlay doors and drawer faces would help with affordability. For additional cost savings, the clients picked up their cabinets from my shop, because the time it takes to drive to their property is significant. They also did the finishing work themselves following a hands-on lesson in my shop, and assisted me with the installation, saving the cost of a hired helper. Finally, we split the project into two phases to allow their budget to catch up after the main investment in constructing the house. First came the island, which is 8-1/2' long and forms the work center of the kitchen; this gave them ample preparation and clean-up space, as well as a place to sit. The following year we tackled the main wall of base and upper cabinets, and the cabinet Jim had planned for storing large items over the fridge.

Cookbook storage. Instead of having a static panel at the end of the island, a small bookcase greets people coming in from the screened porch.

Island work. The island houses a dishwasher and sink, with a bank of four drawers for dish towels, food wrappings and small cooking utensils. A small bookcase at the end facing the screened porch holds cookbooks.

Curtains instead of doors. Not all cabinets need doors. Sherry made a simple curtain to hide the contents of this large cabinet built into the fridge alcove.

Service Providers & Sources

• General contractor: Pritchett Brothers (pritchettbros.com)

• Architect: James Rosenbarger (jamesrosenbarger.com)

• Bar stools: Rejuvenation (rejuvenation.com)

• Pendant light fixtures over island: Rejuvenation (rejuvenation.com)

• Cabinets: NR Hiller Design

• Fabric for curtain over fridge: Spoonflower (spoonflower.com)

• Countertops: Honed granite "Black Pearl" from Quality Surfaces Inc. (qualitysurfaces.com)

Farmhouse style

There's a lot of misinformation out there regarding farmhouse style. On the one hand, you can find meaningless marketing-speak such as the following, in a post billing itself as "The Ultimate Guide to Farmhouse Style:" Farmhouse style is "unpretentious" and "all-American," according to the author. "Nodding to its [sic] homegrown roots, farmhouse style homes have a collected-over-time look, complete with old-school prints, distressed furnishings, and vintage finishes."[12] The kitchens and other rooms provided by way of illustration are indistinguishable from those of suburban condos across the land, although you may find a throw pillow or dish towel made to evoke associations with old flour sacks, or an old panel saw with a barn painted on it mounted over a door.

On the more substantive end of the misinformation spectrum you'll find images of dining rooms with wide-plank floors, exposed beams (whether real or made of high-density polyurethane such as the brand-name product Fypon), vaulted ceilings clad with reclaimed wood and interior walls of exposed brick or stone (again, whether structural or simply applied to the surface – a practice real masons refer to as "lick 'n' stick") as illustrations of farmhouse style. Here, some effort has at least been made to relate to an aesthetic traditionally found on farms. The problem is one of misidentification: The aesthetic is drawn not from the farmhouse, but from the barn.

Historically, farmhouses have simply been houses on farms. They were (and still are) built in the prevailing architectural style of their time and location – a simple 1890s Gothic Revival here, a charming 1920s story-and-a-half bungalow there, a 1915 I-house or a 1950s ranch. There is no such thing as "farmhouse style," other than the mish-mash of superficial farm-evoking tropes that tens of thousands now refer to by that name; the association of farmhouse style with exposed structural elements and a stripped-down, whitewashed aesthetic derives from the culture of barns.

Forget fantasy. The reality behind the marketing of "farmhouse style" is surprisingly prosaic. Farmhouses are simply houses on farms. Their design almost always conforms to architectural styles in fashion when they are constructed, as this selection of farmhouses and one farm-based modular home will attest.

Open view. The kitchen is open to the family room. We discussed pros and cons of having a peninsula or an island. The peninsula, with its uninterrupted stretch of counter, was the winner. The U-shaped workspace faces a wall of pantry-type storage.

DENISE GAUL

Architectural inspiration. Denise and Alice loved the open end of Christine Matheu's peninsula (see "Same Footprint, Different Room"), so I based theirs on that design.
DENISE GAUL

Case Study 7.10

From So-So to Sizzling

The kitchen of Denise Gaul and Alice Collins is a testament to what a woodworker with a grasp of basic materials and techniques can achieve, given patience, determination and problem-solving skills. This contemporary take on mid-century modern style began with an inquiry: Would I work with them to redesign the kitchen, primarily the cabinets and counters, and provide technical advice as needed while they brought the vision to life? A phone call led to a contract, and soon after, I flew to Denver to discuss ideas and take measurements.

As with nearly every kitchen I design, we tossed ideas back and forth until we had a plan, which included scale drawings of the cabinets. Denise and Alice knew they wanted custom-veneered doors, drawers and end panels but didn't have a local supplier in mind, so they paid a visit to Heitink Veneers, where they viewed bundles of the three species they were considering. They decided on quartersawn teak.

They demolished the existing kitchen together, removing the floor tiles with a rented jackhammer. They donated the old cabinets to a local charity and repurposed the countertops as worksurface in their woodworking shop and in Alice's glass art studio. Then began the long process of rebuilding – electrical work, plumbing, drywall, followed by red oak flooring. Denise threw herself into cabinet construction, often with Alice's help. They started by breaking down sheets of 3/4" veneer-core plywood on the table saw, working with the doors of their 14' by 20' shop open to get the necessary space. She assembled the casework in the garage using her newly built Ron Paulk workbench (a knockdown workstation that she stores in the corner when it's not in use; see paulkhomes.com), added solid teak face frames, then turned to building the 40 drawers.

In the middle of this project Denise was laid off from her job. She decided to turn the blow into an opportunity. With enthusiastic support from Alice, she signed up for a nine-month intensive course of study at the Center for Furniture Craftsmanship in Maine. By the time she packed up her truck for the three-day drive, she had installed the drawers. They could finally put things away. In addition to drawers, the kitchen now had counters, plumbing and power.

They worked on the cabinets together over holiday breaks and finally celebrated the installation of the last drawer face in December. All told, it had been a 13-months-long process from the start of demolition – a process that, while sometimes challenging, changed both of their lives for the better. Denise had realized a long-held dream of formal training in furniture making, and together they had created a striking new kitchen.

Before. Commercially manufactured cabinets with full-overlay doors and drawers made less-than-ideal use of the available space. The fashionable yet meaningless variation in cabinet heights to the right of the fridge was one of several features that annoyed Denise and Alice.

Location matters. Changing the kitchen layout to place the range within the U and the refrigerator on the former range wall gave the kitchen a more open feel. It eliminated two solid blocks at each entrance to the kitchen – one where the wall oven had been and another where the refrigerator had stood. Enhancing the greater sense of space is a larger window over the sink; eliminating the upper cabinets over the dishwasher and peninsula area also helped.

A clean view. The fridge wall now has a hardworking bank of floor-to-ceiling cabinets that store pantry goods, pots and pans, espresso maker and coffee grinder, cutting boards, a spice drawer and small appliances. To ease the transition from the den (in the foreground) and living room (visible through the door at left) the end cabinets on the fridge wall are somewhat more open, with a section of counter and a shallower cabinet above. The counter provides an important staging surface for getting things in and out of the fridge.

DENISE GAUL

Easy open. Denise used Blum AVENTOS lift hardware for the counter-height doors. One compartment houses a cappuccino maker; the other incorporates a charging station.
DENISE GAUL

Ready for work. The main work area incorporates a built-in microwave. Denise retrofitted the dishwasher with a teak panel.
DENISE GAUL

Service Providers & Sources

• General contracting, general design and cabinet building and installation: Denise Gaul Design (denisegauldesign.com)

• Layout and cabinet design: NR Hiller Design

• Teak-veneered panels: Heitink Veneers (heitink. us)

• Counters: Brekhus Tile and Stone Inc. (brekhustile.com)

• Floor: red oak, Guy's Floor Service (guysfloor. com)

• Sink and faucet: Kohler (kohler.com)

• Backsplash tile: Realstone Systems Tempered Collection, purchased from Crossville Studios (crossvillestudios.com) and installed by JAM Tile (jamtile.com)

• Stove: Fulgor Milano from Specialty Appliance (buyfromsa.com)

• Hood: Zephyr from Specialty Appliance

• Microwave: JennAir from Specialty Appliance

• Solid teak supplier: Paxton Hardwoods (paxtonwood.com)

• Plywood for the cabinet boxes: prefinished maple ply Rosewood purchased from Austin Hardwoods (austinhardwoods.com)

More horizontal. For the back of the peninsula Denise used solid teak shiplap boards. Next to the wall is a door that allows access to the space that would otherwise have been a hard-to-reach inside corner by the dishwasher.
DENISE GAUL

8

Period Kitchens

*"P*eriod." *From the Greek*
peri 'odos, *a road going around, i.e. a circuit,
revolution, recurrence, course or orbit.*

I am one of those people who dream
about old houses – mysterious places I can't
resist entering, only to find myself tanta-
lized by details: the smell of cedar shakes
when I first walk through the door, the
creak of a floorboard, as dear a sound (to

me) as a kitten's mew, the charm of rooms joined, yet also separated, by divided-light doors hung on beefy ball-tip hinges. My interest in old buildings goes beyond some love of this or that style; it has just as much to do with the way old houses defy current norms and values. Yes, old houses reassure us, people really can live without dishwashers and Keurig coffee makers! Moreover, the very fact of being old, of surviving the wear and tear of generations, is a testament to quality, especially in a world where so many contemporary standards and aesthetic norms are determined by a building-products industry dependent on constant consumption of all things supposedly new and better.

One of my favorite things about old houses is trying to imagine the world as previous inhabitants did – a futile effort, I know, but it reminds me I'm not alone. Others came before. The day I tried to polish the flashed-copper hinges in my 1925 bungalow to remove their aged patina, only to find that the patina was an intentional part of the finish (and exactly the same pattern on every pair of hinges), I experienced an epiphany: Regardless of how long ago they lived, people have always been on the front lines of history. That, for some, is an alarming existential place to be. Surrounding ourselves with things that evoke earlier times – times we know our forebears lived through, successfully – can offer a kind of comfort. There's a sense of solidarity with allies, even if in this case they're unseen. Viewed with this insight, it's no wonder the disruptions of modernism in the 1920s and '30s prompted so many revival styles, from Tudor to Spanish, Colonial, Log Cabin or Colonial.

As soon as I'd established my own business in 1995, I began trying to get work in old houses. Over the years my understanding of old kitchens and the cabinets that furnished them has deepened, partly as a result of reading the books and magazines listed in the bibliography here, but largely because I pay attention to what's in front of my eyes. I've found that some cabinetmakers impose their own understanding of how a face frame or door "should" be onto the way those elements really are. They may see a recessed toe kick where the one before their eyes is flush; instead of noting that the stiles on a sideboard

they're reproducing are a skinny 2" wide, while the top rail is 2-1/4" and the bottom one 3-1/2", they may make all of these parts at 2-1/4". In suggesting that they don't see these details I'm being kind; it may well be that their eyes and minds are working perfectly well and they have simply decided that they know better (and betting that their customer won't notice), especially if efficiency is at stake.

When it comes to kitchens, period (or period-sensitive) design is especially fraught, because kitchens in so many houses of the 1800s through the 1960s were work rooms generally not intended for use by the whole family, let alone guests. As such, they were roughly comparable to garages today. You could have a handsomely decorated dining room and parlor in a three-story Queen Anne and still find plain open shelves and simple cupboards with braced-board doors, along with a worktable, sink and stove in the kitchen.

Until recent decades (and with the notable exception of Shaker kitchens), kitchens were not fitted with cabinets or furniture in the styles we usually associate with particular historical periods. You would never have found a William and Mary highboy storing sieves and colanders in an English kitchen of the late-17th century, nor an elaborate Victorian breakfront in the kitchen of a turreted New England mansion a century later. Aside from a few architect-designed exceptions, early 20th-century houses we call Arts & Crafts in style did not have carved oak sideboards or tables. The overwhelming majority of kitchens in each of these examples would have been kitted out with whatever basic furnishings were typical of kitchens and other utility rooms in their time. The trend of outfitting kitchens with period-style furniture is a far more recent conceit – as, if I'm honest, is the concern with period-authentic kitchens as workrooms. But at least the latter is based on history, not fantasy.

Moreover, houses built in the same neighborhood during the same year can differ greatly. In terms of interior trim and fixtures, some look forward, re-

Catalog resource. Kit home catalogs, such as this example from Aladdin, offer guidance to the original layout of kitchens that may have been modernized.

The Elmhurst :: Priced Including Heating, Lighting, Plumbing

THE Elmhurst is extremely attractive because of the unusual roof lines of the house and porch. Blending in perfect harmony, they lend an atmosphere of charm that never fails to please. It is presented in four excellent floor plans. The exterior appearance and the interior arrangement of the Elmhurst stamp it as an ideal home in every way. The 14′ x 8′ pergola-type porch is a distinctive feature. The porch has a tight, weatherproof roof. Aladdin Certified Lumber insures top notch quality and complete, permanent satisfaction. Remember that Aladdin prices include with your home the plumbing, heating and lighting equipment. See price list enclosed.

Elmhurst No. 1

Elmhurst No. 2

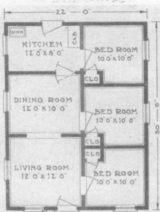

Elmhurst No. 3

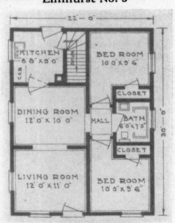

Elmhurst No. 4

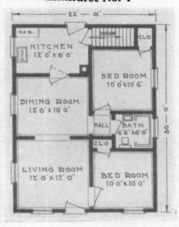

What You Get

Readi-cut materials for "The Elmhurst" Home (see pages 8 and 9).

In addition, the following equipment as shown on pages 6 and 7.

Metropolitan bath-room set.

White enameled bath wall fixtures.

Inset bath wall cabinet.

Aladdin Pipeless Furnace.

"Favorite" Lighting Fixtures.

Built-in kitchen cabinet, one section.

Kitchen Sink No. One.

Freight is paid to your station. Write for Detailed Specifications. Any of the above items will be omitted, if desired, and deduction from the price will be made. We will also make deduction for omitting wall sheathing, or sub-flooring or building paper.

— 18 —

Neighborhood resource. When Lauri Hafvenstein set out to restore her kitchen pantry, she took me to see the surviving original pantry in a neighbor's house. The houses are part of an area developed in the early 20th century with homes of almost identical interior layout.

LAURI HAFVENSTEIN

flecting cutting-edge design in materials affordable by everyman. Others look back, recalling the comfort of homes where people grew up. Many are hybrids of nostalgia and aspiration. I think a good place to start is by looking for clues to the history of your (or your client's) particular house, not some general guide to period style.

That said, don't rely solely on what you can see. As with any raw information, what you see, read or hear requires interpretation. Read widely about the history of your neighborhood, your town, your region. Learn about how houses were built, and where building materials came from. There is no hard and fast guide to period style across the board. Rural houses built in the same year by people of small means will be very different from those built for successful businessmen and judges. Kit houses constitute an entire universe of their own. Old houses,

even more than new ones, show regional differences in windows and window trim, roofing materials, the species of wood used for framing and finished floors and stone. Any building material that is heavy will cost more to transport, so these materials tend to differ widely from one locale to another; hence the common sight of granite in northeastern states where we find limestone in southern Indiana.

Here are some sources of design guidance, along with a few important caveats.

Original Blueprints

Sometimes you get lucky. You buy an old house that was architect-designed and the seller passes along the blueprints. Some blueprints are basic – exterior elevations and a plan view for each floor, along with critical mechanical services such as electric wiring. Even a basic plan view will tell you how the kitchen was laid out, often with a bit more information such as the depth, width and height of built-ins, along with the type of sink. A stove alcove offers insight into the approximate dimensions and type of stove the designer originally envisioned for the space.

Sometimes you get even luckier, with blueprints that include elevations. These are invaluable if you plan to recreate the original kitchen. Most of us don't really want to recreate historical kitchens, many of which had counters at a back-breaking 32" height, not to mention other features out of sync with how most of us live today. Still, even if you're going for 37" counters and want to incorporate a dual-height island with a bar where guests can hang out while you whisk up a roux, original cabinet elevations will provide basic dimensions for door stiles and rails, face frame parts, moulding profiles, hardware and the style of toe kick, to cite just a few examples.

Check the Basement & Garage

In many cases you can find at least some of a house's original cabinets in the basement or garage. Thriftier generations often repurposed cabinets for storing extra canned goods or turned them into shop storage. Even if you don't want to reuse these antiques, you can still base the design of your new cabinets on the old ones.

Neighboring Houses of the Same Vintage & Style

If you live in an urban neighborhood where houses were built on a single basic pattern, often in pairs with mirrored layouts, you may find a neighbor with an intact original kitchen or pantry to guide your kitchen design.

Millwork Catalogs & Booklets From Design Competitions

Another good source of guidance for period kitchens is millwork catalogs. Used catalogs are sometimes available for purchase, though they're precious and relatively rare. Sometimes a millwork catalog is reprinted by a contemporary publisher; Dover's publication of the 1927 "Universal Millwork Catalog" is a rich source of design guidance not only for kitchen cabinets, but all sorts of windows, doors, architectural trim and even telephone niches.

"The Kitchen Plan Book," originally published by the Hoosier Manufacturing Company and republished by *American Bungalow* magazine, is another treasure trove. It's a compilation of plan view and elevation drawings submitted by contestants in a yearly kitchen design contest held by the nation's leading manufacturer of Hoosier cabinets; the point of the contest was to show potential buyers of the cabinets how to incorporate them into a practical kitchen for early 20th-century living. Like the "Universal Millwork Catalog," "The Kitchen Plan Book" is also an excellent source of guidance in other kitchen furnishings such as flooring, counters, appliances, wall tile and hoods.

Existing Built-ins

If your home has surviving built-ins in other rooms, you may find guidance there. Just be aware that a fancy built-in sideboard in a dining room is not a trustworthy guide to the kind of cabinets that originally furnished the kitchen. In old houses, public rooms – those intended for use by extended family and guests – almost always had higher-grade flooring and millwork than rooms used primarily by servants or the women of the house; you'll often find rift- or quartered floorboards and hardwood trim in

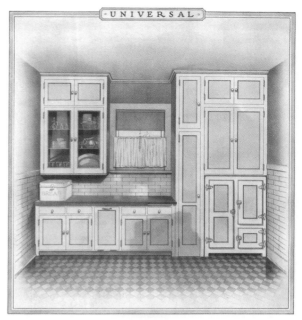

KITCHEN CUPBOARD U2804

IN THIS design several convenient units are combined. It provides space for a refrigerator which can be made with an outside icing door. A large broom closet, flour bin, drawers and storage cupboards are all conveniently grouped, and the work table is well lighted. Give size of refrigerator to be used, as the cabinet above must be made accordingly.

Complete kitchen cupboard includes design as illustrated (except window, room trim and refrigerator), with toe space across bottom, sash doors glazed D. S., two adjustable shelves in each top section, one shelf in each bottom compartment and over broom closet. Countershelf 1⅛" thick. Upper section on left side 3–6 wide and 1–1 deep. Bottom section 7–0 wide and 1–8 deep, with tilting bin and one bread board. Broom closet 1–6 wide and 1–8 deep. Height to top of countershelf 2–10, open space above 1–2. Made for 8–6 ceiling unless other height is given. No backs furnished unless specially ordered. Hardware and bread box not included. Made in other sizes and built of various woods. Always supplied unpainted.

Width and depth given are outside body sizes and do not include projection of moulding and countershelf.

FOR COMPLETE PRICE INFORMATION SEE UNIVERSAL PRICE SUPPLEMENT.

[255]

Lusciously detailed. The illustrations for cabinets and other house components in the Universal Millwork Catalog are a rich source of guidance for designing early 20th-century-style built-ins.
1927 UNIVERSAL MILLWORK CATALOG

the public rooms of houses whose kitchen and bath had linoleum-covered pine or maple floorboards and fir or yellow pine trim.

More reliable guidance for kitchen cabinet design generally comes from utility built-ins such as linen cupboards (often found at the end of a hallway, or recessed into a wall) and pantry cabinets in rooms or hallways adjoining the kitchen.

A Trio of Caveats Concerning Period-style Cabinetry

Some cabinetmakers base kitchen designs on freestanding furniture from other rooms, on the premise that the kitchen in a house of a particular architectural style should reflect that style as popularly

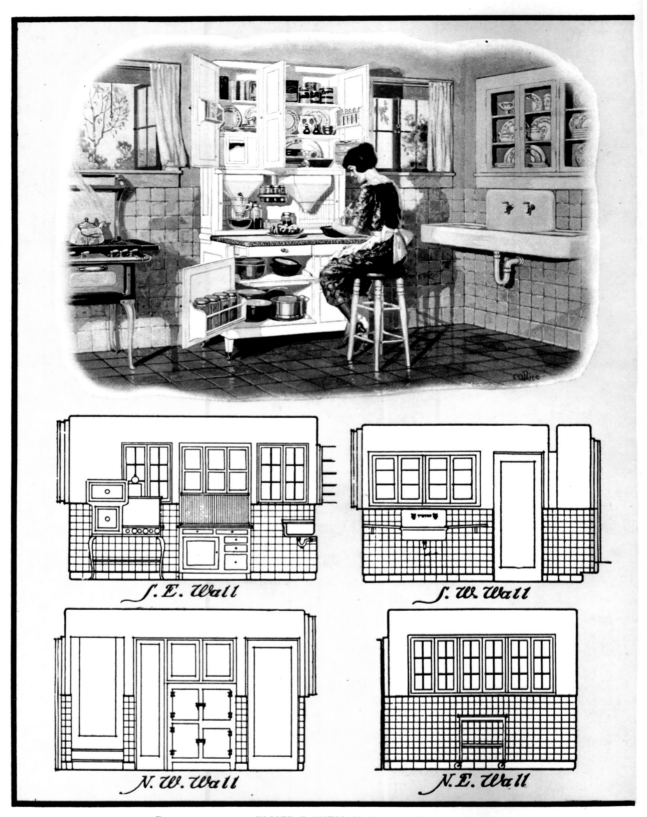

PLAN SUBMITTED BY ELMER E. NIEMAN, COLORADO SPRINGS, COLO.

"Indicates a good relationship between the kitchen and other adjacent parts of the house and a logical sequence of operations within the kitchen. It was felt that the cupboards above the sink were measurably inaccessible The splendid presentation of his design is worthy of favorable comment."—*Quoted from Report of the Jury.*

[10]

understood. So, goes the thinking (or lack thereof), "Victorian" means fretwork and mouldings, fancy feet and inlaid doors. Perhaps, if you're talking about parlors. But not kitchens.

It's always tempting to think that people in the past saw things pretty much as we see things today, but they did not. Western cultures and houses were far more stratified by class and wealth 100 years ago than today. There were also significant differences between urban and rural life, with accompanying differences in the layout and furnishing of kitchens and pantries. In general, if you're even remotely serious about period design in the kitchen, you need to remember that kitchens were basic workrooms, not rooms for show, and their furnishing reflected this.

Second, while magazines such as *Ladies' Home Journal*, *House Beautiful* and *Architectural Digest* (the first two published since the late 19th century; the last since 1920), are chock-full of advertisements for flooring products, counter materials, cleaning supplies, paint and appliances, you should be wary of relying on these ads and the feature articles published alongside them without other sources of guidance. Just as they are today, published designs were often aspirational; they did not reflect how most people lived. Many of the rooms in articles and ads were architect-designed for those who lived the high life. Serious period design is concerned more with paying attention to the history and particularities of your home and those who once lived there than aping some stereotype of period style.

Straight from the horse's mouth. If you're seeking guidance for an early 20th-century kitchen design, one of the best sources is the series of booklets published by the Hoosier Manufacturing Company of Indiana showcasing examples of kitchens designed by architects, designers and homeowners themselves. For several years the company sponsored a competition inviting participants to submit drawings of kitchens that would make optimal use of a Hoosier cabinet. This example from 1923 (left) offers period-authentic guidance to flooring, wall tile, millwork, appliances and other fixtures. (Fireless cooker, anyone?)
COURTESY OF HENRY COUNTY HISTORICAL SOCIETY, NEW CASTLE, IND.

'Salvaging the wartime kitchen.' An article in the June 1943 issue of *Ladies' Home Journal* offered budget-friendly tips on sprucing up the kitchen.

It's not that late. In many respects this kitchen looks like it could be from 1965, but it's from an ad for Armstrong linoleum in *Ladies' Home Journal* from 1942.

ENGLISH CORNER CABINETS, CONSOLES OF MELLOWED PINE, GAY GREEN AND YELLOW CHINTZ—THIS DRAWING ROOM PAINTS THE PORTRAIT OF ITS OWNER

People versus Furniture

BY MARGARET GREEN DARGAN

ROOMS are much more than a mere collection of furniture and fabrics. They are distinct revelations of personality, and are as an open book to one skilled in reading such signs. They are more of an index to one's character than any palm reading could ever show, and make a record not only of the social history of the times in which we live and the influences about us, but of our personal characteristics as well. How we have succumbed to riches or poverty, to inertia or discouragement, or how bravely we have met the challenge of our particular problems in creating an environment for ourselves and our families, is clearly visible. And the case of People versus Furniture is being tried in every room in the land! What would be the verdict in your particular case?

The most beautiful objects will stick out like sore thumbs unless they are related to the other furnishings and unless the carpets and walls—their physical background—are carefully chosen for their benefit. Even homely articles, when made the best of, can assume tranquillity if the rest of the room and things one can control are approached with courage, determination, skill.

In the case of young married people whose budget does not permit a dining room or a guest room, but whose space allows, and their standard of living demands one, there is a great challenge. One delightful young couple were determined to have a dining room in spite of the terrific handicap of a monstrous built-in buffet and some odds and ends of furniture culled from family attics. Undaunted, with all the courage and blitheness in the world, they set out to achieve a room that was daring and amusing and not without a touch of sophistication. Later, as their finances permit they will replace the furniture with things lovely and worth-while, but in the meantime it is arresting and gay, and neither they nor their friends are called upon to endure dreariness, even for a little while. The wall containing the built-in buffet, and the buffet, were painted white, as was a second wall, obliterating thereby some of the most unpleasant features. Then further to lure one's eye away from the things that couldn't be helped, the other two walls were painted a brilliant emerald green. The odds and ends of furniture were painted a uniform white. Then a Victorian sofa was

Before the war. This living room looks as though it could have been decorated for a stylistically conservative family in the early 1960s, '70s or '80s. In fact it's an advertisement from 1935.

This room for two, with pairs of everything, is modern in the best sense because it combines the maximum of beauty and comfort. Notice the indirect lighting at each bedside, the recessed and well-lighted bookcases within easy reach. You'll find several other new decorative ideas, too, as you study this room. And we'll be glad to send you complete specifications upon request.

"Their guest room made me feel at home the moment I stepped into it . . . so comfortably cozy . . . so alive with loveliness." Thus another guest expresses the welcome so carefully built into this room by a smart hostess. She began, as many decorators do today, with the floor . . . a spread of modestly colorful plaid (Armstrong's Embossed Inlaid No. 5470). It's restful and quiet underfoot—and just as kind to the hostess as to the guest. A quick dusting cleans it. Occasional touching up with Armstrong's Linogloss Wax (self-polishing) keeps its colors glowing. What is true of this guest room *can* be true of any room in your home—an Armstrong Floor will help you double its beauty. Your merchant has scores of designs to choose from—and he'll be glad to give you exact prices if you tell him your room measurements.

Decorating Ideas by the Bookful

We have prepared a 36-page book for you, full of ideas that will help you brighten your home. Ask for "Floors That Keep Homes in Fashion," illustrated with room photographs in full natural color. Just send 10¢ (40¢ outside U. S. A.) to Armstrong Cork Products Company, Floor Division, 3606 Mary Street, Lancaster, Pennsylvania. (Makers of cork products since 1860)

The most satisfactory way to install linoleum on wood floors is to insist on a permanent job cemented over felt.

ARMSTRONG'S LINOLEUM FLOORS
for every room Ⓐ in the house

PLAIN • INLAID • EMBOSSED • JASPÉ • PRINTED • ARMSTRONG'S QUAKER RUGS *and* ARMSTRONG'S LINOWALL

Appearances can be deceptive. If I asked you to date the room in this photo, what would you say? Between the clean-lined modern furniture, the mod red and white color scheme and the white-tasseled upholstered chair in the foreground, I would swear it was from the 1960s. But this ad for Armstrong linoleum appeared in the *Ladies' Home Journal* in 1936.

Exchange your present Kitchen for One like this!

YOU can do it . . . quickly and at reasonable cost . . . if you modernize your kitchen with Walls of Carrara. And you'll be surprised how little trouble such a transformation involves . . . for Carrara Walls can usually be installed right over your old walls, without fuss or bother!

Once the old kitchen has disappeared and your new, smart one has taken its place, step into the room and look around you. What a change! Brilliant, shining, reflective walls. Soft, harmonious color-tones, impeccable in taste. A new richness and elegance of atmosphere. A feeling of greater airiness, light and spaciousness.

More than that, you'll know that this new-born beauty will be permanent. For Carrara Walls never check, craze, stain, absorb odors, or fade in color. And you can keep them spotlessly clean by merely wiping them down occasionally with a damp cloth!

Find out about Carrara, the modern structural glass . . . how it can transform your present kitchen, how surprisingly little it costs. Let us send you our folder containing complete information and colored illustrations of bathroom and kitchen installations. Pittsburgh Plate Glass Company, 2269 Grant Building, Pittsburgh, Penna.

Here is an example of how Carrara Walls can assist in the transformation of a kitchen, giving the room new life, new beauty, new personality. A gleaming wainscoting of Ivory Carrara, with base trim of Black Carrara, assures sanitation, good looks and easy cleaning. Upper walls are finished in Suntone Wallhide. The "Vitolized Oil" Paint, and the ceiling in a contrasting shade of Wallhide. Table and cabinets are finished in appropriate colors of Waterspar Quick-Drying Enamel.

CARRARA
The modern structural glass

A product of

PITTSBURGH
PLATE GLASS COMPANY

Mixed messages. It would be hard to date this kitchen based on looks alone. The cabinets could have been manufactured in the early 1960s. The floor looks more 1950s. I saw draperies like this one in houses right up to the 1980s. But that wall-mounted sink without a cabinet? So much more at home in the 1910s or '20s. Ads for glass tile such as this one were published in the 1930s and '40s.

Finally, just because a house was built in 1910 or 1920 doesn't mean it has to have a kitchen that looks original to the time of its construction. Houses, like all buildings, evolve. There are reasons why few houses that have been inhabited constantly for over a century retain their original kitchen. Family needs change. Parts wear out. Appliances may no longer be repairable. Conventional norms for cooking and cleaning are always shifting. Even in the homes of modest families who have done no other remodeling, the kitchen may have been redone, because of the kitchen's importance to family life. As articles and advertisements from the early and mid-20th century attest, prior to the women's liberation

movement in the 1960s and '70s, the kitchen was the central point around which women's lives revolved. Of course there were exceptions, most notably during wartime, but the cult of domesticity was still largely an ideal, if not always a reality, and keeping mama happy with a kitchen she found functional and attractive made sense for the entire family.

So if you find a 1912 house that's period-perfect in every way other than the campy teal green kitchen added in 1948, don't be too quick with the crowbar and sledge hammer. Some changes to a house are worth saving; after all, they're integral to the house's history.

A stylish look back. This mid-century kitchen remodel in Nancy Rutkowski's 1920s house brings the pages of culinary classic "The Joy of Cooking" to life. The cabinets are plywood with half-inset doors. Counters and backsplash on the far walls are pale pink laminate with stainless steel mouldings; those barely visible at the left of this image are stainless steel. The swooping peninsula has an overhanging laminate counter; there's a storage cabinet on the working side not visible here. The bulkhead with integral lighting echoes the curve. The cream, grey and pink wallpaper patterned with stylized roosters, plants and flowers is the icing on the cake.
SPECTRUM CREATIVE GROUP

Proper proportions. *This Shaker classic is one of the best examples of how frame components can influence the character of a cabinet. While the board between the doors does not exactly qualify as a face frame stile, that is one of its functions. Contrast its extreme width with the single-board thickness of the rails between the drawers.*
PRIVATE COLLECTION, PAUL ROCHELEAU

Cabinet Details to Note when Designing a Period-Style Kitchen

1. Widths of door stiles & rails

Bottom rails are almost always wider than top rails on old cabinet and furniture doors. Sometimes stiles are the same width as the top rail (before material is removed for fitting the doors), sometimes not – and sometimes they are dramatically different.

2. Dimensions of face frame stiles and rails (in addition to where they appear)

For example, a true period look for cabinets predating the widespread use of mechanical drawer slides requires intermediate drawer rails. Even if you plan to mount your drawers on full-extension slides, you should incorporate rails between them to evoke the look of those that once supported web frames.

3. Hardware

What kind of hinges were used, and how were they attached? If the doors were hung on butt hinges, were they mortised into the door and face frame, or only into the door? What is the length of the hinge? How wide are the leaves? Are the pins removable or fixed, and do they have finials? What is the finish?

4. Hardware position

Note the distance of the top and bottom (and center, if applicable) hinges from the ends of the door. Note the position of drawer pulls, doorknobs or latches; door hardware was commonly installed approximately halfway or two-thirds to three-quarters of the way up on base cabinet doors and similarly spaced in the opposite direction for upper doors. They were not usually located in the upper or lower corner, as is typical of cabinet doors today.

5. Are doors and drawers inset, overlay or half inset?

Drawer faces were sometimes half inset even though the doors in the same set of cabinets were fully inset.

Set correctly. *When we recreated the pantry in Lauri Hafvenstein's 1917 house, I followed the original pattern Lauri had seen in a neighbor's kitchen, with inset doors and half-inset drawer faces.*
LAURI HAFVENSTEIN

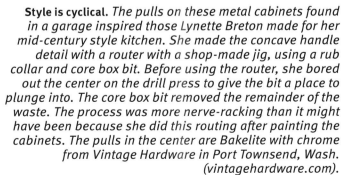

Style is cyclical. *The pulls on these metal cabinets found in a garage inspired those Lynette Breton made for her mid-century style kitchen. She made the concave handle detail with a router with a shop-made jig, using a rub collar and core box bit. Before using the router, she bored out the center on the drill press to give the bit a place to plunge into. The core box bit removed the remainder of the waste. The process was more nerve-racking than it might have been because she did this routing after painting the cabinets. The pulls in the center are Bakelite with chrome from Vintage Hardware in Port Townsend, Wash. (vintagehardware.com).*
MARGARET STEVENS BECKSVOORT

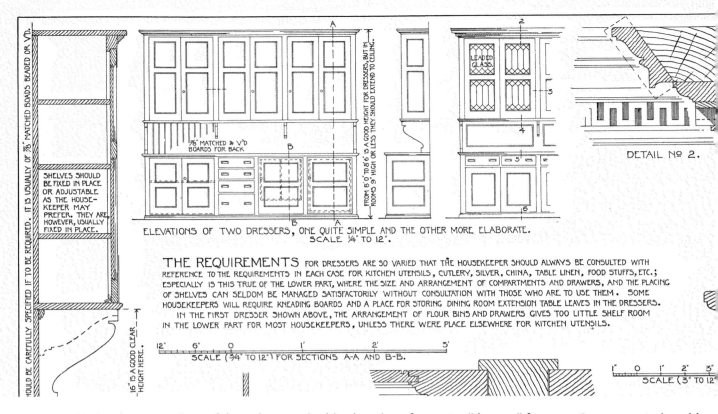

Graduated. *Notice the proportions of door elements in this elevation of a pantry "dresser" from an 1899 carpenter's guide.*
A GIFT TO THE AUTHOR FROM CHARLES BICKFORD

6. Moulding profiles

It should go without saying that moulding profiles are important. They can vary enormously and are one of the most distinctive and delightful details in a period kitchen. If you cannot replicate a profile yourself, you can usually have it done in the species of your choice by a millwork shop willing to custom-grind knives. Just be sure you order extra, as there will usually be a hefty set-up charge along with the grinding fee, and different batches can have dimensional variations invisible to the eye but great enough to cause headaches during installation.

7. Edge treatment of half inset drawer faces

These may be eased, quarter-round, beveled or moulded

8. Proportions of graduated drawers

Along with the proportions of face frames and door components, one of the least-noticed and most critical aspects of historic kitchens is the proportions of drawer faces. Many cabinetmakers make the mistake of building all the drawer faces in a stack to the same size. Not only does this look terrible, because when viewed from above (i.e., from normal standing height), the bottom drawer will inevitably look smaller than the rest, and so, out of scale. It's also not how drawers were traditionally sized. You can make as many adverse comparisons as you like between 19th-century cabinetmakers and the furniture made by those who worked in the golden zone of northeastern American states during the late 18th century, but even oft-maligned Victorians worked with a tradition grounded in classical proportions. This was one of the first and most important lessons I learned from Roy Griffiths in 1980.

9. Toe kicks

Are they flush (i.e., does the bottom rail of the face frame go all the way to the floor) or recessed? If the toe kick is partially recessed – i.e., if the face frame stiles extend down to the floor with inset toe kicks between them – note the rhythm of this variation. In some cases the stiles are full-length only at the end of each cabinet run, with the kick recessed everywhere else. In others, the stiles may run down to the floor on each cabinet.

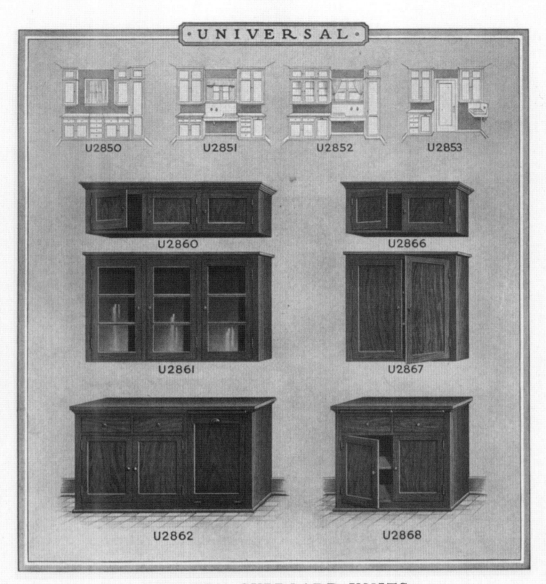

KITCHEN CUPBOARD UNITS

MANY combinations are possible with these cupboard units as the variety of sizes makes them adaptable to almost any space. A few arrangements are suggested in the small illustrations at top.

Body Sizes of Units

DESIGN	WIDE	HIGH	DEEP		DESIGN	WIDE	HIGH	DEEP
U2860	4 – 8 x 1 – 6 x 1 – 1				U2866	3 – 0 x 1 – 6 x 1 – 1		
U2861	4 – 8 x 3 – 0 x 1 – 1				U2867	3 – 0 x 3 – 0 x 1 – 1		
U2862	4 – 8 x 2 –10 x 1 – 6				U2868	3 – 0 x 2 –10 x 1 – 6		

Complete units include fronts, doors, drawers, drawer slides, tilting bin, bread boards, ends, tops, bottoms, shelves and mouldings (except shoe) as illustrated. Sash doors glazed plain. Countershelves $1\frac{1}{16}''$ thick. Furnished K. D. with fronts, drawers and bin put together. No backs included unless ordered. Hardware never supplied. Wood brackets to support top sections can be furnished extra. A long countershelf, made to cover two or more units in place of individual tops shown, will be supplied on special order.

FOR COMPLETE PRICE INFORMATION SEE UNIVERSAL PRICE SUPPLEMENT.

[264]

Toe kicks. *Flush toe kicks were an option in 1927, and still are today.*
1927 UNIVERSAL MILLWORK CATALOG

Cold pantry. The cold pantry serves as extra storage and prep space. David has furnished it with antique kitchen tools and appliances such as this circa-1950 Hobart C100 stand mixer and a 1953 Frigidaire butter pre-server (a mechanical slicer). The ceiling light is a Benjamin Electric Co. cluster light with a 14" milk glass shade.

Case Study 8.1

Shingle Style

You could be forgiven for feeling more than a tinge of envy on encountering David Berman's kitchen, with its original 1910 cabinets, restored antique appliances, salvaged lighting, ceramic crown and chair mouldings. Did I mention the pantries, plural? But before you succumb to all-out lust, bear in mind that this luscious study in period style wasn't always as pulled together as it appears today.

Get to work. Barely visible here, the worktable in the kitchen's center is from a school laboratory and likely dates to the 1920s or '30s; there is no maker's mark. It's fitted with two swing-out seats. The Windsor style chair is by Haywood Wakefield.

In 1994, when David moved into the house, which he calls a hybrid Shingle Style/Colonial Revival, these portions of the servants' quarters were considerably less lovely. The cabinets, built of Southern yellow pine, were there, but their tops were covered in sturdy battleship blue linoleum. The wooden floors were terribly worn, the ceiling in one of the pantries had collapsed and a good portion of the sink surround had rotted away. What you see in these images reflects years of devoted labor.

David stripped the linoleum from the pantry counters, removed the mastic and refinished the pine with Varathane oil-based floor finish. Amazingly, the finish on the rest of the cabinetry is origi-nal. Because the wood floors were in such bad shape (and also because he did not want to worry about the kind of damage a softwood floor would suffer with daily use), he installed commercial-grade vinyl composition tile in a black and white checkerboard. After living for many years with regular modern appliances, he recently replaced them. The fridge is a restored Frigidaire built in 1929 (it now runs on modern refrigerant instead of its original sulfur dioxide), the stove a 1928 Glenwood SNJ Super Capacity Range. As for the ceramic mouldings, they're fake – a bit of trompe l'oeil by David, who designs and prints period-style wallpapers for his business, Trustworth Studios.

My kingdom for a butler. Just off the dining room, the butler's pantry stores dishware and glasses, and offers a convenient staging area for elaborate dinner parties. David based the dancing mice wallpaper pattern on a Silver Studio design.

Wallpaper. Inspired by the food halls at Harrods department store in London, David designed crown and chair mouldings to go with his kitchen wallpaper. The detail of shadow and light makes for a deceit so masterful that the two-dimensional reality is undetectable until you look carefully at the room's outside corners.

Carefully chosen accoutrements. The 1930s Telechron "Consort" is the perfect complement to the wallpaper. David designed the paper based on British architect C.F.A. Voysey's "Laborate et Amate" tiles. (The title is Latin for the imperative "Love and Work!")

Period appliances. David has outfitted his restored 1929 Frigidaire with several of the green glass storage containers that originally came with this model. The 1910 house would have had an icebox when it was first constructed, but even David thought that would be taking things too far.

Service Providers & Sources

• Design and general contracting: David Berman, Trustworth Studios (trustworth.com)

• Wallpaper: Trustworth Studios

• Antique stove: Glenwood

• Antique refrigerator: Frigidaire

Evening view. The small section of cabinetry with the main kitchen sink faces west. The sink is original, though the taps are not.

Recessed shelves create space. A chase that could not be removed protruded from the corner at the left of the sink. Instead of relocating the sink about a foot to the right, we extended the plane of the chase a few feet to create a shallow bump-out that allowed for recessed shelves above. Framing out this small section of wall also made it easier to run wiring for sconces and a switch than it would otherwise have been, since the wall on this side of the kitchen is brick.
LAURI HAFVENSTEIN

Let us eat cake. Use period-evocative decoration. This framed advertisement for Gold Medal Flour came from a 1917 magazine.
LAURI HAFVENSTEIN

Case Study 8.2

Happy Hundredth

Lauri Hafvenstein introduced herself to me at the end of a talk I presented in Baltimore in 2009 about designing kitchens for old houses. She'd recently bought a 1917 house in Washington, D.C., and was hoping to redo the kitchen in time for her home's hundredth birthday. A couple of years later she got back in touch and hired me for a design consultation. I arrived to find her dining table covered in original catalogs from 1917 and knew right away that I was dealing with someone who was intensely interested in period authenticity.

Long view. The kitchen is minimally furnished, as it would have been when the house was originally constructed. Instead of filling the space with conventional built-ins, we took Lauri's storage needs and aesthetic preferences into account when planning the cabinets. The cabinets now are fewer and better. Large drawers on full-extension slides hold pots and pans, utensils, silverware and linens. The upper cabinet stores dishes and glasses.

LAURI HAFVENSTEIN

False Economy. When previous homeowners removed the wall between the kitchen and pantry to open up the space, they turned a workhorse pantry into a relatively useless hallway. In view of the shallow space available for cabinets on the wall at right in what had been the pantry, they installed a run of conventional-depth cabinets several feet in from the entrance to the room, using angled cabinets at each end and a heavily radiused counter to compensate for the awkward protrusion.

LAURI HAFVENSTEIN

We discussed her ideas and I shared my own, along with resources. We also visited a neighbor's house that still had its original pantry so we could recreate the one that had been in her kitchen.

A few years later Lauri was ready to take the plunge. To make the job affordable, we did the work in stages. I built the cabinetry in my shop; then, with my husband, Mark, a builder, drove everything to D.C. in 2015. We installed the cabinetry and recreated the wall that had originally separated the kitchen from the pantry. Next, Lauri's brother, Larry, made several trips from out of state to repair plaster, install trim and paint. I returned the following year to install the newly painted cabinets' doors and drawers, add open shelving in the pantry, build a recessed niche over the sink (which Lauri's neighbor Brian trimmed out) and assemble a small worktable I'd built in pieces and brought in my luggage on the plane.

Lauri's images document the dramatic transformation of her kitchen, a true labor of love that took several years, along with a lot of patience, research and hard work. She is now a partner in D.C.-area design business Old House Loves.

Salvaged hardware. Lauri collected antique hinges, latches and drawer pulls, buying them online whenever she spotted them for sale. She sorted them to come up with matching lots for the cabinet in the pantry and kitchen proper, respectively. For a period-authentic look, she bought new slotted oval head screws and aged them in antiquing solution to match the old hardware.
LAURI HAFVENSTEIN

Pantry, after. In the restored pantry, open shelves on wooden battens face a wall of shallow built-in storage designed to make optimal use of available space. Lauri and I based the design of the cabinetry on a surviving pantry in a neighbor's home. Lauri found salvaged wavy glass and stripped it of old paint and glazing compound. The glass had come from different buildings; the pieces most special to her came from windows that her next-door neighbor had replaced, so the glass was from the same year as that in her own windows. Some pieces had a bluish cast, while others were more green. Before cutting them to size, Lauri sorted them by shade so that those in the pantry and kitchen proper, respectively, would be of a piece. She and her brother, Larry, cleaned and cut the glass together, "holding our breath for every stroke because there was no room for error," she remembers.
LAURI HAFVENSTEIN

Sink and stove wall, after. The sink and stove were salvaged from the homes in which they were originally installed – the sink near Pittsburgh, the stove in Baltimore County. Lauri wanted to incorporate an Oriole stove in view of the manufacturer's long history with her locale – Oriole stoves were made in Baltimore. She bought this one restored; it runs on natural gas. Between the sink and stove a small table provides a work surface and storage for small items used at the sink.

LAURI HAFVENSTEIN

Sink & stove wall, before. The kitchen's previous iteration had plentiful storage on the wall with the sink and stove, but the sink corner was dark and uninviting.

LAURI HAFVENSTEIN

Restored appliances. The fridge is a circa-1929 Frigidaire W-5 with the compressor in the compartment at the bottom. Lauri bought it on eBay from the nephew of the original owner. Like all pre-modern refrigerators, it has to be defrosted regularly – a chore Lauri completes gladly in exchange for the opportunity to have this glorious antique appliance in her kitchen. Auxiliary refrigeration comes from a modern fridge that used to be in the kitchen and is now in the basement.

LAURI HAFVENSTEIN

Vitamix drawer. Among Lauri's priorities was storage for her Vitamix blender that would allow her to use it on a daily basis without having to move it. Together, we designed a drawer with low sides, full-extension slides and an electrical receptacle in the back of the cabinet, which allows her to use the appliance in place, then remove the carafe for cleaning. The drawer stores all of the machine's parts in one convenient location.

LAURI HAFVENSTEIN

Service Providers & Sources

• General contractor and designer: Lauri Hafvenstein, Old House Loves (oldhouseloves.com)

• Painting: Larry Hafvenstein

• Design consultation and cabinetry: NR Hiller Design

• Carpentry: Mark Longacre Construction and Larry Hafvenstein

• Stove restoration: The Good Time Stove Company (goodtimestove.com)

• Sink: Architectural Emporium in Canonsburg, Pennsylvania architectural-emporium.com; legs, purchased separately, came from Caravati's Architectural Salvage in Virginia (caravatis.com)

• Paint: Benjamin Moore Advance (cabinets), Aura (walls), and Regal Select (trim)

• Plumbing and electrical work: Larry Hafvenstein

• Heart pine counters: Goodwin Heart Pine (heartpine.com)

• Counter finish: Waterlox Original Satin Finish Tung Oil (waterlox.com)

• Cabinet hinges: salvaged

• Drawer pulls: Ed Donaldson Hardware Restorations (eddonaldson.com)

Movement. To accommodate the dramatic slope of the ceiling in some areas of the room, I widened the top section of the new crown moulding to allow for scribing. Although the fit was snug when we installed the cabinets in 2014, the crown has shrunken a little over the years, opening up a small gap. (These photos are from 2018.)
SPECTRUM CREATIVE GROUP

Baker's cabinet. The small cabinet to the left of the fridge is a turn-of-the-century baker's cabinet based on one in a photo of Tasha's great-grandmother, Maud Hamar, in a cooking class around the same time as this original kitchen was built. A framed print of that photograph hangs on the wall at the right of the fridge, the perfect meta-accessory.

SPECTRUM CREATIVE GROUP

Case Study 8.3

Former Servants' Quarters

Tasha Vorderstrasse and Brian Muhs, owners of this 1915 flat in Chicago, are scholars with a passionate interest in material culture. When they bought their home in 2014, they wanted to replace the kitchen's hodge-podge of modular particleboard cabinets and makeshift furniture with something more sensitive to the flat's history. They had spoken with other builders, most of whom urged them to demolish the wall between the kitchen and dining room, the very thought of which was anathema to them.

Interpreting original cabinet details. The cabinet at far right in this view is original to the kitchen. Although its face frame extends to the floor, my clients wanted the new cabinets to have recessed toe kicks. To relate the new design clearly to the old, I extended the face frame stiles to the floor and recessed the kicks between them.

The original upper cabinets' sides go all the way to the counter, but the clients decided against this detail for the new cabinets. We also reduced the width of the face frame stiles for the new cabinets to avoid wasting space. I made the new shelves adjustable and mounted the new drawers on full-extension slides instead of wooden runners; again, this decision was the product of careful discussion.

The latches and bin pulls are salvaged.

The narrow table to the left of the stove, so skinny that we called it "the giraffe," hides the radiator while providing additional workspace. It's topped with soapstone.

SPECTRUM CREATIVE GROUP

Mahogany counters and an unconventional table. An antique scroll saw table paired with old stools makes a compact spot for breakfast or coffee. The counters are solid mahogany with a dark stain and oil-based polyurethane finish.
SPECTRUM CREATIVE GROUP

The flat still had many of its original architectural features – leaded glass windows, wonderful hallway built-ins, a barrel-vaulted dining room ceiling and original bathrooms, to name a few. Most surprising was the intact arrangement of a suite at the back that had originally been the servant's quarters. A swinging doorway from the dining room led into the kitchen: turn hard left for a sweet little bathroom with a tiny clawfoot tub and corner sink, diagonally left for the servant's bedroom. Enter the kitchen proper and there's a pantry on the exterior wall – perfect for keeping foodstuffs cool, and fitted with a handy pass-through for ice deliveries. Even the original hard maple floor in the main part of the kitchen was still in good condition.

Luckily, the pair of original cabinets flanking the doorway to the dining room was also still there. I incorporated many of their details into the new cabinets. This kitchen has a number of idiosyncratic elements, such as two different counter heights and discontinuous upper cabinets (the narrow spaces between which will admittedly be a bear to paint when the time comes). Each of these details resulted from protracted discussion, with the clients as the final arbiters, which is as it should be.

Unconventional hinge installation. The original cabinets have inset doors with 2-1/2" ball-tipped butt hinges, but unlike most installations in the United States, the hinges were mortised into the door stile alone and simply screwed to the edge of the face frame. I replicated this detail in the new cabinets.

SPECTRUM CREATIVE GROUP

Service Providers & Sources

• Backsplash: Heritage Tile (heritagetile.com)
• Stove: Wedgewood, restored by Savon Appliances (savonappliance.com)

Stove repairs: Retro Stove and Gas Works (retrostoveandgasworks.com)

• Fridge restoration: Antique Appliances (antiqueappliances.com)

• Design and cabinetry: NR Hiller Design; Duncan Campbell, retired director of the graduate program in historical preservation at Ball State University, worked on wall repair, cabinet installation and painting

• Cabinet hinges: Rejuvenation (rejuvenation.com)
• Latches and bin pulls: salvaged
• Sink: salvaged

Stove cabinet area with upper. A base cabinet next to the stove holds pots, pans and other cookware in addition to keeping storage containers right next to the fridge. After much discussion, Jane opted to scale down the height of the upper cabinet (patterned after the original one on the opposite wall) in keeping with the other elements on this side of the room.

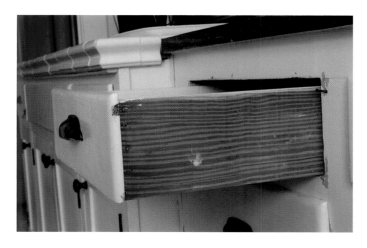

Basic joinery. The original built-in's drawers were rabbeted and nailed, so I built the new drawers with the same type of joinery (though I used poplar instead of softwood and mounted the drawers on Blum Tandem slides, as a result of which I added a drawer face instead of rabbeting the sides directly into the face).

Case Study 8.4

Grad-School Style to Grown Up

During the 15 years Jane Goodman had lived in her 1912 gable-ell house, she'd worked her way through nearly every room, restoring plaster and trim, then painting each in a luminous palette of blue-green, lavender and pale rose. When it was time to turn her attention to the kitchen, her goals were three: replace what she calls the grad-school workbench with a built-in cabinet, widen the doorway between the kitchen and dining room for wheelchair

325

Before. Original cabinet. The original built-in had inset doors and half-inset drawer faces. Note the plastic-like coating applied to the original yellow pine counter. Not only was the coating a visual crime; it was also coming unbonded from the wood, because whoever applied it had not adequately prepped the original varnish to receive additional coating.

access and generally make the room more functional and attractive.

At 15' long by 9'3" wide, it's a relatively small kitchen. The fundamental efficiency of the galley-like layout was decreased by the existence of four doorways. At one end of the room there's a door to a pantry closet and another leading out to a porch; opposite, there were two doorways separated by a narrow strip of wall – one to the dining room, the other to a small hallway leading to the basement stairs. While having two doorways to essentially the same hallway reduced the space available for cabinets, it did bring natural light into the kitchen from

a south-facing bedroom, as well as keeping the kitchen from feeling cramped.

Mark and his crew widened the opening of the door to the dining room, reusing as much original trim as possible, and enclosed the doorway to the south so that a new sink base could go all the way to the end. Instead of completely doing away with the second doorway, they made a cased opening that functions as a window. We replaced the grad-school bench with base and upper cabinets patterned on the kitchen's original built-in, designing every detail with Jane's storage needs in mind.

Counter revolution. Stripped and refinished, the wood gleams with renewed life.

Vitamin drawer. Jane wanted a handy place to keep vitamins without having them on the counter. Simple shop-made inserts of 1/4" prefinished plywood keep bottles organized with their labels easy to read.

Custom curtains. When she removed the original cabinet's tip-out flour bin, Jane discovered a piece of original linoleum in a vaguely Moorish pattern – a nice coincidence, given that her research as an anthropologist has focused on Algeria. She bought fabric in a similar print and had curtains made by a local company.

Service Providers & Sources

• General contractor: Mark Longacre Construction (marklongacre.com)

• Design and cabinetry: NR Hiller Design

• Stone counters: Quality Surfaces (qualitysurfaces.com)

• Electrical: Homeowner Service Electric (homeownerserviceelectric.com)

• Painting: Roath Custom Coatings, Bloomington, Ind.

• Plumbing: Mann Plumbing (mannplumbinginc.com)

• Custom sewing: The Tailored Fit (thetailoredfit.com)

Before. One door too many. Having two doorways into essentially the same space wasted precious storage and workspace in the kitchen.

After. Room with a view. Instead of closing off the wall completely, Jane decided to keep an opening between the kitchen and a bedroom with southeast exposure. Enclosing the lower portion of the opening freed up enough space for a dishwasher, one of Jane's longed-for improvements.

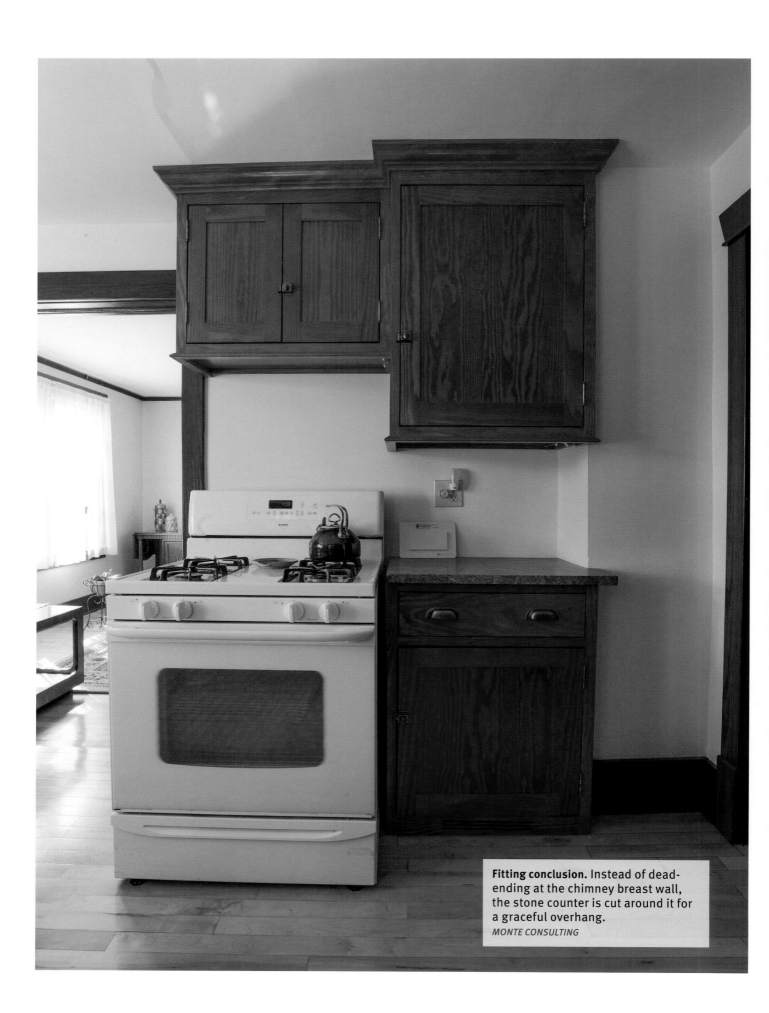

Fitting conclusion. Instead of dead-ending at the chimney breast wall, the stone counter is cut around it for a graceful overhang.
MONTE CONSULTING

Subtle detail. A simple moulding added to the underside of the upper cabinets relates to the window and door trim. It also hides a recess with task lighting on a rheostat switch.
MONTE CONSULTING

Case Study 8.5

Tiny & Mighty

"Hello Ms. Hiller,

"My name is Kathleen Funkey, I own a house in Houghton, Michigan, built in 1895 and remodeled in 1930. I bought the property eight years ago and hired two craftsmen, skilled in restoration, to go through the house room-by-room – plastering, painting and restoring. Beautiful work.

"The kitchen is a whole different story. It's small, dirty, and has doors and windows on every wall. I use the back door, as do guests, to enter and exit the house and am committed to improving this space this year. I've seen samples of your work online and am very impressed. I don't know enough to say why I liked it so much but I did.

"Would you be interested in consulting on this project? Scope being kitchen design, era-appropriate cabinets, hardware, countertop, appliances and material selections. Please contact via email or call to discuss. I've attached some pictures and have many more. Thank you.

"Sincerely,

"Kathleen Funkey"

So began one of few kitchen design jobs I have done from a distance without seeing the site in person. I strongly prefer to visit; it's the best way to assess a space, not just to get measurements (and locate important features that need to be worked around, such as oddly placed electrical receptacles, flues and HVAC vents), but to gain insight into the character of the space that comes from less tangible elements such as views through doors and windows, or how the natural light changes through the day. In this case the distance from my home base to the client's house is significant – 650 miles – and there is no major airport nearby. Complicating matters, the client wasn't living in the house at the time, but working on the East Coast. She hoped I would be able to design the kitchen in conversation with her general contractor and cabinetmaker, Jake Korpela.

At 13' x 9', a total of about 117 square feet, the space is small, and the usable space is further limited by the presence of – count them! – four doorways, as with Jane Goodman's kitchen, along with two substantial windows, which ate up a lot of wall area. One doorway opens onto the dining room, one to the backyard and one to the basement. Most significant, the fourth door leads directly to the front entryway – the kitchen is literally the first thing you see when you come through the front door.

Understandably, Kathleen wanted the kitchen to fit in with the rest of the house. I referred her to oldhouseonline.com, a website chock-full of content from *Old-House Interiors*, *Old-House Journal*, *Arts &*

Framed by the doorway. When your front door opens directly onto a view of the kitchen, it's especially important to make that view attractive. Kathleen wanted the kitchen to be in sync with the other rooms, which have fir trim and maple floors, while still being clearly identifiable as a kitchen.
MONTE CONSULTING

Every inch counts. The cabinet over the stove is shallower to keep the cook from feeling cramped. There is 30" of vertical clearance between its underside and the top of the cooking surface. Stoves and exhaust hoods come with specifications regarding minimum and maximum clearance between the cooking surface and fixtures above it for fire prevention and effective ventilation, respectively.

The upper cabinet to the right of the stove is 16" deep. The base cabinet is 20", a compromise between standard depth base (24") and the depth of the recess formed by the chimney breast (12-1/2"). The relatively shallow base cabinet allows for easy access to contents on shelves without the need for pullouts; hence the single drawer.

MONTE CONSULTING

Change in plane. The sink cabinet bumps out 3" beyond the face of the adjacent chest of drawers, a change in plane that breaks up the wall, reducing the sense that these are regimented built-ins. Glazing the side of the upper cabinet next to the window adds a bit of charm and allows light to come through the cabinet's doors. Note that the glazed side's top and bottom rails are wider so that they continue the horizontal line of the door rails around.

MONTE CONSULTING

Crafts Homes and related magazines published under the expert eye of Patricia Poore. There she found a Kennebec kitchen in fir with stone counters that would serve as a guide for the basic look she wanted.

Kathleen had sent me rough dimensions based on measurements made by another cabinetmaker, but they had far too little detail for me to produce the scale drawings she wanted. I scheduled a call with one of her old friends in Houghton, who took detailed measurements to my specifications while we were on the phone.

The kitchen that resulted has fewer cabinets but significantly more usable storage space than before. The layout is practical; the room feels peaceful and spacious. Kathleen says it's a pleasure to work in, and it blends well with the rest of the house.

More windows and doors than wall space. Four doors and two large windows added to the challenge of fitting sufficient storage and preparation space into this small room.

MONTE CONSULTING

Service Providers & Sources

• General contractor: World of Wood (worldofwoodmi.com)

• Cabinetry: World of Wood (worldofwoodmi.com)

• Counters: M. Teixeira Soapstone (soapstones.com)

• Sink: Kohler (kohler.com)

• Faucet: Lefroy Brooks (usa.lefroybrooks.com)

• Lighting and cabinet hardware: Rejuvenation (rejuvenation.com)

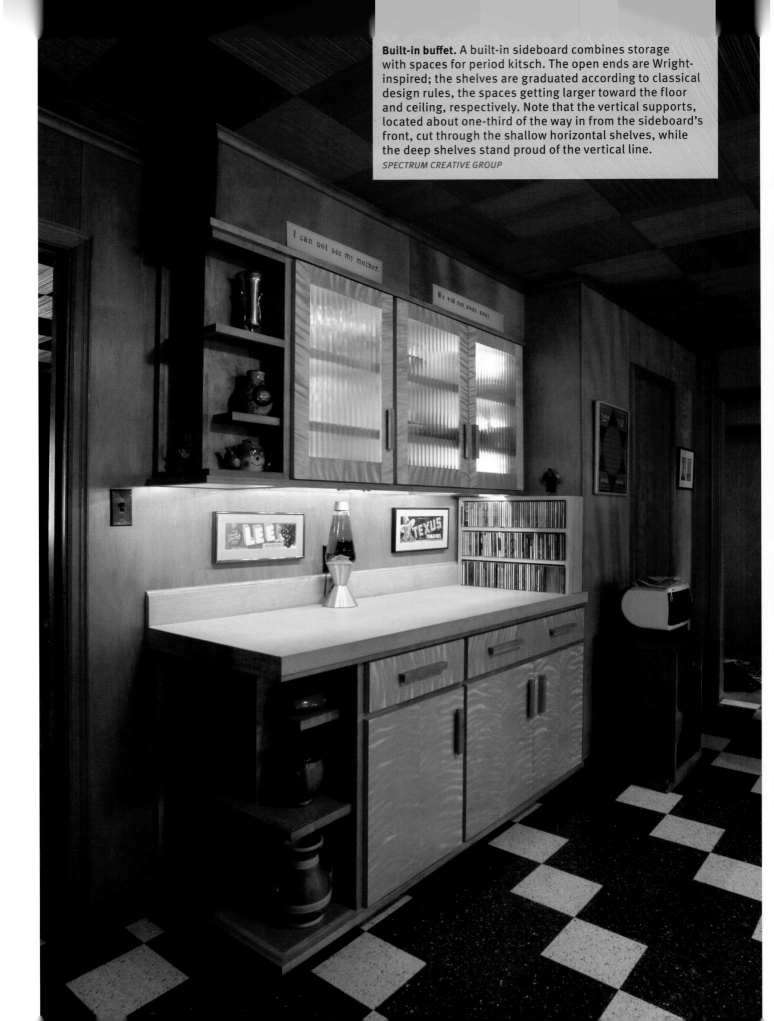

Built-in buffet. A built-in sideboard combines storage with spaces for period kitsch. The open ends are Wright-inspired; the shelves are graduated according to classical design rules, the spaces getting larger toward the floor and ceiling, respectively. Note that the vertical supports, located about one-third of the way in from the sideboard's front, cut through the shallow horizontal shelves, while the deep shelves stand proud of the vertical line.
SPECTRUM CREATIVE GROUP

Selectively exposed joinery. A good portion of the face frame stiles' width is exposed at the ends of each cabinet run, to emphasize the cabinets' structure. Daniel O'Grady made the upper face frames with bridle joints and left the tenons exposed for what Eric called a "carpentery" effect.

Case Study 8.6

Elevating a Mid-Century Kitchen

Lee and Eric Sandweiss fell in love with their house the moment they stepped through the door in January 2002. The 1951 ranch, built by Indiana University business professor Nate Silverstein, had remained in the family the entire time and had been treated with great care. The only room to have been remodeled significantly was the kitchen, which had been updated in the 1970s with dark brown "colonial" style cabinets and yellow laminate counters; stainless steel appliances were added in the 1990s. Fortunately, the room still had its original textured cedar tile ceiling, resilient tile floor and veneered walls.

337

A bit of investigation revealed that the '70s cabinets followed the original cabinets' footprint. There were even some of the original cabinets left in the house; painted steel topped with metal-edged laminate, the cheerful units had been removed to an adjacent workroom. When Lee and Eric hired me to work with them on the kitchen design, my first question was whether they might want to reuse the old cabinets. No, they replied, then took me on a tour of the house's two bathrooms. With rolled glass dividers, Vitrolite tile and hardware in Lucite and chrome, these "necessary rooms" were more Hollywood than Hoosier. My brief was to elevate the kitchen's aesthetic to something nearer that of the bathrooms. Curly birch veneer, painstaking attention to proportions and an illuminated sideboard with glass that echoes that in the master bath did the trick.

Open-ended. The working side of the island has three capacious drawers without faces for unimpeded access. The drawer heights are carefully lined up with the shelves on the open end. For these shelves, I took design cues from an old mid-century table that Lee and Eric had found at a garage sale; instead of solid dividers, a sturdy leg notched around the shelves gives vertical support.

Quintessentially mid-mod style. Apart from the cabinets and appliances, most of the kitchen's features are original. A checkerboard ceiling formed of textured cedar tiles appears about to converge with a green and white resilient tile floor. The walls are finished with veneered panels.
SPECTRUM CREATIVE GROUP

Buffet corner view. This kitchen has counters of locally quarried limestone sealed with paste wax. I made custom door and drawer pulls based on an original mid-century example, ripping lengths of cherry in L-section, then cutting them to length for sanding and finishing. Wood screws run through the drawer face hold the pulls in place.

With enthusiastic support from Lee and Eric, we had some fun with the interplay of vertical and horizontal cabinet elements. As you can see here, the horizontal face frame member that divides the top drawers from the doors or drawers below comes all the way through the vertical face frame stiles. The trim immediately beneath the stone is cherry, stained to provide a subtle horizontal accent.

Copper footrest. The island has a footrest made of copper pipe with copper caps from a local plumbing supply house. I used handrail holders, commonly used for stair rails, to affix it in place. Because the walls of the pipe are a little too thin to hold the screws firmly, I inserted a length of wooden closet rod for extra bite; although the rod is slightly smaller in diameter than the inside diameter of the pipe, the tightened screws pulled it down against the pipe's inside wall.

Subtle shifts in tone. The cabinets are built primarily of birch with cherry details. The cherry is left natural for the pulls but stained for the trim below the counter, to accentuate the cabinets' horizontal lines. Recessed toe kicks are painted black.

Service Providers & Sources

- Design and cabinetry: NR Hiller Design; primary cabinetmaker Daniel O'Grady
- Limestone: 3-D Stone (3dstoneinc.com)
- Plumbing: Mann Plumbing Inc. (mannplumbinginc.com)
- Electrical: Bloomington Heating, Cooling, Refrigeration and Electrical (bloomingtonhvac.com)
- Veneer: Certainly Wood (certainlywood.com)
- Veneering work: Ted Stahly, Bloomington, Ind.
- Maple island counter: Boos (butcherblockco.com)
- Ceiling tile: original, but similar tile is available through vintageplywood.com
- Floor tile: original

Focal post. Christine used the structural elements of her post-and-beam house to guide her design. She turned the central post of the wall that originally divided the kitchen from the dining area into a pivotal feature around which other elements articulate. The sink and dishwasher are concealed behind a backsplash that supports a bar. The section of counter that houses the sink continues beyond the post and wraps around to the public side, below the bar. An open shelf unit at the end holds ceramic pitchers, bowls and bakeware, a dynamic punctuation to the bank of cabinets that makes an ideal transition between the spaces for production and relaxation, respectively. She continued the line of the post-and-beam structure through other planes, with a maple "post" between a pair of upper cabinets, a band of darker counter across the light and a walnut panel set vertically between base cabinets.

Materials matter. Instead of drywalling the dining room side of the wall behind the oven housing, Christine specified a maple panel that identifies the space unmistakably with the kitchen. Ben Sturbaum of Golden Hands Construction fabricated the maple vent for the HVAC return.

Case Study 8.7

Same Footprint, Different Room

Architect Christine Matheu bought her home with her husband, William Cohen, in 1989. The split-level modernist residence had been designed in 1958 by Indianapolis architect Ed James. A spacious living/dining space takes up most of the upper level; a massive brick chimney with a fireplace open to both sides creates a subtle division between the two areas.

Subtly highlighting structure. Christine shadowed her home's post-and-beam structural elements with a maple panel in the bank of upper cabinets that flows through a dark line of horizontal counter and on to a vertical walnut rail.

Hidden utility. The sink and dishwasher are built into the cabinets on the kitchen side of the peninsula. The window looks out on forest to the south.

The house still had its original kitchen 31 years after construction, shoehorned into a 16'-long x just over 8'-wide space just off the dining area and accessed by means of an accordion-style door. A pass-through was the only other opening between the kitchen and public space. Not surprisingly, the room was cramped and dark, with just one window on the south wall. The original plywood cabinets were intact, along with the stove, by then sufficiently old to have some heavy retro charm. The layout was streamlined and compact, if uninviting.

In 2006, when Christine started planning her kitchen remodel in earnest, she considered expanding several feet out the south wall. In the end, she decided to retain the kitchen's footprint and open it to the dining room. The way she did this is a brilliant example of working with the space you have — and transforming how it looks, feels and functions.

Multitasking space. The oven housing incorporates storage spaces for cookware. Overlooking the short flight of steps from the entryway to the living area, as well as the stone steps that lead to the door, this window also affords insight into a portion of the house's architecture that was formerly hidden from view.

Flooded with light. Christine dramatically increased her kitchen's natural illumination by adding a pair of skylights and installing a floor-to-ceiling window (inoperable) in the north wall, which lets in light from the main entry side of the house.

To maximize the usefulness of the narrow space next to the oven cabinet Christine switched the orientation, making a wide, shallow cabinet with adjustable shelves that are ideal for storing wine, in the lower section, and coffee, tea, olive oil, vinegar, carafes etc., above.

The cabinets are faced with maple and Peruvian walnut veneers.

Service Providers & Sources

- Design: Christine Matheu, AIA (matheuarchitects. com)

- General contractor: Golden Hands Construction (goldenhandsco.com)

- Cabinetry: NR Hiller Design; primary cabinetmaker Daniel O'Grady

- Counters: Tremain Tile and Marble (tre-main.com)

- Aluminum-framed doors: Maplecraft USA (maplecraftusa.com)

- Veneers: Certainly Wood (certainlywood.com)

- Veneer cutting and pressing: Ted Stahly, Bloomington, Ind.

- Peninsula feet, door and drawer pulls: Hafele (hafele.com)

- Back-painted glass: Thickstun Glass (trtglass. com)

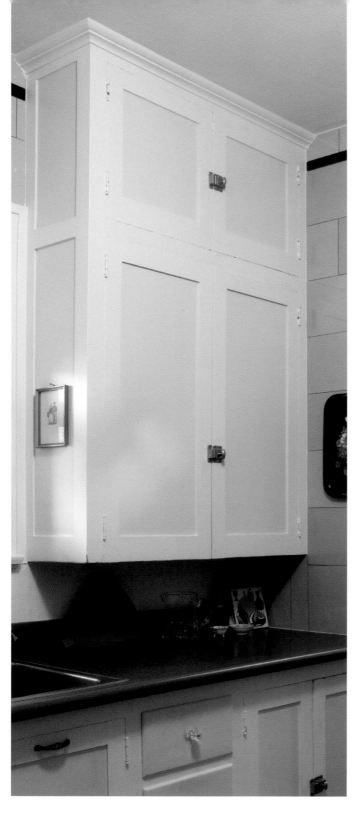

'Shaker' doors that didn't know their own name. *1926 built-ins made by the Hoosier Manufacturing Company in the kitchen of Linda Handelsman have inset doors with flat panels and square edges on their door frames.*

Shaker Style

Mother Ann Lee must be exhausted from rolling over in her grave. The English-born leader of the religious sect commonly known as the Shakers[13] would be distressed to learn that the band of zealous followers she led across the Atlantic in 1774 are now most widely associated with a popular style of kitchen cabinet door.

In 1990 I was a student of Stephen J. Stein, professor of American religious history and the scholar behind the authoritative volume "The Shaker Experience in America." Four years earlier, The Whitney Museum of New York had organized an exhibit of Shaker furniture, tools and other artifacts that went on to the Corcoran Gallery in Washington, D.C. Newspapers across the country (at a time when they still had the healthy support of subscribers) were falling over themselves to publish articles on Shaker architecture and design. Interest in Shaker furniture was at its zenith, and woodworkers across the nation were making chairs, pencil post beds, tables, seed boxes and oval boxes based on original Shaker examples. Given this popularity, it wasn't surprising that Professor Stein took the opportunity to prompt an easy laugh when he introduced the segment of his American Religious History course on the Shakers by noting drily that "the sect's official name was The United Society of Believers in Christ's Second Coming, but you could be forgiven for thinking they were The United Society of Furniture Makers."

Despite their accomplishments in agriculture and construction, their widespread business of selling packaged seeds, and their fabrication and sale of diverse items – baskets, brushes, leather goods, carpet, yarn and more – not to mention their well-ordered communal living (even if the celibacy they demanded

Community kitchen. *Real Shaker kitchens were designed to cook for communities, not a few members of a nuclear family. In this kitchen at Pleasant Hill, Kentucky, large kitchen-related tools hang from a peg rail. Barely visible is a corner of a recessed press with storage shelves.*
TIMOTHY BROWN

all but guaranteed the communities' eventual demise), we know them primarily as makers of furniture. A recent internet search for "Shaker style" produced more than 100 million results, most related to kitchens. And the overwhelming majority of these have nothing to do with an actual Shaker kitchen.

What led to this phenomenon is the identification of doors that have square-edged frames and flat panels with the simple, restrained design of historical Shaker furniture and buildings. Few seem to have looked carefully enough at original Shaker cabinets to notice that many of their doors were made with thumbnail mouldings on the frames' inside edges and often had raised panels on their outside faces.[14] (Oops.) Since the mid-1990s, I've seen plain inset doors referred to as Shaker style. Today this association has become so galactically divorced from its historical origins that there

Open fire. *As was typical of kitchens in the Midwest through many years of the 19th century, much cooking was done at the hearth.*
MARK LONGACRE

East Coast Shaker. *The 1830-31 basement-level kitchen of the Brick Dwelling at Hancock Shaker Village.*
PHOTO COURTESY HANCOCK SHAKER VILLAGE

Authentic Shaker. This stepback would make a fine model for cabinets in a Shaker-style kitchen. Note the recessed shelves in the wall at right, another Shaker storage mode.
CHRISTOPHER SCHWARZ

are companies using the term "Shaker style" to market built-in cabinets with full-overlay doors and drawers opened by means of pot-metal pulls. Others invoke the name to sell live-edge slab tables with metal bases and contemporary versions of Danish modern sideboards.

Chris Becksvoort is among the nation's foremost makers of furniture in the Shaker style. Although he prefers to spend his time building furniture, he has also done a few kitchens over the course of his career. The best, a kitchen he did for clients in Washington, D.C., in 1992, was furnished with freestanding Shaker furniture pieces – a tall cupboard, a workcounter with a maple top, an Enfield cupboard – but the house changed hands long ago, and sadly, he has no photos. The pictures here show one piece from Chris's most recent book, "Shaker Inspiration"; the book includes scale drawings of this and many others.

What Chris does have is access to the home of a client in New Gloucester, Maine. The cabinets shown here are part of a well-used kitchen in one of the town's older homes, dating from the turn of the 19th century. He built the cabinets shown here in 1985. The case con-

Direct inspiration. *Chris and his clients came up with the cabinet plan, which includes this broom cupboard.*
MARGARET STEVENS-BECKSVOORT

Slender storage. *A tall cupboard by Chris Becksvoort based on an example at the Shaker community in Mt. Lebanon, N.Y.*
DENNIS GRIGGS

Could work in the kitchen. Tailor's or work counter painted blue, used in the Canterbury, N.H., meeting house, circa 1815.
SHAKER MUSEUM | MOUNT LEBANON 1955.7366.1.

struction is all local white pine, as are the face frames, doors and drawers. The drawers are dovetailed by hand. The finish is a latex paint in a color called "Ox-blood" made by Gagnon & Haskell (no longer in business), with interiors in white. The hinges are extruded brass butts; knobs are hand-turned in black walnut.

The occasional kitchen you'll find online is based on historical Shaker built-ins or freestanding furniture. But the most important feature of an actual Shaker kitchen seems to have escaped nearly everyone who claims this style as inspiration: The Shakers did not live in single-family units. Celibacy and communal living were integral dimensions of their culture from the earliest days of the sect. Historically speaking, a Shaker kitchen doesn't just differ from those called Shaker today in terms of the furnishings it contains – a large central worktable, freestanding cabinets and flour bins, wood-fired ovens and cupboards known as presses built into recesses within walls. Shaker kitchens were places to cook for large groups of residents.

Just as with any school of design popularized to the point where the ideals and values that gave it life are forgotten, we ourselves are diminished by reducing material culture to mere "style."

Drawn from furniture. *Details drawn from pieces of Shaker furniture in this kitchen I did for Nancy Hiestand in the 1990s include graduated drawers, a hard maple counter with bullnose edge and cherry cove moulding below.*
SPECTRUM CREATIVE GROUP

Sleight of hand. *What appear to be two slim drawers at the top of this stack are actually one; the applied fronts are joined together with a false rail between them in the interest of stylistic faithfulness.*
SPECTRUM CREATIVE GROUP

End Notes

From Introduction

1. Cott, Nancy, et al. "Root of Bitterness," p.361.
2. Hiller, Nancy. "The Hoosier Cabinet in Kitchen History," p.39.
3. Beecher, Catharine. "Miss Beecher's Domestic Receipt-Book," p.213.
4. Much of this history is documented in my book "The Hoosier Cabinet in Kitchen History."

Chapter 1

5. While it's true that today we once again see people spinning wool, weaving fabric, making clothing and curtains, soap and furniture, cultivating crops and raising animals on small-scale farms, such production is not the norm and can rarely, if ever, compete with mass-produced equivalents (not that they can in any meaningful way be considered equivalent) on price.

Chapter 3

6. See Ruskin, John. "The Nature of Gothic."

Chapter 4

7. I am indebted to Craig Regan for pointing out the existence of this type of hardware.

Chapter 5

8. For a good survey see Johnny Grey, "The Art of Kitchen Design." For additional insight, see Hiller, "The Hoosier Cabinet in Kitchen History."
9. Source: Retrorenovation.com/2013/07/01/monel-sink-counter-top

Chapter 7

10. Grey, Johnny. "The Art of Kitchen Design," p.113.
11. The kitchen that served as inspiration for this one has since been remodeled. The illustrations from Jan's kitchen in Chapter 5, "Elements of Design," show the new iteration.
12. https://www.wayfair.com/ideas-and-advice/decorate-with-farmhouse-style-S6007.html

Chapter 8

13. Short for Shaking Quakers, due to their shaking and dancing during worship.
14. As with most solid-wood doors and panels in furniture and cabinetry before the widespread use of mechanized saws and planers, doors typically had one surface raised, which required less handwork to get the panel to the desired thickness and also reduced the panel's surface area, for enhanced stability. In many cases the raised surface was installed toward the cabinet interior, with the flat surface facing out.

Bibliography

Alexander, Christopher, et al. "A Pattern Language" (New York: Oxford University Press, 1977).

Bascom, Mansfield. "Wharton Esherick: The Journey of a Creative Mind" (New York: Abrams, 2010).

Becksvoort, Christian. "Shaker Inspiration: Five Decades of Fine Craftsmanship" (Fort Mitchell KY: Lost Art Press, 2018).

Beecher, Catharine. "Miss Beecher's Domestic Receipt-Book" (Mineola NY: Dover, 2001).

Cott, Nancy et al. "Root of Bitterness: Documents of the Social History of American Women" (Boston: Northeastern University Press, 1996).

DeChiara, Joseph et al. "Time-Saver Standards for Interior Design and Space Planning" (New York: McGraw-Hill, Inc. 1991).

Dresser, Christopher. "Studies in Design" (Layton, UT: Gibbs Smith, 2002).

Gellner, Arrol. "Red Tile Style: America's Spanish Revival Architecture" (New York: Viking Studio, 2002).

Grey, Johnny. "The Art of Kitchen Design: Planning for Comfort and Style" (London: Cassell, 1994).

Grey, Johnny. "Kitchen Culture: Reinventing Kitchen Design" (Buffalo NY: Firefly Books, 2004).

Hiller, Nancy. "The Hoosier Cabinet in Kitchen History" (Bloomington IN: Indiana University Press, 2009).

Innes, Jocasta. "Country Kitchens" (New York: Universe Publishing, 1996).

Lupton, Ellen and Miller, J. Abbott. "The Bathroom, the Kitchen and the Aesthetics of Waste: A Process of Elimination" (New York: Kiosk, 1992).

Martin, Clarence. "Details of Building Construction" (Boston: Bates & Guild Company, 1905).

Panero, Julius and Martin Zelnik. "Human Dimension & Interior Space: A Source Book of Design Reference Standards" (New York: Watson-Guptill Publications, 1979).

Plante, Ellen. "The American Kitchen 1700 to the Present: From Hearth to Highrise" (New York NY: Facts on File, 1995).

Poore, Patricia, ed. "Kitchen Classics: The Essential Kitchen Guide" (El Segundo CA: Cruz Bay Publishing, 2011).

Powell, Jane. "Bungalow Kitchens" (Salt Lake City: Gibbs Smith, 2000).

Powell, Jane. "Linoleum" (Salt Lake City: Gibbs Smith, 2003).

Ruskin, John. "Unto This Last and Other Writings" (New York: Penguin Classics, 1985).

Stein, Stephen J. "The Shaker Experience in America" (New Haven CT: Yale University Press, 1992).

"The Shorter Oxford English Dictionary on Historical Principles" (London: Oxford University Press 1973).

Tolpin, Jim. "Building Traditional Kitchen Cabinets" (Newtown CT: Taunton Press, 1994).

"Universal Millwork Catalog 1927" (Mineola NY: Dover, 2003).

Wearing, Robert. "The Solution at Hand: Jigs & Fixtures to Make Benchwork Easier" (Covington KY: Lost Art Press, 2019).

Winter, Robert. "American Bungalow Style" (New York: Simon & Schuster, 1996).

"The Kitchen Plan Book" (Newcastle IN: Hoosier Manufacturing Co. c.1917; republished by *American Bungalow*, 1997).

Magazines & Online Sources

Also see *Old-House Journal* and *Arts & Crafts Homes and the Revival* magazines.

oldhouseonline.com

retrorenovation.com

Acknowledgments

This book had its genesis in a late-evening text exchange. It was November 2016, and I was just about to get into a hot bath when my phone pinged. "Hey Nancy," said the note from Chris Schwarz. "Next time you are in Cincinnati let me know and we can get lunch or a drink if you like. Maybe talk about books if you like." Talk about books? With Chris Schwarz? That made my day/week/month.

We ended up talking by phone instead of in person. He wanted to know whether I'd be interested in writing a book about English Arts and Crafts furniture. I thought he was joking – Megan Fitzpatrick had already asked me to do a book on that subject for Popular Woodworking, and I'd started work on the project. Ack, said Chris (here I'm going from memory). I would never poach an author from those guys. I thought the book you were doing for them was about kitchens. In the end we agreed that I would write a book about kitchens for Lost Art Press.

It's an honor to have my work published by an operation I hold in such high regard for many reasons, in addition to their production of high-quality books. I'm grateful to Chris for treating me as a genuine partner in this project. Throughout the various stages of editing and book design he and Megan have been focused on the task, even as other necessary projects for business and family have vied for their attention, and shockingly prompt at communicating. Each of them made suggestions that improved the finished product, and I'm thrilled with Chris's book design. I am also grateful to Megan and Kara Gebhart Uhl for securing various images and the permission to publish them.

Sincere thanks to my former woodworking employers, from whom I learned so much: Roy Giffiths and his wife, Mimi Van der Franzen; Martin Short and Steve of Millside Cabinet Makers; David Haber, Chris Wall and Michael Goldfinger; and to the late Kent Perelman.

Thanks also go to others who have seen the value in my sometimes-unconventional methods, especially Kelly Mehler, who invited me to teach cabinetmaking courses at his school for several years, and Phil Huber at *Woodsmith Magazine*, who invited me to work with his crew on a video series about building custom cabinets.

I could not have supported myself without my clients, some of whose kitchens appear here. Daniel O'Grady was my right-hand man for almost three years, as well as the principal cabinetmaker on a few of the jobs in this book. Daniel also read and offered constructive suggestions for Chapter 4. Jerry Nees worked with us on a few of the kitchens. Stephen J. Stein and Christian Becksvoort read the short section on Shakers. I am also grateful to all of the general contractors, materials suppliers and other individuals whose work appears here – and I hope I have acknowledged them all by name in the right spots – along with the photographers: Kendall Reeves, Matt Monte, Margaret Stevens-Becksvoort, Benedict Grey and Lauri Hafvenstein. Thanks also to Estela Vieira and Johannes Türk.

Last, I am blessed to have Mark Longacre, a poet, gardener, sailor and carpenter who prides himself on meticulous work, as my partner in life.